# Gates of Prayer

## for Shabbat and Weekdays

A Gender Sensitive Prayerbook

Chaim Stern, Editor

CENTRAL CONFERENCE OF AMERICAN RABBIS
5755   NEW YORK   1994

Library of Congress Cataloging-in-Publication Data


Siddur (Reform, Central Conference of American Rabbis, New York
Gates of Prayer for Shabbat and Weeekdays: a gender sensitive prayerbook
/ Chaim Stern, editor.
        p.        cm.
English and Hebrew.
    ISBN 0-88123-063-4 (Heb. op.) : $12.95.    --ISBN ISBN 0-88123-064-2
(Eng. op.) : $12.95
        1. Siddurim--Texts.     2. Reform Judaism--Liturgy--Texts.
I. Stern, Chaim.    II. Central Conference of American Rabbis.
III. Title.      IV. Title: Gender sensitive prayerbook.
BM674.34.C46     1994
296.4--dc20                                    94-15419
                                               CIP

# Contents

Preface                                                          iv

On Usage                                                         vi

Weekday Evening Service                                          1

Weekday Morning Service                                          9

Weekday T'filah                                                  22

Shabbat Evening Service I                                        38

Shabbat Evening Service II                                       65

Shabbat Evening Service III                                      82

Shabbat Morning Service                                          98

Alternative Opening Prayers                                      99

Afternoon Service                                                125

For the Reading of the Torah                                     141

Concluding Prayers                                               148

Aleinu I                                                         148

Aleinu II                                                        149

Before the Kaddish                                               151

Songs                                                            156

Supplementary Prayers                                            162

For the New Month                                                162

Bar and Bar Mitzvah Prayers                                      163

At Home and in the Synagogue                                     164

Candle Lighting                                                  165

Kiddush for the Eve of Shabbat                                   165

Kiddush for the Morning of Shabbat                               167

Short Thanksgiving after the Meal                                168

Havdalah                                                         172

Short Hallel                                                     176

Chanukah                                                         177

The Sabbath before Purim                                         181

The Sabbath before Yom Ha-atzmaut                                182

The Sabbath before Yom Ha-shoah                                  184

For our People, our Congregation and our Nation                  186

# Preface

This volume replaces a number of interim volumes published by the Central Conference in recent years. These are: *Gates of Prayer for Shabbat, Gates of Prayer for Weekdays.* and *Gates of Prayer for Assemblies*. With the publication of *Gates of Prayer for Shabbat and Weekdays*, we in the Reform Movement can now present a gender-sensitive liturgy to stand alongside the more comprehensive original *Gates of Prayer*. It includes the services and prayers published in the aforementioned volumes, and in some respects goes beyond them.

Just before Gates of Prayer went to press in late 1974, the Editor changed all English-language references to human beings in general that on their face excluded women, to gender-neutral terms. Thus, 'mankind' became 'humankind,' 'fathers' became 'ancestors' or 'fathers and mothers,' and so on. He did not at that time change language referring to God and he made no attempt to emend the Hebrew texts. Now, nineteen years later, we present several services for weekdays and Shabbat in which the gender-neutral approach is extended to English-language references to God, and, in some degree, to the Hebrew.

We thank the many colleagues whose helpful suggestions and criticisms have been gratefully received and carefully considered. This revised edition would have been the poorer without their help. Rabbis H. Leonard Poller and Donna Berman, and Cantor Edward Graham formed, with the Editor, a working group that studied the Editor's almost-final draft, and helped decide on many matters. To them, a particular word of thanks. Later, the Editor had the benefit of help from Rabbi A. Stanley Dreyfus, whose detailed study of the text helped eliminate many errors, and whose suggestions for improvements were generously offered. It should be noted that the publication of *Gates of Prayer for Shabbat*, one of the volumes incorporated into the present prayerbook, was made possible by the contribution of James Nathaniel Dreyfus and Richard Baeck Dreyfus in honor of their father, Rabbi A. Stanley Dreyfus. In its latter stages, Rabbi David Katz, Rabbi Morley T. Feinstein, Rabbi Robert Klensin and Rabbi Simeon J. Maslin improved the present work by their suggestions. As always, Rabbi Elliot Stevens,

Publications Director of the Conference, was a source of unstinting support. Several prayers were adapted by the Editor from *Forms of Prayer for Jewish Worship,* © Reform Synagogues of Gt. Britain, 1977, to whom we are grateful. Finally, the Editor wishes to express his gratitude to Rabbi John D. Rayner, friend and collaborator over many years, whose influence for good will be evident on many pages of the present volume.

*Chaim Stern*

CHAPPAQUA, NEW YORK

# On Usage

We utilize a number of conventions in this prayer book, which we suggest you note carefully.

\* The type–style of this paragraph is used whenever we suggest the English be read by the person leading the service. When this style is a point smaller, it suggests that the preceding Hebrew may be sung or chanted.

*\* The oblique type style of this paragraph is used whenever we suggest that the congregation as a whole might read the English. In those congregations where unison reading is not the norm, this type–style might identify passages to be read by diverse individuals.*

\* This sans–serif type–style is used for transliterations, to assist those who have not yet learned to read Hebrew.

The Hebrew reader will note a symbol used to designate the *kamatz katan* ( ָ ). In the past the *kamatz* ( ָ ). was used universally, despite the difference in pronunciation required in some instances. Thus: בָּרוּךְ is pronounced b **a**-ruch, whereas כָּל is pronounced k **o**l.

Where the English accompanying a Hebrew passage does not translate that Hebrew, we utilize two symbols to inform the worshipper who is not adequately Hebrew–literate to know this without help:

° This signifies that the English is a variation on the theme of the Hebrew. Hewing to the theme of the Hebrew, the English may come to that theme from a [sometimes very] different perspective.

• This signifies that the English is a paraphrase or loose translation of the Hebrew.

Your greatness, Eternal One, surpasses our understanding, yet at times we feel Your nearness.

Overwhelmed by awe and wonder as we behold the signs of Your presence, still we feel within us a kinship with the Divine.

And so we turn to You, O God, looking at the world about us, and inward to the world within us, there to find You, and from Your presence gain life and strength.

or

God, You give meaning to our days, to our struggles and strivings. Without You we are lost, our lives empty. Then we turn to You! And then, in the stillness of the night, when the outer darkness enters the soul; in the press of the crowd, when we walk alone though yearning for companionship; and when in agony we are bystanders to our own confusion, we look to You for hope and peace.

We do not ask for a life of ease, for happiness without alloy. Instead, we ask You to teach us to be uncomplaining and unafraid. In our darkness help us to find Your light, and in our loneliness to discover the many spirits akin to our own. Give us strength to face life with hope and courage, that even from its discords and conflicts we may draw blessing, as we learn to exult in heights gained after the toil of climbing.

*Let our darkness be dispelled by Your love, that we may rise above fear and failure, our steps sustained by faith. God, You give meaning to our days; You are our support and our trust.*

## MEDITATION

There are moments when we hear the call of our higher selves, the call that links us to the Divine. Then we know how blessed we are with life and love. May this be a moment of such vision, a time of deeper attachment to the godlike in us and in our world, for which we shall give thanks and praise!

### All rise

**The Sh'ma and its Blessings**　　　　　　שמע וברכותיה

בָּרְכוּ אֶת־יי הַמְבֹרָךְ!

Praise the One to whom our praise is due!

בָּרוּךְ יי הַמְבֹרָךְ לְעוֹלָם וָעֶד!

*Ba-ruch Adonai ha-m'vo-rach l'o-lam va-ed!*

*Praised be the One to whom our praise is due, now and for ever!*

CREATION　　　　　　　　　　　　　　מעריב ערבים

בָּרוּךְ אַתָּה יי, אֱלֹהֵינוּ מֶלֶךְ הָעוֹלָם, אֲשֶׁר בִּדְבָרוֹ
מַעֲרִיב עֲרָבִים, בְּחָכְמָה פּוֹתֵחַ שְׁעָרִים, וּבִתְבוּנָה מְשַׁנֶּה
עִתִּים, וּמַחֲלִיף אֶת־הַזְּמַנִּים, וּמְסַדֵּר אֶת־הַכּוֹכָבִים
בְּמִשְׁמְרוֹתֵיהֶם בָּרָקִיעַ כִּרְצוֹנוֹ.
בּוֹרֵא יוֹם וָלַיְלָה, גּוֹלֵל אוֹר מִפְּנֵי חֹשֶׁךְ וְחֹשֶׁךְ מִפְּנֵי אוֹר,
וּמַעֲבִיר יוֹם וּמֵבִיא לָיְלָה, וּמַבְדִּיל בֵּין יוֹם וּבֵין לָיְלָה,
יי צְבָאוֹת שְׁמוֹ.
אֵל חַי וְקַיָּם, תָּמִיד יִמְלוֹךְ עָלֵינוּ לְעוֹלָם וָעֶד.
בָּרוּךְ אַתָּה יי, הַמַּעֲרִיב עֲרָבִים.

2

We praise You, Eternal God, Sovereign of the universe, whose word brings on the evening. With wisdom You open heaven's gates, and with understanding You make the ages pass and the seasons alternate; Your will controls the stars as they travel through the skies.

*You are Creator of day and night, rolling light away from darkness, and darkness from light; You cause day to pass and bring on the night, separating day from night; You command the hosts of heaven! May the living and eternal God rule us always, to the end of time! We praise You, O God, whose word makes evening fall.*

REVELATION                                      אהבת עולם

אַהֲבַת עוֹלָם בֵּית יִשְׂרָאֵל עַמְּךָ אָהֳבְתָּ.
תּוֹרָה וּמִצְוֹת, חֻקִּים וּמִשְׁפָּטִים אוֹתָנוּ לִמַּדְתָּ.
עַל־כֵּן, יְיָ אֱלֹהֵינוּ, בְּשָׁכְבֵנוּ וּבְקוּמֵנוּ נָשִׂיחַ בְּחֻקֶּיךָ,
וְנִשְׂמַח בְּדִבְרֵי תוֹרָתֶךָ וּבְמִצְוֹתֶיךָ לְעוֹלָם וָעֶד.
כִּי הֵם חַיֵּינוּ וְאֹרֶךְ יָמֵינוּ, וּבָהֶם נֶהְגֶּה יוֹמָם וָלָיְלָה.
וְאַהֲבָתְךָ אַל־תָּסוּר מִמֶּנּוּ לְעוֹלָמִים!
בָּרוּךְ אַתָּה יְיָ, אוֹהֵב עַמּוֹ יִשְׂרָאֵל.

Unending is Your love for Your people, the House of Israel: Torah and Mitzvot, laws and precepts have You taught us.

*Therefore, O God, when we lie down and when we rise up, we will meditate on Your laws and rejoice in Your Torah and Mitzvot for ever.*

*Day and night we will reflect on them, for they are our life and the length of our days. Then Your love shall never depart from our hearts! We praise You, O God: You love Your people Israel.*

3

שְׁמַע יִשְׂרָאֵל: יהוה אֱלֹהֵינוּ, יהוה אֶחָד!

Sh'ma Yis-ra-eil: Adonai Eh-lo-hei-nu, Adonai Eh-chad!

*Hear, O Israel: the Eternal One is our God,*
*the Eternal God alone!*

בָּרוּךְ שֵׁם כְּבוֹד מַלְכוּתוֹ לְעוֹלָם וָעֶד!

Ba-ruch shem k'vod mal-chu-to l'o-lam va–ed!

*Blessed is God's glorious majesty for ever and ever!*

## All are seated

וְאָהַבְתָּ אֵת יהוה אֱלֹהֶיךָ בְּכָל־לְבָבְךָ וּבְכָל־נַפְשְׁךָ וּבְכָל־מְאֹדֶךָ:
וְהָיוּ הַדְּבָרִים הָאֵלֶּה אֲשֶׁר אָנֹכִי מְצַוְּךָ הַיּוֹם עַל־לְבָבֶךָ:
וְשִׁנַּנְתָּם לְבָנֶיךָ וְדִבַּרְתָּ בָּם בְּשִׁבְתְּךָ בְּבֵיתֶךָ וּבְלֶכְתְּךָ בַדֶּרֶךְ
וּבְשָׁכְבְּךָ וּבְקוּמֶךָ: וּקְשַׁרְתָּם לְאוֹת עַל־יָדֶךָ וְהָיוּ לְטֹטָפֹת בֵּין
עֵינֶיךָ: וּכְתַבְתָּם עַל־מְזוּזֹת בֵּיתֶךָ וּבִשְׁעָרֶיךָ:

לְמַעַן תִּזְכְּרוּ וַעֲשִׂיתֶם אֶת־כָּל־מִצְוֹתָי וִהְיִיתֶם קְדֹשִׁים
לֵאלֹהֵיכֶם: אֲנִי יהוה אֱלֹהֵיכֶם אֲשֶׁר הוֹצֵאתִי אֶתְכֶם
מֵאֶרֶץ מִצְרַיִם לִהְיוֹת לָכֶם לֵאלֹהִים אֲנִי יהוה אֱלֹהֵיכֶם:

V'a–hav–ta et Adonai Eh–lo–heh–cha b'chol l'va–v'cha u–v'chol naf–
sh'cha u–v'chol m'o–deh–cha. V'ha–yu ha–d'va–rim ha–ei–leh a–sher a–
no–chi m'tza–v'cha ha–yom al l'va–veh–cha. V'shi–nan–tam l'va–neh–cha
v'di–bar–ta bam b'shiv–t'cha b'vei–teh–cha u–v'lech–t'cha va–deh–rech u–
v'shoch–b'cha u–v'ku–meh–cha. U–k'shar–tam l'ot al ya–deh–cha v'ha–yu
l'to–ta–fot bein ei–neh–cha; u–ch'tav–tam al m'zu–zot bei–teh–cha u–vi–
sh'a–reh–cha.

L'ma–an tiz–k'ru va–a–si–tem et kol mitz–vo–tai, vi–h'yi–tem k'do–shim
lei–lo–hei–chem. Ani Adonai Eh–lo–hei–chem a–sher ho–tzei–ti et–chem
mei–eh–retz mitz–ra–yim li–h'yot la–chem lei–lo–him. Ani Adonai Eh–lo–
hei–chem.

4

*You shall love your Eternal God with all your heart, with all your mind, with all your being. Set these words, which I command you this day, upon your heart. Teach them faithfully to your children; speak of them in your home and on your way, when you lie down and when you rise up. Bind them as a sign upon your hand; let them be symbols before your eyes; inscribe them on the doorposts of your house, and on your gates.*

*Be mindful of all My Mitzvot, and do them: so shall you consecrate yourselves to your God. I am your Eternal God who led you out of Egypt to be your God; I am your Eternal God.*

REDEMPTION                                                          גאולה

אֱמֶת וֶאֱמוּנָה כָּל־זֹאת, וְקַיָּם עָלֵינוּ, כִּי הוּא יְיָ אֱלֹהֵינוּ,
וְאֵין זוּלָתוֹ, וַאֲנַחְנוּ יִשְׂרָאֵל עַמּוֹ. הַפּוֹדֵנוּ מִיַּד מְלָכִים, הַגּוֹאֲלֵנוּ
מִכַּף כָּל־הֶעָרִיצִים, וַיּוֹצֵא אֶת־עַמּוֹ יִשְׂרָאֵל מִמִּצְרַיִם לְחֵרוּת
עוֹלָם. וְרָאוּ בָנָיו גְּבוּרָתוֹ; שִׁבְּחוּ וְהוֹדוּ לִשְׁמוֹ. וּמַלְכוּתוֹ בְּרָצוֹן
קִבְּלוּ עֲלֵיהֶם. לְךָ עָנוּ שִׁירָה בְּשִׂמְחָה רַבָּה, וְאָמְרוּ כֻלָּם:

All this we hold to be true and sure: You alone are our God; there is none else, and we are Israel Your people.

*You are our Sovereign: You deliver us from the hand of oppressors, and save us from the fist of tyrants.*

You do wonders without number, marvels that pass our understanding.

*You give us our life; by Your help we survive all who seek our destruction.*

You did wonders for us in the land of Egypt, miracles and marvels in the land of Pharaoh,

*You led Your people Israel out, forever to serve You in freedom.*

5

When Your children witnessed Your power, they extolled You
and gave You thanks; willingly they enthroned You; and, full of
joy, Moses, Miriam, and all Israel sang this song:

מִי־כָמְכָה בָּאֵלִם, יהוה? מִי כָּמְכָה, נֶאְדָּר בַּקֹּדֶשׁ,
נוֹרָא תְהִלֹּת, עֹשֵׂה פֶלֶא?

מַלְכוּתְךָ רָאוּ בָנֶיךָ, בּוֹקֵעַ יָם לִפְנֵי מֹשֶׁה; זֶה אֵלִי!
עָנוּ וְאָמְרוּ: יהוה יִמְלֹךְ לְעֹלָם וָעֶד!

וְנֶאֱמַר: כִּי פָדָה יהוה אֶת־יַעֲקֹב, וּגְאָלוֹ מִיַּד חָזָק מִמֶּנּוּ.
בָּרוּךְ אַתָּה יי, גָּאַל יִשְׂרָאֵל.

Mi cha–mo–cha ba–ei–lim, Adonai?
Mi ka–mo–cha, neh–dar ba–ko–desh, no–ra t'hi–lot, o–sei feh–leh?
Mal–chu–t'cha ra–u va–neh–cha, bo–kei–a yam li–f'nei Mo–sheh; zeh Ei–li!
    A–nu v'a–m'ru: Adonai yim–loch l'o–lam va–ed!
V'neh–eh–mar: Ki fa–da Adonai et Ya–a–kov, u–g'a–lo mi–yad cha–zak
    mi–meh–nu.
Ba–ruch a–ta Adonai, ga–al Yis–ra–eil.

Who is like You, Eternal One, among the gods that are worshipped?
Who is like You, majestic in holiness, awesome in splendor, doing
wonders?

In their escape from the sea, Your children saw Your sovereign might
displayed. "This is my God!" they cried. "The Eternal will reign for
ever and ever!"

And it has been said: The Eternal One delivered Jacob, and redeemed us
from the hand of one stronger than ourselves.

We praise You, O God, Redeemer of Israel.

6

DIVINE PROVIDENCE                                        הַשְׁכִּיבֵנוּ

הַשְׁכִּיבֵנוּ, יי אֱלֹהֵינוּ, לְשָׁלוֹם, וְהַעֲמִידֵנוּ, מַלְכֵּנוּ, לְחַיִּים. וּפְרֹשׂ
עָלֵינוּ סֻכַּת שְׁלוֹמֶךָ, וְתַקְּנֵנוּ בְּעֵצָה טוֹבָה מִלְּפָנֶיךָ, וְהוֹשִׁיעֵנוּ
לְמַעַן שְׁמֶךָ, וְהָגֵן בַּעֲדֵנוּ. וְהָסֵר מֵעָלֵינוּ אוֹיֵב דֶּבֶר וְחֶרֶב וְרָעָב
וְיָגוֹן; וְהָסֵר שָׂטָן מִלְּפָנֵינוּ וּמֵאַחֲרֵינוּ, וּבְצֵל כְּנָפֶיךָ תַּסְתִּירֵנוּ,
כִּי אֵל שׁוֹמְרֵנוּ וּמַצִּילֵנוּ אָתָּה, כִּי אֵל מֶלֶךְ חַנּוּן וְרַחוּם אָתָּה.
וּשְׁמוֹר צֵאתֵנוּ וּבוֹאֵנוּ לְחַיִּים וּלְשָׁלוֹם מֵעַתָּה וְעַד עוֹלָם.
בָּרוּךְ אַתָּה יי, שׁוֹמֵר עַמּוֹ יִשְׂרָאֵל לָעַד.

Grant that we may lie down in peace, Eternal God, and raise us up, O Sovereign, to life renewed. Spread over us the shelter of Your peace; guide us with Your good counsel; and for Your name's sake, be our Help.

*Shield us from hatred and plague; keep us from war and famine and anguish; subdue our inclination to evil. O God, our Guardian and Helper, our gracious and merciful Sovereign, give us refuge in the shadow of Your wings. O guard our coming and our going, that now and always we have life and peace.*

*We praise You, O God, the Guardian of Israel.*

∼∼

## All rise

READER'S KADDISH     חצי קדיש

יִתְגַּדַּל וְיִתְקַדַּשׁ שְׁמֵהּ רַבָּא בְּעָלְמָא דִי־בְרָא כִרְעוּתֵהּ,
וְיַמְלִיךְ מַלְכוּתֵהּ בְּחַיֵּיכוֹן וּבְיוֹמֵיכוֹן וּבְחַיֵּי דְכָל־בֵּית
יִשְׂרָאֵל, בַּעֲגָלָא וּבִזְמַן קָרִיב, וְאִמְרוּ: אָמֵן.

יְהֵא שְׁמֵהּ רַבָּא מְבָרַךְ לְעָלַם וּלְעָלְמֵי עָלְמַיָּא.

יִתְבָּרַךְ וְיִשְׁתַּבַּח, וְיִתְפָּאַר וְיִתְרוֹמַם וְיִתְנַשֵּׂא, וְיִתְהַדָּר
וְיִתְעַלֶּה וְיִתְהַלָּל שְׁמֵהּ דְּקֻדְשָׁא, בְּרִיךְ הוּא,
לְעֵלָּא מִן־כָּל־בִּרְכָתָא וְשִׁירָתָא, תֻּשְׁבְּחָתָא וְנֶחֱמָתָא
דַּאֲמִירָן בְּעָלְמָא, וְאִמְרוּ: אָמֵן.

Yit-ga-dal v'yit–ka–dash sh'mei ra-ba b'al-ma di-v'ra chi-r'u'tei, v'yam-lich mal-chu-tei b'cha-yei-chon u-v'yo-mei-chon u-v'cha-yei d'chol beit Yis-ra-eil, ba-a-ga-la u-vi-z'man ka-riv, v'i-m' ru: A-mein.

Y'hei sh'mei ra-ba m'va-rach l'a-lam u-l'al-mei al-ma-ya.

Yit-ba-rach v'yish-ta-bach, v'yit-pa-ar v'yit-ro-mam v'yit-na-sei, v'yit-ha-dar v'yit-a-leh v'yit-ha-lal sh'mei d'kud-sha, b'rich hu,

l'ei-la min kol bir-cha-ta v'shi-ra-ta, tush-b'cha-ta v'neh-cheh-ma-ta da-a-mi-ran b'al-ma, v'i-m' ru: A-mein.

## The weekday T'filah is on page 22

8

FOR THOSE WHO WEAR A TALLIT

בָּרְכִי נַפְשִׁי אֶת־יהוה! יהוה אֱלֹהַי, גָּדַלְתָּ מְּאֹד!
הוֹד וְהָדָר לָבָשְׁתָּ, עֹטֶה־אוֹר כַּשַּׂלְמָה, נוֹטֶה שָׁמַיִם כַּיְרִיעָה.

Praise the Eternal One, O my soul!
O God, You are very great!
Arrayed in glory and majesty, You wrap Yourself in light as with a
garment, and stretch out the heavens like a curtain.

בָּרוּךְ אַתָּה יי, אֱלֹהֵינוּ מֶלֶךְ הָעוֹלָם,
אֲשֶׁר קִדְּשָׁנוּ בְּמִצְוֹתָיו וְצִוָּנוּ לְהִתְעַטֵּף בַּצִּיצִית.

We praise You, Eternal God, Sovereign of the universe:
You hallow us with Your Mitzvot, and teach us to wrap ourselves
in the fringed Tallit.

～～

## FOR THOSE WHO WEAR TEFILLIN

*On the hand*

בָּרוּךְ אַתָּה יי, אֱלֹהֵינוּ מֶלֶךְ הָעוֹלָם, אֲשֶׁר קִדְּשָׁנוּ בְּמִצְוֹתָיו
וְצִוָּנוּ לְהָנִיחַ תְּפִלִּין.

We praise You, Eternal God, Sovereign of the universe: You
hallow us with Your Mitzvot, and teach us to put on Tefillin.

*On the head*

בָּרוּךְ אַתָּה יי, אֱלֹהֵינוּ מֶלֶךְ הָעוֹלָם, אֲשֶׁר קִדְּשָׁנוּ בְּמִצְוֹתָיו
וְצִוָּנוּ עַל־מִצְוַת תְּפִלִּין.

We praise You, Eternal God, Sovereign of the universe: You
hallow us with Your Mitzvot, and teach us concerning the
Mitzvah of Tefillin.

~ ~

"I will betroth you to Me for
ever; I will betroth you to Me in
righteousness and justice, in
love and compassion; I will betroth you to Me in faithfulness,
and you shall know the Eternal
One."

וְאֵרַשְׂתִּיךְ לִי לְעוֹלָם;
וְאֵרַשְׂתִּיךְ לִי בְּצֶדֶק וּבְמִשְׁפָּט,
וּבְחֶסֶד וּבְרַחֲמִים.
וְאֵרַשְׂתִּיךְ לִי בֶּאֱמוּנָה,
וְיָדַעַתְּ אֶת־יהוה.

~ ~

10

## Morning Blessings

ברכות השחר

FOR THE BLESSING OF WORSHIP

מה טבו

מַה־טֹּבוּ אֹהָלֶיךָ, יַעֲקֹב, מִשְׁכְּנֹתֶיךָ, יִשְׂרָאֵל!
וַאֲנִי, בְּרֹב חַסְדְּךָ אָבוֹא בֵיתֶךָ,
אֶשְׁתַּחֲוֶה אֶל־הֵיכַל קָדְשְׁךָ בְּיִרְאָתֶךָ.

יהוה, אָהַבְתִּי מְעוֹן בֵּיתֶךָ, וּמְקוֹם מִשְׁכַּן כְּבוֹדֶךָ.
וַאֲנִי אֶשְׁתַּחֲוֶה וְאֶכְרָעָה, אֶבְרְכָה לִפְנֵי־יהוה עֹשִׂי.

וַאֲנִי תְפִלָּתִי־לְךָ, יהוה, עֵת רָצוֹן.
אֱלֹהִים, בְּרָב־חַסְדֶּךָ, עֲנֵנִי בֶּאֱמֶת יִשְׁעֶךָ.

Mah to-vu o-ha-leh-cha, Ya-a-kov, mish-k'no-teh-cha, Yis-ra-eil!
Va-a-ni, b'rov chas-d'cha a-vo vei-teh-cha,
esh-ta-cha-veh el hei-chal kod-sh'cha b'yir-a-teh-cha.

Adonai, a-hav-ti m'on bei-teh-cha u-m'kom mish-kan k'vo-deh-cha.
Va-a-ni esh-ta-cha-veh v'ech-ra-ah, ev-r'cha li-f'nei Adonai o-si.

Va-a-ni t'fi-la-ti l'cha, Adonai, eit ra-tzon.
Eh-lo-him, b'rov chas-deh-cha, a-nei-ni beh-eh-met yish-eh-cha.

How lovely are your tents, O Jacob, your dwelling-places, O Israel!
As for me, O God abounding in grace,
I enter your house to worship with awe in Your sacred place.

I love Your house, Eternal One, the dwelling-place of Your glory;
humbly I worship You, humbly I seek blessing from God my Maker.

To You, Eternal One, goes my prayer: may this be a time of Your favor.
In Your great love, O God, answer me with Your saving truth.

11

FOR THE BODY            אשר יצר

בָּרוּךְ אַתָּה יְיָ, אֱלֹהֵינוּ מֶלֶךְ הָעוֹלָם, אֲשֶׁר יָצַר אֶת־הָאָדָם
בְּחָכְמָה, וּבָרָא בוֹ נְקָבִים נְקָבִים, חֲלוּלִים חֲלוּלִים. גָּלוּי
וְיָדוּעַ לִפְנֵי כִסֵּא כְבוֹדֶךָ, שֶׁאִם יִפָּתֵחַ אֶחָד מֵהֶם, אוֹ
יִסָּתֵם אֶחָד מֵהֶם, אִי אֶפְשָׁר לְהִתְקַיֵּם וְלַעֲמוֹד לְפָנֶיךָ.
בָּרוּךְ אַתָּה יְיָ, רוֹפֵא כָל־בָּשָׂר וּמַפְלִיא לַעֲשׂוֹת.

*We praise You, Eternal God, Sovereign of the universe. With divine wisdom You have made our bodies, combining veins, arteries, and vital organs into a finely balanced network.*

*Were one of them to fail, O wondrous Maker and Sustainer of life, —how well we are aware!—we would lack the strength to stand in life before You.*

*Source of our health and strength, we give You thanks and praise.*

FOR TORAH            לעסוק בדברי תורה

בָּרוּךְ אַתָּה יְיָ, אֱלֹהֵינוּ מֶלֶךְ הָעוֹלָם, אֲשֶׁר קִדְּשָׁנוּ בְּמִצְוֹתָיו
וְצִוָּנוּ לַעֲסוֹק בְּדִבְרֵי תוֹרָה.

We praise You, Eternal God, Sovereign of the universe: You hallow us with the gift of Torah and command us to immerse ourselves in its words.

*Eternal our God, make the words of Your Torah sweet to us, and to the House of Israel, Your people, that we and our children may be lovers of Your name and students of Your Torah. We praise You, O God, Teacher of Torah to Your people Israel.*

12

These are duties whose worth cannot be measured:

*honoring one's father and mother,*

*acts of love and kindness,*

*diligent pursuit of knowledge and wisdom,*

*hospitality to strangers,*

*visiting the sick,*

*celebrating with bride and groom,*

*consoling the bereaved,*

*praying with sincerity,*

*and making peace where there is strife.*

*And the study of Torah leads to them all.*

אֵלּוּ דְבָרִים שֶׁאֵין לָהֶם שִׁעוּר:

כִּבּוּד אָב וָאֵם,

וּגְמִילוּת חֲסָדִים,

וְהַשְׁכָּמַת בֵּית הַמִּדְרָשׁ

שַׁחֲרִית וְעַרְבִית,

וְהַכְנָסַת אוֹרְחִים,

וּבִקּוּר חוֹלִים,

וְהַכְנָסַת כַּלָּה,

וּלְוָיַת הַמֵּת,

וְעִיּוּן תְּפִלָּה,

וַהֲבָאַת שָׁלוֹם בֵּין אָדָם

לַחֲבֵרוֹ.

וְתַלְמוּד תּוֹרָה כְּנֶגֶד כֻּלָּם.

FOR THE SOUL          אלהי נשמה

אֱלֹהַי, נְשָׁמָה שֶׁנָּתַתָּ בִּי טְהוֹרָה הִיא! אַתָּה בְרָאתָהּ, אַתָּה
יְצַרְתָּהּ, אַתָּה נְפַחְתָּהּ בִּי, וְאַתָּה מְשַׁמְּרָהּ בְּקִרְבִּי. כָּל־זְמַן
שֶׁהַנְּשָׁמָה בְקִרְבִּי, מוֹדֶה אֲנִי לְפָנֶיךָ, יְיָ אֱלֹהַי וֵאלֹהֵי אֲבוֹתַי
וְאִמּוֹתַי, רִבּוֹן כָּל־הַמַּעֲשִׂים, אֲדוֹן כָּל־הַנְּשָׁמוֹת.
בָּרוּךְ אַתָּה יְיָ, אֲשֶׁר בְּיָדוֹ נֶפֶשׁ כָּל־חָי וְרוּחַ כָּל־בְּשַׂר־אִישׁ.

The soul that You have given me, O God, is pure! You created and formed it, breathed it into me, and within me You sustain it. So long as I have breath, therefore, I will give thanks to You, my God and the God of all ages, Source of all being, loving Guide of every human spirit.

13

We praise You, O God, in whose hands are the souls of all the living and the spirits of all flesh.

FOR OUR BLESSINGS נסים בכל יום

בָּרוּךְ אַתָּה יְיָ, אֱלֹהֵינוּ מֶלֶךְ הָעוֹלָם,

אֲשֶׁר נָתַן לַשֶּׂכְוִי בִינָה לְהַבְחִין בֵּין יוֹם וּבֵין לָיְלָה.

*Praised be the Eternal God, who has implanted mind and instinct within every living being.*

בָּרוּךְ אַתָּה יְיָ, אֱלֹהֵינוּ מֶלֶךְ הָעוֹלָם, שֶׁעָשַׂנִי יִשְׂרָאֵל.

*Praised be the Eternal God, who has made me a Jew.*

בָּרוּךְ אַתָּה יְיָ, אֱלֹהֵינוּ מֶלֶךְ הָעוֹלָם, שֶׁעָשַׂנִי בֶּן חוֹרִין.

*Praised be the Eternal God, who has made me to be free.*

בָּרוּךְ אַתָּה יְיָ, אֱלֹהֵינוּ מֶלֶךְ הָעוֹלָם, פּוֹקֵחַ עִוְרִים.

*Praised be the Eternal God, who helps the blind to see.*

בָּרוּךְ אַתָּה יְיָ, אֱלֹהֵינוּ מֶלֶךְ הָעוֹלָם, מַלְבִּישׁ עֲרֻמִּים.

*Praised be the Eternal God, who clothes the naked.*

בָּרוּךְ אַתָּה יְיָ, אֱלֹהֵינוּ מֶלֶךְ הָעוֹלָם, מַתִּיר אֲסוּרִים.

*Praised be the Eternal God, who frees the captive.*

בָּרוּךְ אַתָּה יְיָ, אֱלֹהֵינוּ מֶלֶךְ הָעוֹלָם, זוֹקֵף כְּפוּפִים.

*Praised be the Eternal God, who lifts up the fallen.*

בָּרוּךְ אַתָּה יְיָ, אֱלֹהֵינוּ מֶלֶךְ הָעוֹלָם, הַמֵּכִין מִצְעֲדֵי־גָבֶר.

*Praised be the Eternal God, who makes firm our steps.*

בָּרוּךְ אַתָּה יְיָ, אֱלֹהֵינוּ מֶלֶךְ הָעוֹלָם, אוֹזֵר יִשְׂרָאֵל בִּגְבוּרָה.

*Praised be the Eternal God, who girds our people Israel with strength.*

14

בָּרוּךְ אַתָּה יְיָ, אֱלֹהֵינוּ מֶלֶךְ הָעוֹלָם, עוֹטֵר יִשְׂרָאֵל בְּתִפְאָרָה.

*Praised be the Eternal God, who crowns Israel with glory.*

בָּרוּךְ אַתָּה יְיָ, אֱלֹהֵינוּ מֶלֶךְ הָעוֹלָם, הַנּוֹתֵן לַיָּעֵף כֹּחַ.

*Praised be the Eternal God, who gives strength to the weary.*

בָּרוּךְ אַתָּה יְיָ, אֱלֹהֵינוּ מֶלֶךְ הָעוֹלָם, הַמַּעֲבִיר שֵׁנָה מֵעֵינַי
וּתְנוּמָה מֵעַפְעַפָּי.

*Praised be the Eternal God, who removes sleep from the eyes, slumber from the eyelids.*

FOR CONSCIENCE                                           תורה ומצוות

יְהִי רָצוֹן מִלְּפָנֶיךָ, יְיָ אֱלֹהֵינוּ וֵאלֹהֵי אֲבוֹתֵינוּ, שֶׁתַּרְגִּילֵנוּ
בְּתוֹרָתֶךָ, וְדַבְּקֵנוּ בְּמִצְוֹתֶיךָ, וְאַל תְּבִיאֵנוּ לֹא לִידֵי חֵטְא,
וְלֹא לִידֵי עֲבֵרָה וְעָוֹן, וְלֹא לִידֵי נִסָּיוֹן, וְלֹא לִידֵי בִזָּיוֹן,
וְאַל תַּשְׁלֶט־בָּנוּ יֵצֶר הָרָע, וְהַרְחִיקֵנוּ מֵאָדָם רָע וּמֵחָבֵר
רָע, וְדַבְּקֵנוּ בְּיֵצֶר הַטּוֹב וּבְמַעֲשִׂים טוֹבִים, וְכֹף אֶת־
יִצְרֵנוּ לְהִשְׁתַּעְבֶּד־לָךְ, וּתְנֵנוּ הַיּוֹם וּבְכָל־יוֹם לְחֵן וּלְחֶסֶד
וּלְרַחֲמִים בְּעֵינֶיךָ וּבְעֵינֵי כָל־רוֹאֵינוּ, וְתִגְמְלֵנוּ חֲסָדִים
טוֹבִים.

בָּרוּךְ אַתָּה יְיָ, גּוֹמֵל חֲסָדִים טוֹבִים לְעַמּוֹ יִשְׂרָאֵל.

Eternal One, our God and God of all ages, school us in Your Torah and bind us to Your Mitzvot.

Help us to keep far from sin, to master temptation, and to avoid falling under its spell. May our darker passions not rule us, nor evil companions lead us astray.

*Strengthen in us the voice of conscience; prompt us to deeds of goodness; and bend our every impulse to Your service, so that this day and always we may know Your love and the*

15

*good will of all who behold us. We praise You, O God: You bestow love and kindness on Your people Israel.*

~ ~

At all times revere God inwardly as well as outwardly, acknowledge the truth and speak it in your heart.

All rise

READER'S KADDISH                                         חֲצִי קַדִּישׁ

יִתְגַּדַּל וְיִתְקַדַּשׁ שְׁמֵהּ רַבָּא בְּעָלְמָא דִי־בְרָא כִרְעוּתֵהּ,
וְיַמְלִיךְ מַלְכוּתֵהּ בְּחַיֵּיכוֹן וּבְיוֹמֵיכוֹן וּבְחַיֵּי דְכָל־בֵּית
יִשְׂרָאֵל, בַּעֲגָלָא וּבִזְמַן קָרִיב, וְאִמְרוּ: אָמֵן.

יְהֵא שְׁמֵהּ רַבָּא מְבָרַךְ לְעָלַם וּלְעָלְמֵי עָלְמַיָּא.

יִתְבָּרַךְ וְיִשְׁתַּבַּח, וְיִתְפָּאַר וְיִתְרוֹמַם וְיִתְנַשֵּׂא, וְיִתְהַדָּר
וְיִתְעַלֶּה וְיִתְהַלָּל שְׁמֵהּ דְּקוּדְשָׁא, בְּרִיךְ הוּא,
לְעֵלָּא מִן־כָּל־בִּרְכָתָא וְשִׁירָתָא, תֻּשְׁבְּחָתָא וְנֶחֱמָתָא
דַּאֲמִירָן בְּעָלְמָא, וְאִמְרוּ: אָמֵן.

Yit-ga-dal v'yit–ka–dash sh'mei ra-ba b'al-ma di-v'ra chi-r'u'tei, v'yam-lich mal-chu-tei b'cha-yei-chon u-v'yo-mei-chon u-v'cha-yei d'chol beit Yis-ra-eil, ba-a-ga-la u-vi-z'man ka-riv, v'i-m' ru: A-mein.

Y'hei sh'mei ra-ba m'va-rach l'a-lam u-l'al-mei al-ma-ya.

Yit-ba-rach v'yish-ta-bach, v'yit-pa-ar v'yit-ro-mam v'yit-na-sei, v'yit-ha-dar v'yit-a-leh v'yit-ha-lal sh'mei d'kud-sha, b'rich hu,

l'ei-la min kol bir-cha-ta v'shi-ra-ta, tush-b'cha-ta v'neh-cheh-ma-ta da-a-mi-ran b'al-ma, v'i-m' ru: A-mein.

16

The Sh'ma and its Blessings                                שמע וברכותיה

בָּרְכוּ אֶת־יְיָ הַמְבֹרָךְ!

Praise the One to whom our praise is due!

בָּרוּךְ יְיָ הַמְבֹרָךְ לְעוֹלָם וָעֶד!

*Ba-ruch Adonai ha-m'vo-rach l'o-lam va-ed!*

*Praised be the One to whom our praise is due, now and for ever!*

CREATION                                                            יוצר

בָּרוּךְ אַתָּה יְיָ, אֱלֹהֵינוּ מֶלֶךְ הָעוֹלָם, יוֹצֵר אוֹר וּבוֹרֵא חֹשֶׁךְ,
עֹשֶׂה שָׁלוֹם וּבוֹרֵא אֶת־הַכֹּל. הַמֵּאִיר לָאָרֶץ וְלַדָּרִים
עָלֶיהָ בְּרַחֲמִים, וּבְטוּבוֹ מְחַדֵּשׁ בְּכָל־יוֹם תָּמִיד מַעֲשֵׂה
בְרֵאשִׁית. מָה רַבּוּ מַעֲשֶׂיךָ, יְיָ! כֻּלָּם בְּחָכְמָה עָשִׂיתָ,
מָלְאָה הָאָרֶץ קִנְיָנֶךָ. תִּתְבָּרַךְ, יְיָ אֱלֹהֵינוּ, עַל־שֶׁבַח מַעֲשֵׂה יָדֶיךָ,
וְעַל־מְאוֹרֵי־אוֹר שֶׁעָשִׂיתָ: יְפָאֲרוּךָ. סֶלָה
בָּרוּךְ אַתָּה יְיָ, יוֹצֵר הַמְּאוֹרוֹת.

• We praise You, Eternal God, Sovereign of the universe.
Your mercy makes light to shine over the earth and all its
inhabitants, and Your goodness renews day by day the work
of creation.

*How manifold are Your works, O God! In wisdom You have
made them all. The heavens declare Your glory. The earth
reveals Your creative power. You form light and darkness, bring
harmony into nature, and peace to the human heart.*

*We praise You, O God, Creator of light.*

אַהֲבָה רַבָּה אֲהַבְתָּנוּ, יי אֱלֹהֵינוּ, חֶמְלָה גְדוֹלָה וִיתֵרָה חָמַלְתָּ
עָלֵינוּ. אָבִינוּ מַלְכֵּנוּ, בַּעֲבוּר אֲבוֹתֵינוּ וְאִמּוֹתֵינוּ שֶׁבָּטְחוּ בְךָ
וַתְּלַמְּדֵם חֻקֵּי חַיִּים, כֵּן תְּחָנֵּנוּ וּתְלַמְּדֵנוּ. אָבִינוּ, הָאָב הָרַחֲמָן,
הַמְרַחֵם, רַחֵם עָלֵינוּ וְתֵן בְּלִבֵּנוּ לְהָבִין וּלְהַשְׂכִּיל, לִשְׁמֹעַ,
לִלְמֹד וּלְלַמֵּד, לִשְׁמֹר וְלַעֲשׂוֹת וּלְקַיֵּם אֶת־כָּל־דִּבְרֵי תַלְמוּד
תוֹרָתֶךָ בְּאַהֲבָה. וְהָאֵר עֵינֵינוּ בְּתוֹרָתֶךָ, וְדַבֵּק לִבֵּנוּ בְּמִצְוֹתֶיךָ,
וְיַחֵד לְבָבֵנוּ לְאַהֲבָה וּלְיִרְאָה אֶת־שְׁמֶךָ. וְלֹא־נֵבוֹשׁ לְעוֹלָם וָעֶד,
כִּי בְשֵׁם קָדְשְׁךָ הַגָּדוֹל וְהַנּוֹרָא בָּטָחְנוּ. נָגִילָה וְנִשְׂמְחָה
בִּישׁוּעָתֶךָ, כִּי אֵל פּוֹעֵל יְשׁוּעוֹת אָתָּה, וּבָנוּ בָחַרְתָּ וְקֵרַבְתָּנוּ
לְשִׁמְךָ הַגָּדוֹל סֶלָה בֶּאֱמֶת, לְהוֹדוֹת לְךָ וּלְיַחֶדְךָ בְּאַהֲבָה.
בָּרוּךְ אַתָּה יי, הַבּוֹחֵר בְּעַמּוֹ יִשְׂרָאֵל בְּאַהֲבָה.

• *Deep is Your love for us, abiding Your compassion. From of old we have put our trust in You, and You have taught us the laws of life. Be gracious now to us, that we may understand and fulfill the teachings of Your word.*

*Enlighten our eyes in Your Torah, that we may cling to Your Mitzvot. Unite our hearts to love and revere Your name.*

*We trust in You and rejoice in Your saving power, for You are the Source of our help. You have called us and drawn us near to You in faithfulness.*

*Joyfully we lift up our voices and proclaim Your unity, O God. In love, You have called us to Your service.*

שְׁמַע יִשְׂרָאֵל: יהוה אֱלֹהֵינוּ, יהוה אֶחָד!

Sh'ma Yis-ra-el: Adonai Eh-lo-hei-nu, Adonai Eh-chad!

*Hear, O Israel: the Eternal One is our God,*
*the Eternal God alone!*

בָּרוּךְ שֵׁם כְּבוֹד מַלְכוּתוֹ לְעוֹלָם וָעֶד!

Ba-ruch shem k'vod mal-chu-to l'o-lam va–ed!

*Blessed is God's glorious majesty for ever and ever!*

## All are seated

וְאָהַבְתָּ אֵת יְהֹוָה אֱלֹהֶיךָ בְּכָל־לְבָבְךָ וּבְכָל־נַפְשְׁךָ וּבְכָל־מְאֹדֶךָ:
וְהָיוּ הַדְּבָרִים הָאֵלֶּה אֲשֶׁר אָנֹכִי מְצַוְּךָ הַיּוֹם עַל־לְבָבֶךָ:
וְשִׁנַּנְתָּם לְבָנֶיךָ וְדִבַּרְתָּ בָּם בְּשִׁבְתְּךָ בְּבֵיתֶךָ וּבְלֶכְתְּךָ בַדֶּרֶךְ
וּבְשָׁכְבְּךָ וּבְקוּמֶךָ: וּקְשַׁרְתָּם לְאוֹת עַל־יָדֶךָ וְהָיוּ לְטֹטָפֹת בֵּין
עֵינֶיךָ: וּכְתַבְתָּם עַל־מְזוּזֹת בֵּיתֶךָ וּבִשְׁעָרֶיךָ:
לְמַעַן תִּזְכְּרוּ וַעֲשִׂיתֶם אֶת־כָּל־מִצְוֹתָי וִהְיִיתֶם קְדֹשִׁים
לֵאלֹהֵיכֶם: אֲנִי יְהֹוָה אֱלֹהֵיכֶם אֲשֶׁר הוֹצֵאתִי אֶתְכֶם
מֵאֶרֶץ מִצְרַיִם לִהְיוֹת לָכֶם לֵאלֹהִים אֲנִי יְהֹוָה אֱלֹהֵיכֶם:

V'a–hav–ta et Adonai Eh–lo–heh–cha b'chol l'va–v'cha u–v'chol naf–sh'cha u–v'chol m'o–deh–cha. V'ha–yu ha–d'va–rim ha–ei–leh a–sher a–no–chi m'tza–v'cha ha–yom al l'va–veh–cha. V'shi–nan–tam l'va–neh–cha v'di–bar–ta bam b'shiv–t'cha b'vei–teh–cha u–v'lech–t'cha va–deh–rech u–v'shoch–b'cha u–v'ku–meh–cha. U–k'shar–tam l'ot al ya–deh–cha v'ha–yu l'to–ta–fot bein ei–neh–cha; u–ch'tav–tam al m'zu–zot bei–teh–cha u–vi–sh'a–reh–cha.

L'ma–an tiz–k'ru va–a–si–tem et kol mitz–vo–tai, vi–h'yi–tem k'do–shim lei–lo–hei–chem. Ani Adonai Eh–lo–hei–chem a–sher ho–tzei–ti et–chem mei–eh–retz mitz–ra–yim li–h'yot la–chem lei–lo–him. Ani Adonai Eh–lo–hei–chem.

*You shall love your Eternal God with all your heart, with all your mind, with all your being. Set these words, which I command you this day, upon your heart. Teach them faithfully to your children; speak of them in your home and on your*

19

*way, when you lie down and when you rise up. Bind them as a sign upon your hand; let them be symbols before your eyes; inscribe them on the doorposts of your house, and on your gates.*

*Be mindful of all My Mitzvot, and do them: so shall you consecrate yourselves to your God. I am your Eternal God who led you out of Egypt to be your God; I am your Eternal God.*

REDEMPTION                                                    גְּאוּלָה

אֱמֶת וְיַצִּיב וְיָשָׁר וְקַיָּם וְטוֹב וְיָפֶה הַדָּבָר הַזֶּה עָלֵינוּ לְעוֹלָם
וָעֶד. אֱמֶת שָׁאַתָּה הוּא יי אֱלֹהֵינוּ וֵאלֹהֵי אֲבוֹתֵינוּ וְאִמּוֹתֵינוּ,
יוֹצְרֵנוּ צוּר יְשׁוּעָתֵנוּ, פּוֹדֵנוּ וּמַצִּילֵנוּ מֵעוֹלָם הוּא שְׁמֶךָ, אֵין
אֱלֹהִים זוּלָתֶךָ. אֱמֶת אַתָּה הוּא רִאשׁוֹן וְאַתָּה הוּא אַחֲרוֹן,
וּמִבַּלְעָדֶיךָ אֵין לָנוּ מוֹשִׁיעַ. מִמִּצְרַיִם גְּאַלְתָּנוּ, יי אֱלֹהֵינוּ,
וּמִבֵּית עֲבָדִים פְּדִיתָנוּ. מֹשֶׁה וּמִרְיָם וּבְנֵי יִשְׂרָאֵל לְךָ עָנוּ
שִׁירָה בְּשִׂמְחָה רַבָּה, וְאָמְרוּ כֻלָּם:

• Eternal truth it is that You alone are God,
and there is none else.
*May all the world rejoice in Your love*
*and exult in Your justice.*

Let them beat their swords into plowshares;
*let them beat their spears into pruning–hooks.*

Let nation not lift up sword against nation;
let them study war no more.
*You shall not hate another in your heart;*
*you shall love your neighbor as yourself.*

Let the stranger in your midst be to you as the native;
for you were strangers in the land of Egypt.
*From the house of bondage we went forth to freedom,*
*so let all be free to sing with joy:*

20

מִי־כָמְכָה בָּאֵלִם, יהוה? מִי כָּמְכָה, נֶאְדָּר בַּקֹּדֶשׁ,
נוֹרָא תְהִלֹת, עֹשֵׂה פֶלֶא?
שִׁירָה חֲדָשָׁה שִׁבְּחוּ גְאוּלִים לְשִׁמְךָ עַל־שְׂפַת הַיָּם;
יַחַד כֻּלָּם הוֹדוּ וְהִמְלִיכוּ וְאָמְרוּ:
יהוה יִמְלֹךְ לְעֹלָם וָעֶד.

Mi cha–mo–cha ba–ei–lim, Adonai? Mi ka–mo–cha, neh–dar ba–ko–desh,
no–ra t'hi–lot, o–sei feh–leh?
Shi–ra cha–da–sha shi–b'chu g'u–lim l'shi–m'cha al s'fat ha–yam;
ya–chad ku–lam ho–du v'him–li–chu v'a–m'ru:
Adonai Yim–loch l'o–lam va–ed!

צוּר יִשְׂרָאֵל, קוּמָה בְּעֶזְרַת יִשְׂרָאֵל,
וּפְדֵה כִנְאֻמֶךָ יְהוּדָה וְיִשְׂרָאֵל.
גֹּאֲלֵנוּ, יי צְבָאוֹת שְׁמוֹ, קְדוֹשׁ יִשְׂרָאֵל.
בָּרוּךְ אַתָּה יי, גָּאַל יִשְׂרָאֵל.

Tzur Yis-ra-eil, ku-mah b'ez-rat Yis-ra-eil,
u-f'dei ki-n'u-meh-cha Y'hu-da v'yis-ra-eil.
Go-a-lei-nu, Adonai Tz'va-ot sh'mo, k'dosh Yis-ra-eil.
Ba-ruch a-ta Adonai, ga-al Yis-ra-eil.

Who is like You, Eternal One, among the gods that are worshipped?
Who is like You, majestic in holiness, awesome in splendor, doing
wonders?

A new song the redeemed sang to Your name. At the shore of the sea,
saved from destruction, they proclaimed Your sovereign power: "The
Eternal One will reign for ever and ever!"

O Rock of Israel, come to Israel's help. Our Redeemer is God Most
High, the Holy One of Israel. We praise You, O God, Redeemer of Israel.

21

## All rise

אֲדֹנָי, שְׂפָתַי תִּפְתָּח, וּפִי יַגִּיד תְּהִלָּתֶךָ.

Eternal God, open my lips, that my mouth may declare Your glory.

GOD OF ALL GENERATIONS         אבות ואמהות

בָּרוּךְ אַתָּה יי, אֱלֹהֵינוּ וֵאלֹהֵי אֲבוֹתֵינוּ וְאִמּוֹתֵינוּ:
אֱלֹהֵי אַבְרָהָם, אֱלֹהֵי יִצְחָק, וֵאלֹהֵי יַעֲקֹב.
אֱלֹהֵי שָׂרָה, אֱלֹהֵי רִבְקָה, אֱלֹהֵי לֵאָה וֵאלֹהֵי רָחֵל.
הָאֵל הַגָּדוֹל הַגִּבּוֹר וְהַנּוֹרָא, אֵל עֶלְיוֹן, גּוֹמֵל חֲסָדִים
טוֹבִים וְקוֹנֵה הַכֹּל, וְזוֹכֵר חַסְדֵי אָבוֹת וְאִמָּהוֹת,
וּמֵבִיא גְאֻלָּה לִבְנֵי בְנֵיהֶם, לְמַעַן שְׁמוֹ בְּאַהֲבָה.

BETWEEN ROSH HASHANAH AND YOM KIPPUR ADD:

זָכְרֵנוּ לְחַיִּים, מֶלֶךְ חָפֵץ בַּחַיִּים,
וְכָתְבֵנוּ בְּסֵפֶר הַחַיִּים, לְמַעַנְךָ אֱלֹהִים חַיִּים.

מֶלֶךְ עוֹזֵר וּמוֹשִׁיעַ וּמָגֵן.
בָּרוּךְ אַתָּה יי, מָגֵן אַבְרָהָם וְעֶזְרַת שָׂרָה.

Ba–ruch a–ta Adonai, Eh–lo–hei–nu vei–lo–hei a–vo–tei–nu v'i–mo–tei–nu:
Eh–lo–hei Av–ra–ham, eh–lo–hei Yitz–chak, vei–lo–hei Ya–a–kov.
Eh–lo–hei Sa–ra, Eh–lo–hei Riv–ka, Eh–lo–hei Lei–a vei–lo–hei Ra–cheil.
Ha–eil ha–ga–dol ha–gi–bor v'ha–no–ra, Eil el–yon, go–meil cha–sa–dim
to–vim, v'ko–nei ha–kol, v'zo–cheir cha–s'dei a–vot v'i–ma–hot,
u–mei–vi g'u–la  li–v'nei v'nei–hem, l'ma–an sh'mo, b'a–ha–va.
Meh–lech o–zeir u–mo–shi–a u–ma–gein.
Ba–ruch a–ta Adonai, ma–gein Av–ra–ham v'ez–rat Sa–ra.

Praised be our God, the God of our fathers and our mothers:
God of Abraham, God of Isaac, and God of Jacob; God of Sarah,

22

God of Rebekah, God of Leah and God of Rachel; great, mighty, and awesome, God supreme.

Ruler of all the living, Your ways are ways of love. You remember the faithfulness of our ancestors, and in love bring redemption to their children's children for the sake of Your name.

> BETWEEN ROSH HASHANAH AND YOM KIPPUR ADD:
> Remember us unto life, Sovereign who delights in life, and inscribe us in the Book of Life, that Your will may prevail, O God of life.

You are our Sovereign and our Help, our Redeemer and our Shield. We praise You, Eternal One, Shield of Abraham, Protector of Sarah.

GOD'S POWER

גְּבוּרוֹת

אַתָּה גִּבּוֹר לְעוֹלָם, אֲדֹנָי, מְחַיֵּה הַכֹּל אַתָּה, רַב לְהוֹשִׁיעַ.
מְכַלְכֵּל חַיִּים בְּחֶסֶד, מְחַיֵּה הַכֹּל בְּרַחֲמִים רַבִּים. סוֹמֵךְ
נוֹפְלִים, וְרוֹפֵא חוֹלִים, וּמַתִּיר אֲסוּרִים, וּמְקַיֵּם אֱמוּנָתוֹ
לִישֵׁנֵי עָפָר. מִי כָמְוֹךָ בַּעַל גְּבוּרוֹת, וּמִי דְּוֹמֶה לָּךְ,
מֶלֶךְ מֵמִית וּמְחַיֶּה וּמַצְמִיחַ יְשׁוּעָה?

> BETWEEN ROSH HASHANAH AND YOM KIPPUR ADD:
> מִי כָמְוֹךָ, אַב הָרַחֲמִים, זוֹכֵר יְצוּרָיו לְחַיִּים בְּרַחֲמִים?

וְנֶאֱמָן אַתָּה לְהַחֲיוֹת הַכֹּל. בָּרוּךְ אַתָּה יי, מְחַיֵּה הַכֹּל.

A–ta gi–bor l'o–lam, Adonai, m'cha–yei ha–kol a–ta, rav l'ho–shi–a.
M'chal–keil cha–yim b'cheh–sed, m'cha–yei ha–kol b'ra–cha–mim ra–bim.
So–meich no–f'lim, v'ro–fei cho–lim, u–ma–tir a–su–rim, u–m'ka–yeim eh–mu–na–to li–shei–nei a–far. Mi cha–mo–cha ba–al g'vu–rot, u–mi do–meh lach, meh–lech mei–mit u–m'cha–yeh u–matz–mi–ach y'shu–a?
V'neh–eh–man a–ta l'ha–cha–yot ha–kol. Ba–ruch a–ta Adonai, m'cha–yei ha–kol.

23

*Eternal is Your might, O God; all life is Your gift; great is Your power to save!*

*With love You sustain the living, with great compassion give life to all. You send help to the falling and healing to the sick; You bring freedom to the captive and keep faith with those who sleep in the dust.*

*Who is like You, Mighty One, Author of life and death, Source of salvation?*

BETWEEN ROSH HASHANAH AND YOM KIPPUR ADD:

*Who is like You, Source of mercy? In compassion You sustain the life of Your children.*

*We praise You, O God, the Source of life.*

FOR AN EVENING SERVICE

THE HOLINESS OF GOD                                    קְדוּשַׁת הַשֵּׁם

אַתָּה קָדוֹשׁ וְשִׁמְךָ קָדוֹשׁ, וּקְדוֹשִׁים בְּכָל־יוֹם יְהַלְלוּךָ, סֶּלָה.
\* בָּרוּךְ אַתָּה יי, הָאֵל הַקָּדוֹשׁ.

\*   BETWEEN ROSH HASHANAH AND YOM KIPPUR CONCLUDE:

בָּרוּךְ אַתָּה יי, הַמֶּלֶךְ הַקָּדוֹשׁ.

You are holy, Your name is holy, and those who strive to be holy declare Your glory day by day.
\* We praise You, Eternal One, the holy God.

\*   BETWEEN ROSH HASHANAH AND YOM KIPPUR CONCLUDE:

We praise You, Eternal One: You rule in holiness.

## All are seated

We continue on page 26

24

## FOR A MORNING OR AFTERNOON SERVICE

SANCTIFICATION                קְדוּשָׁה

נְקַדֵּשׁ אֶת־שִׁמְךָ בָּעוֹלָם, כְּשֵׁם שֶׁמַּקְדִּישִׁים אוֹתוֹ בִּשְׁמֵי מָרוֹם,

כַּכָּתוּב עַל־יַד נְבִיאֶךָ: וְקָרָא זֶה אֶל־זֶה וְאָמַר:

We sanctify Your name on earth, even as all things, to the ends
of time and space, proclaim Your holiness, and in the words of
the prophet we say:

קָדוֹשׁ, קָדוֹשׁ, קָדוֹשׁ יהוה צְבָאוֹת, מְלֹא כָל־הָאָרֶץ כְּבוֹדוֹ.

Ka–dosh, Ka–dosh, Ka–dosh Adonai tz'va–ot, m'lo chol ha–a–retz k'vo–do.

*Holy, Holy, Holy is the God of all being! The whole earth is
filled with Your glory!*

לְעֻמָּתָם בָּרוּךְ יֹאמֵרוּ:

All being recounts Your praise:

בָּרוּךְ כְּבוֹד־יהוה מִמְּקוֹמוֹ!

Ba–ruch k'vod Adonai mi-m'ko-mo.

*Praised be the glory of God in heaven and earth.*

וּבְדִבְרֵי קָדְשְׁךָ כָּתוּב לֵאמֹר:

And this is Your sacred word:

יִמְלֹךְ יהוה לְעוֹלָם, אֱלֹהַיִךְ צִיּוֹן, לְדֹר וָדֹר. הַלְלוּיָהּ!

Yim–loch Adonai l'o–lam, Eh–lo–ha–yich tzi–yon, l'dor va–dor.
Halleluyah!

*The Eternal One shall reign for ever; your God, O Zion, from
generation to generation. Halleluyah!*

לְדוֹר וָדוֹר נַגִּיד גָּדְלֶךָ, וּלְנֵצַח נְצָחִים קְדֻשָּׁתְךָ נַקְדִּישׁ.
וְשִׁבְחֲךָ, אֱלֹהֵינוּ, מִפִּינוּ לֹא יָמוּשׁ לְעוֹלָם וָעֶד.
\* בָּרוּךְ אַתָּה יְיָ, הָאֵל הַקָּדוֹשׁ.

\* BETWEEN ROSH HASHANAH AND YOM KIPPUR CONCLUDE:

בָּרוּךְ אַתָּה יְיָ, הַמֶּלֶךְ הַקָּדוֹשׁ.

To all generations we will make known Your greatness, and to
all eternity proclaim Your holiness. Your praise, O God, shall
never depart from our lips.

\* We praise You, Eternal One, the holy God.

> \* BETWEEN ROSH HASHANAH AND YOM KIPPUR CONCLUDE:
> We praise You, Eternal One: You rule in holiness.

### All are seated

### FOR ALL SERVICES

(The Intermediate Benedictions, through
page 30, may be recited silently or together)

WISDOM          בינה

אַתָּה חוֹנֵן לְאָדָם דַּעַת וּמְלַמֵּד לֶאֱנוֹשׁ בִּינָה. חָנֵּנוּ מֵאִתְּךָ
דֵּעָה, בִּינָה וְהַשְׂכֵּל. בָּרוּךְ אַתָּה יְיָ, חוֹנֵן הַדָּעַת.

By Your grace we have the power to gain knowledge and to
learn wisdom. Favor us with knowledge, wisdom, and insight, for
You are their Source.

*We praise You, O God, gracious Giver of knowledge.*

REPENTANCE          תשובה

הֲשִׁיבֵנוּ אָבִינוּ לְתוֹרָתֶךָ, וְקָרְבֵנוּ מַלְכֵּנוּ לַעֲבוֹדָתֶךָ, וְהַחֲזִירֵנוּ
בִּתְשׁוּבָה שְׁלֵמָה לְפָנֶיךָ. בָּרוּךְ אַתָּה יְיָ, הָרוֹצֶה בִּתְשׁוּבָה.

26

Help us, our Creator, to return to Your Teaching; draw us near, our Sovereign, to Your service; and bring us back into Your presence in perfect repentance.

*We praise You, O God: You delight in repentance.*

FORGIVENESS                                                                    סליחה

סְלַח־לָנוּ אָבִינוּ כִּי חָטָאנוּ, מְחַל־לָנוּ מַלְכֵּנוּ כִּי פָשָׁעְנוּ, כִּי מוֹחֵל
וְסוֹלֵחַ אָתָּה. בָּרוּךְ אַתָּה יְיָ, חַנּוּן הַמַּרְבֶּה לִסְלוֹחַ.

Forgive us, our Creator for we have sinned; pardon us, our Sovereign, for we have transgressed; for You are One who pardons and forgives.

*We praise You, O God, gracious and quick to forgive.*

REDEMPTION                                                                  גאולה

רְאֵה בְעָנְיֵנוּ וְרִיבָה רִיבֵנוּ, וּגְאָלֵנוּ מְהֵרָה לְמַעַן שְׁמֶךָ,
כִּי גּוֹאֵל חָזָק אָתָּה. בָּרוּךְ אַתָּה יְיָ, גּוֹאֵל יִשְׂרָאֵל.

Look upon our affliction and help us in our need; O mighty Redeemer, redeem us speedily for Your name's sake.

*We praise You, O God, Redeemer of Israel.*

HEALTH                                                                      רפואה

רְפָאֵנוּ יְיָ וְנֵרָפֵא, הוֹשִׁיעֵנוּ וְנִוָּשֵׁעָה, וְהַעֲלֵה רְפוּאָה שְׁלֵמָה
לְכָל־מַכּוֹתֵינוּ. בָּרוּךְ אַתָּה יְיָ, רוֹפֵא הַחוֹלִים.

Heal us, O God, and we shall be healed; save us, and we shall be saved; grant us a perfect healing for all our infirmities.

(A personal prayer for one who is ill may be added here.)

*We praise You, O God, Healer of the sick.*

27

ABUNDANCE                                                    ברכת השנים

בָּרֵךְ עָלֵינוּ, יי אֱלֹהֵינוּ, אֶת־הַשָּׁנָה הַזֹּאת וְאֶת־כָּל־מִינֵי תְבוּאָתָהּ

לְטוֹבָה. וְתֵן בְּרָכָה עַל־פְּנֵי הָאֲדָמָה, וְשַׂבְּעֵנוּ מִטּוּבֶךָ.

בָּרוּךְ אַתָּה יי, מְבָרֵךְ הַשָּׁנִים.

Bless this year for us, Eternal God: may its produce bring us
well-being. Bestow Your blessing on the earth, that all Your
children may share its abundance in peace.

*We praise You, O God, for You bless earth's seasons from year*
*to year.*

FREEDOM                                                           חרות

תְּקַע בְּשׁוֹפָר גָּדוֹל לְחֵרוּתֵנוּ, וְשָׂא נֵס לִפְדוֹת עֲשׁוּקֵינוּ, וְקוֹל

דְּרוֹר יִשָּׁמַע בְּאַרְבַּע כַּנְפוֹת הָאָרֶץ.

בָּרוּךְ אַתָּה יי, פּוֹדֶה עֲשׁוּקִים.

Sound the great shofar to proclaim freedom, raise high the
banner of liberation for the oppressed, and let the song of liberty
be heard in the four corners of the earth.

*We praise You, O God, Redeemer of the oppressed.*

JUSTICE                                                         משפט

עַל שׁוֹפְטֵי אֶרֶץ שְׁפוֹךְ רוּחֶךָ, וְהַדְרִיכֵם בְּמִשְׁפְּטֵי צִדְקֶךָ,

וּמְלוֹךְ עָלֵינוּ אַתָּה לְבַדֶּךָ, בְּחֶסֶד וּבְרַחֲמִים.

בָּרוּךְ אַתָּה יי, מֶלֶךְ אוֹהֵב צְדָקָה וּמִשְׁפָּט.

Bestow your spirit upon the rulers of all lands; guide them that
they may govern justly. Thus shall love and compassion be
enthroned among us.

*We praise You, Eternal One, the Sovereign God who loves*
*righteousness and justice.*

28

ON EVIL · עַל הָרִשְׁעָה

וְלָרִשְׁעָה עַל־תְּהִי תִקְוָה, וְהַתּוֹעִים אֵלֶיךָ יָשׁוּבוּ, וּמַלְכוּת זָדוֹן
מְהֵרָה תְשַׁבֵּר. תַּקֵּן מַלְכוּתְךָ בְּתוֹכֵנוּ, בְּקָרוֹב בְּיָמֵינוּ לְעוֹלָם
וָעֶד. בָּרוּךְ אַתָּה יְיָ, הַמַּשְׁבִּית רֶשַׁע מִן־הָאָרֶץ.

Let the reign of evil afflict us no more. May every errant heart
find its way back to You. O help us to shatter the dominion of
arrogance, to raise up a better world where virtue will ennoble
the life of Your children.

We praise You, O God, whose will it is that evil may vanish
from the earth.

THE RIGHTEOUS · עַל הַצַּדִּיקִים

עַל־הַצַּדִּיקִים וְעַל־הַחֲסִידִים וְעַל גֵּרֵי הַצֶּדֶק וְעָלֵינוּ יֶהֱמוּ
רַחֲמֶיךָ, יְיָ אֱלֹהֵינוּ, וְתֵן שָׂכָר טוֹב לְכָל הַבּוֹטְחִים בְּשִׁמְךָ
בֶּאֱמֶת, וְשִׂים חֶלְקֵנוּ עִמָּהֶם לְעוֹלָם.
בָּרוּךְ אַתָּה יְיָ, מִשְׁעָן וּמִבְטָח לַצַּדִּיקִים.

For the righteous and faithful of all humankind, for all who
join their lives to ours, for all who put their trust in You, and for
all honest men and women, we ask Your favor, Eternal God.
Grant that we may always be numbered among them.

We praise You, O God, Staff and Support of the righteous.

JERUSALEM · בּוֹנֵה יְרוּשָׁלַיִם

שְׁכוֹן, יְיָ אֱלֹהֵינוּ, בְּתוֹךְ יְרוּשָׁלַיִם עִירֶךָ, וִיהִי שָׁלוֹם בִּשְׁעָרֶיהָ,
וְשַׁלְוָה בְּלֵב יוֹשְׁבֶיהָ, וְתוֹרָתְךָ מִצִּיּוֹן תֵּצֵא, וּדְבָרְךָ מִירוּשָׁלָיִם.
בָּרוּךְ אַתָּה יְיָ, בּוֹנֵה יְרוּשָׁלָיִם.

Let your presence be manifest in Jerusalem, Your city. Establish
peace in her gates and quietness in the hearts of all who dwell

29

there. Let Your Torah go forth from Zion, Your word from Jerusalem.

We praise You, O God, Builder of Jerusalem.

DELIVERANCE ישועה

אֶת־צֶמַח צְדָקָה מְהֵרָה תַצְמִיחַ, וְקֶרֶן יְשׁוּעָה תָּרוּם כִּנְאֻמֶךָ, כִּי לִישׁוּעָתְךָ קִוְּינוּ כָּל־הַיּוֹם. בָּרוּךְ אַתָּה יי, מַצְמִיחַ קֶרֶן יְשׁוּעָה.

Let the plant of righteousness blossom and flourish, and let the light of deliverance shine forth according to Your word: we await Your deliverance all the day.

We praise You, O God: You will cause the light of deliverance to dawn for all the world.

PRAYER שומע תפלה

שְׁמַע קוֹלֵנוּ, יי אֱלֹהֵינוּ, חוּס וְרַחֵם עָלֵינוּ, וְקַבֵּל בְּרַחֲמִים וּבְרָצוֹן אֶת־תְּפִלָּתֵנוּ, כִּי אֵל שׁוֹמֵעַ תְּפִלּוֹת וְתַחֲנוּנִים אָתָּה. בָּרוּךְ אַתָּה יי, שׁוֹמֵעַ תְּפִלָּה.

Hear our voice, Eternal God; have compassion upon us, and accept our prayer with favor and mercy, for You are a God who hears prayer and supplication.

We praise You, O God: You hearken to prayer.

(The Intermediate Benedictions end here.)

30

WORSHIP עבודה

רְצֵה, יְיָ אֱלֹהֵינוּ, בְּעַמְּךָ יִשְׂרָאֵל, וּתְפִלָּתָם בְּאַהֲבָה תְקַבֵּל, וּתְהִי לְרָצוֹן תָּמִיד עֲבוֹדַת יִשְׂרָאֵל עַמֶּךָ. אֵל קָרוֹב לְכָל־ קֹרְאָיו, פְּנֵה אֶל עֲבָדֶיךָ וְחָנֵּנוּ; שְׁפוֹךְ רוּחֲךָ עָלֵינוּ, וְתֶחֱזֶינָה עֵינֵינוּ בְּשׁוּבְךָ לְצִיּוֹן בְּרַחֲמִים. בָּרוּךְ אַתָּה יְיָ, הַמַּחֲזִיר שְׁכִינָתוֹ לְצִיּוֹן.

Be gracious, Eternal God, to Your people Israel, and receive our prayers with love. O may our worship always be acceptable to You.

*Fill us with the knowledge that You are near to all who seek You in truth. Let our eyes behold Your presence in our midst and in the midst of our people in Zion. We praise You, O God, whose presence gives life to Zion and all Israel.*

ON ROSH CHODESH AND CHOL HAMOEID :

אֱלֹהֵינוּ וֵאלֹהֵי אֲבוֹתֵינוּ וְאִמּוֹתֵינוּ, יַעֲלֶה וְיָבֹא וְיִזָּכֵר זִכְרוֹנֵנוּ וְזִכְרוֹן כָּל־עַמְּךָ בֵּית יִשְׂרָאֵל לְפָנֶיךָ לְטוֹבָה לְחֵן לְחֶסֶד וּלְרַחֲמִים, לְחַיִּים וּלְשָׁלוֹם בְּיוֹם

● רֹאשׁ הַחֹדֶשׁ הַזֶּה.

● חַג הַמַּצּוֹת הַזֶּה.

● חַג הַסֻּכּוֹת הַזֶּה.

● הָעַצְמָאוּת הַזֶּה.

| | |
|---|---|
| זָכְרֵנוּ, יְיָ אֱלֹהֵינוּ, בּוֹ לְטוֹבָה. | אָמֵן. |
| וּפָקְדֵנוּ בוֹ לִבְרָכָה. | אָמֵן. |
| וְהוֹשִׁיעֵנוּ בוֹ לְחַיִּים. | אָמֵן. |

Our God, God of our fathers and our mothers, be mindful of Your people Israel on this

• first day of the new month,

- festival of Pesach,
- festival of Sukkot,
- day of Independence,

and renew in us love and compassion, goodness, life, and peace.

This day remember us for well–being.     *Amen.*

This day bless us with Your nearness.     *Amen.*

This day help us to a fuller life.     *Amen.*

THANKSGIVING                                                   הוֹדָאָה

מוֹדִים אֲנַחְנוּ לָךְ, שָׁאַתָּה הוּא יי אֱלֹהֵינוּ וֵאלֹהֵי אֲבוֹתֵינוּ
וְאִמּוֹתֵינוּ לְעוֹלָם וָעֶד. צוּר חַיֵּינוּ, מָגֵן יִשְׁעֵנוּ, אַתָּה הוּא
לְדוֹר וָדוֹר. נוֹדֶה לְךָ וּנְסַפֵּר תְּהִלָּתֶךָ, עַל־חַיֵּינוּ הַמְּסוּרִים
בְּיָדֶךָ, וְעַל־נִשְׁמוֹתֵינוּ הַפְּקוּדוֹת לָךְ, וְעַל־נִסֶּיךָ שֶׁבְּכָל־יוֹם
עִמָּנוּ, וְעַל־נִפְלְאוֹתֶיךָ וְטוֹבוֹתֶיךָ שֶׁבְּכָל־עֵת, עֶרֶב וָבֹקֶר
וְצָהֳרָיִם. הַטּוֹב: כִּי לֹא־כָלוּ רַחֲמֶיךָ, וְהַמְרַחֵם: כִּי־לֹא תַמּוּ
חֲסָדֶיךָ, מֵעוֹלָם קִוִּינוּ לָךְ.
וְעַל כֻּלָּם יִתְבָּרַךְ וְיִתְרוֹמַם שִׁמְךָ, מַלְכֵּנוּ, תָּמִיד לְעוֹלָם וָעֶד.

BETWEEN ROSH HASHANAH AND YOM KIPPUR ADD:

וּכְתוֹב לְחַיִּים טוֹבִים כָּל־בְּנֵי בְרִיתֶךָ.

וְכֹל הַחַיִּים יוֹדוּךָ סֶּלָה, וִיהַלְלוּ אֶת־שִׁמְךָ בֶּאֱמֶת, הָאֵל
יְשׁוּעָתֵנוּ וְעֶזְרָתֵנוּ סֶלָה.

בָּרוּךְ אַתָּה יי, הַטּוֹב שִׁמְךָ וּלְךָ נָאֶה לְהוֹדוֹת.

We gratefully acknowledge that You are our God and the God
of our people, the God of all  generations. You are the Rock of our
life, the Power that shields us in every age.

*We thank You and sing Your praises: for our lives, which are
in Your hand; for our souls, which are in Your keeping; for the
signs of Your presence we encounter every day; and for Your*

*wondrous gifts at all times, morning, noon, and night. You are Goodness: Your mercies never end; You are Compassion: Your love will never fail. You have always been our hope.*

*For all these things, O Sovereign God, let Your name be for ever exalted and blessed.*

BETWEEN ROSH HASHANAH AND YOM KIPPUR ADD:

*Let life abundant be the heritage of all the children of Your covenant.*

*O God our Redeemer and Helper, let all who live affirm You and praise Your name in truth. Eternal God, whose nature is Goodness, we give You thanks and praise.*

ON CHANUKAH ADD:

עַל הַנִּסִּים, וְעַל הַפֻּרְקָן, וְעַל הַגְּבוּרוֹת, וְעַל הַתְּשׁוּעוֹת, וְעַל הַנֶּחָמוֹת שֶׁעָשִׂיתָ לַאֲבוֹתֵינוּ וּלְאִמּוֹתֵינוּ בַּיָּמִים הָהֵם וּבַזְּמַן הַזֶּה.

בִּימֵי מַתִּתְיָהוּ בֶּן־יוֹחָנָן כֹּהֵן גָּדוֹל, חַשְׁמוֹנַאי וּבָנָיו, כְּשֶׁעָמְדָה מַלְכוּת יָוָן הָרְשָׁעָה עַל עַמְּךָ יִשְׂרָאֵל, לְהַשְׁכִּיחָם תּוֹרָתֶךָ וּלְהַעֲבִירָם מֵחֻקֵּי רְצוֹנֶךָ. וְאַתָּה בְּרַחֲמֶיךָ הָרַבִּים עָמַדְתָּ לָהֶם בְּעֵת צָרָתָם. מַסְרְתָּ גִּבּוֹרִים בְּיַד חַלָּשִׁים, וְרַבִּים בְּיַד מְעַטִּים, וְזֵדִים בְּיַד עוֹסְקֵי תוֹרָתֶךָ. וּלְךָ עָשִׂיתָ שֵׁם גָּדוֹל וְקָדוֹשׁ בְּעוֹלָמֶךָ, וּלְעַמְּךָ יִשְׂרָאֵל עָשִׂיתָ תְּשׁוּעָה גְדוֹלָה וּפֻרְקָן כְּהַיּוֹם הַזֶּה. וְאַחַר כֵּן בָּאוּ בָנֶיךָ לִדְבִיר בֵּיתֶךָ, וּפִנּוּ אֶת־הֵיכָלֶךָ, וְטִהֲרוּ אֶת־מִקְדָּשֶׁךָ, וְהִדְלִיקוּ נֵרוֹת בְּחַצְרוֹת קָדְשֶׁךָ, וְקָבְעוּ שְׁמוֹנַת יְמֵי חֲנֻכָּה אֵלּוּ, לְהוֹדוֹת וּלְהַלֵּל לְשִׁמְךָ הַגָּדוֹל.

In days of old, at this season, You saved our people by wonders and mighty deeds. In the days of Mattathias the Hasmonean, the tyrannic Empire sought to destroy our people Israel by making them forget their Torah, and by forcing them to abandon their ancient way of life.

Through the power of Your spirit the weak defeated the strong, the few prevailed over the many, and the righteous were victorious. Then Your

33

children returned to Your House to purify the sanctuary and to kindle its lights.

And they dedicated these days to give thanks and praise to Your majestic glory.

ON PURIM ADD:

עַל הַנִּסִּים וְעַל הַפֻּרְקָן, וְעַל הַגְּבוּרוֹת וְעַל הַתְּשׁוּעוֹת, וְעַל הַמִּלְחָמוֹת שֶׁעָשִׂיתָ לַאֲבוֹתֵינוּ וּלְאִמּוֹתֵינוּ בַּיָּמִים הָהֵם וּבַזְּמַן הַזֶּה. בִּימֵי מָרְדְּכַי וְאֶסְתֵּר בְּשׁוּשַׁן הַבִּירָה, כְּשֶׁעָמַד עֲלֵיהֶם הָמָן הָרָשָׁע, בִּקֵּשׁ לְהַשְׁמִיד לַהֲרוֹג וּלְאַבֵּד אֶת־כָּל־הַיְּהוּדִים, מִנַּעַר וְעַד־זָקֵן, טַף וְנָשִׁים, בְּיוֹם אֶחָד, בִּשְׁלוֹשָׁה עָשָׂר לְחֹדֶשׁ שְׁנֵים־עָשָׂר, הוּא־ חֹדֶשׁ אֲדָר, וּשְׁלָלָם לָבוֹז. וְאַתָּה בְּרַחֲמֶיךָ הָרַבִּים הֵפַרְתָּ אֶת־ עֲצָתוֹ וְקִלְקַלְתָּ אֶת־מַחֲשַׁבְתּוֹ.

In days of old, at this season, You saved our people by wonders and mighty deeds.

In the days of Mordechai and Esther, the wicked Haman arose in Persia, plotting the destruction of all the Jews, young and old alike. He planned to destroy them in a single day, the thirteenth of Adar, and to plunder their possessions.

But through Your great mercy his plan was thwarted, his scheme frustrated. We therefore thank and bless You, the great and gracious God!

PEACE                                                 ברכת שלום

FOR AN EVENING SERVICE

שָׁלוֹם רָב עַל־יִשְׂרָאֵל עַמְּךָ תָּשִׂים לְעוֹלָם, כִּי אַתָּה הוּא מֶלֶךְ אָדוֹן לְכָל־הַשָּׁלוֹם. וְטוֹב בְּעֵינֶיךָ לְבָרֵךְ אֶת־עַמְּךָ יִשְׂרָאֵל וְאֶת־כָּל־הָעַמִּים בְּכָל־עֵת וּבְכָל־שָׁעָה בִּשְׁלוֹמֶךָ. * בָּרוּךְ אַתָּה יְיָ, הַמְבָרֵךְ אֶת־עַמּוֹ יִשְׂרָאֵל בַּשָּׁלוֹם.

34

* BETWEEN ROSH HASHANAH AND YOM KIPPUR CONCLUDE:

בְּסֵפֶר חַיִּים וּבְרָכָה נִכָּתֵב לְחַיִּים טוֹבִים וּלְשָׁלוֹם.

בָּרוּךְ אַתָּה יי, עוֹשֵׂה הַשָּׁלוֹם.

O Sovereign Source of peace, let Israel Your people know enduring peace, for it is good in Your sight to bless Israel and all peoples continually with Your peace.

* *We praise You, O God, for You bless Israel with peace.*

* BETWEEN ROSH HASHANAH AND YOM KIPPUR CONCLUDE:

*Inscribe us in the Book of life, blessing, and peace.*

*We praise You, O God, the Source of peace.*

Sha-lom rav al Yis-ra-eil a-m'cha ta-sim l'o-lam, ki a-ta hu meh-lech a-don l'chol ha-sha-lom. V'tov b'ei-neh-cha l'va-reich et a-m'cha Yis-ra-eil v'et kol ha-a-mim b'chol eit u-v'chol sha-a bi-sh'lo-meh-cha. Ba-ruch a-ta Adonai, ha-m'va-reich et a-mo Yis-ra-eil ba-sha-lom.

## We continue on page 36

### FOR A MORNING OR AFTERNOON SERVICE

שִׂים שָׁלוֹם, טוֹבָה וּבְרָכָה, חֵן וָחֶסֶד וְרַחֲמִים, עָלֵינוּ וְעַל כָּל־יִשְׂרָאֵל עַמֶּךָ. בָּרְכֵנוּ, אָבִינוּ, כֻּלָּנוּ כְּאֶחָד בְּאוֹר פָּנֶיךָ, כִּי בְאוֹר פָּנֶיךָ נָתַתָּ לָּנוּ, יי אֱלֹהֵינוּ, תּוֹרַת חַיִּים, וְאַהֲבַת חֶסֶד, וּצְדָקָה וּבְרָכָה וְרַחֲמִים וְחַיִּים וְשָׁלוֹם. וְטוֹב בְּעֵינֶיךָ לְבָרֵךְ אֶת־עַמְּךָ יִשְׂרָאֵל וְאֶת־כָּל־הָעַמִּים בְּכָל־עֵת וּבְכָל־שָׁעָה בִּשְׁלוֹמֶךָ.

* בָּרוּךְ אַתָּה יי, הַמְבָרֵךְ אֶת־עַמּוֹ יִשְׂרָאֵל בַּשָּׁלוֹם.

* BETWEEN ROSH HASHANAH AND YOM KIPPUR CONCLUDE:

בְּסֵפֶר חַיִּים וּבְרָכָה נִכָּתֵב לְחַיִּים טוֹבִים וּלְשָׁלוֹם.

בָּרוּךְ אַתָּה יי, עוֹשֶׂה הַשָּׁלוֹם.

Sim sha-lom, to-va u-v'ra-cha, chein va-cheh-sed v'ra-cha-mim, a-lei-nu v'al kol Yis-ra-eil a-meh-cha.

Ba-r'chei-nu, a-vi-nu, ku-la-nu k'eh-chad b'or pa-neh-cha, ki v'or pa-neh-cha na-ta-ta la-nu, Adonai Eh-lo-hei-nu, To-rat cha-yim, v'a-ha-vat cheh-sed, u-tz'da-ka u-v'ra-cha v'ra-cha-mim v'cha-yim v'sha-lom. V'tov b'ei-neh-cha l'va-reich et a-m'cha Yis-ra-eil v'et kol ha-a-mim b'chol eit u-v'chol sha-ah bi-sh'lo-meh-cha. Ba-ruch a-ta Adonai, ha-m'va-reich et a-mo Yis-ra-eil ba-sha-lom.

° Grant us peace, Your most precious gift, O Eternal Source of peace, and give us the will to proclaim its message to all the peoples of the earth.

Bless our country, that it may always be a stronghold of peace, and its advocate among the nations.

May contentment reign within its borders, health and happiness within its homes.

Strengthen the bonds of friendship among the inhabitants of all lands, and may the love of Your name hallow every home and every heart. We praise You, O God, the Source of peace. *

* BETWEEN ROSH HASHANAH AND YOM KIPPUR CONCLUDE:

Inscribe us in the Book of life, blessing, and peace.
We praise You, O God, the Source of peace.

### SILENT PRAYER

אֱלֹהַי, נְצֹר לְשׁוֹנִי מֵרָע, וּשְׂפָתַי מִדַּבֵּר מִרְמָה. וְלִמְקַלְלַי נַפְשִׁי תִדֹּם וְנַפְשִׁי כֶּעָפָר לַכֹּל תִּהְיֶה. פְּתַח לִבִּי בְּתוֹרָתֶךָ, וּבְמִצְוֹתֶיךָ תִּרְדֹּף נַפְשִׁי. וְכָל־הַחוֹשְׁבִים עָלַי רָעָה, מְהֵרָה הָפֵר עֲצָתָם וְקַלְקֵל מַחֲשַׁבְתָּם. עֲשֵׂה לְמַעַן שְׁמֶךָ, עֲשֵׂה לְמַעַן יְמִינֶךָ, עֲשֵׂה לְמַעַן קְדֻשָּׁתֶךָ, עֲשֵׂה לְמַעַן תּוֹרָתֶךָ; לְמַעַן יֵחָלְצוּן יְדִידֶיךָ, הוֹשִׁיעָה יְמִינְךָ וַעֲנֵנִי.

O God, keep my tongue from evil and my lips from deceit. Help me to be silent in the face of derision, humble in the presence of all. Open my heart to Your Torah, that I may hasten to do Your Mitzvot. Save me with Your power; in time of trouble be my answer, that those who love You may rejoice.

~~

יִהְיוּ לְרָצוֹן אִמְרֵי־פִי וְהֶגְיוֹן לִבִּי לְפָנֶיךָ, יהוה, צוּרִי וְגֹאֲלִי.

Yi-h'yu l'ra-tzon i-m'rei fi v'heg-yon li-bi l'fa-neh-cha, Adonai tzu-ri v'go-a-li.

May the words of my mouth and the meditations of my heart be acceptable to You, O God, my Rock and my Redeemer.

~

עֹשֶׂה שָׁלוֹם בִּמְרוֹמָיו, הוּא יַעֲשֶׂה שָׁלוֹם עָלֵינוּ וְעַל־כָּל־יִשְׂרָאֵל, וְאִמְרוּ: אָמֵן.

O-seh sha-lom bi-m'ro-mav, hu ya-a-seh sha-lom a-lei-nu v'al kol Yis-ra-eil, v'i-m'ru: A-mein.

• May the One who causes peace to reign in the high heavens cause peace to reign among us, all Israel, and all the world.

For the Reading of the Torah, continue on page 141

Aleinu is on page 148 and page 149

37

אֵל הָרַחֲמִים, אָנָּא מְשֹׁךְ חַסְדְּךָ עָלֵינוּ וְעַל קְרוֹבֵינוּ הָאֲהוּבִים. וְזַכֵּנוּ
לָלֶכֶת בְּדַרְכֵי יְשָׁרִים לְפָנֶיךָ, דְּבֵקִים בַּתּוֹרָה וּבְמַעֲשִׂים טוֹבִים.

Source of mercy, continue Your loving care for us and our loved
ones. Give us strength to walk in Your presence on the paths of
the righteous, loyal to Your Torah, steadfast in goodness.

וְהַרְחֵק מֵעָלֵינוּ כָּל־חֶרְפָּה, תּוּגָה וְיָגוֹן. וְשִׂים שָׁלוֹם, אוֹרָה וְשִׂמְחָה

בִּמְעוֹנֵנוּ. כִּי עִמְּךָ מְקוֹר הַחַיִּים. בְּאוֹרְךָ נִרְאֶה אוֹר. אָמֵן.

*Keep us far from all shame, grief, and anguish; fill our homes*
*with peace, light, and joy. O God, Fountain of Life, by Your*
*light shall we see light.*

~ ~

Ba-ruch a-ta Adonai, Eh-lo-hei-nu
meh-lech ha-o-lam, a-sher ki-d'sha-
nu b'mitz-vo-tav v'tzi-va-nu l'had-
lik ner shel Shabbat.

בָּרוּךְ אַתָּה יְיָ, אֱלֹהֵינוּ מֶלֶךְ
הָעוֹלָם, אֲשֶׁר קִדְּשָׁנוּ בְּמִצְוֹתָיו
וְצִוָּנוּ לְהַדְלִיק נֵר שֶׁל שַׁבָּת.

We praise You, Eternal God, Sovereign of the universe: You
hallow us with Your Mitzvot, and command us to kindle the lights
of Shabbat.

May we be blessed with Shabbat joy. *Amen.*
May we be blessed with Shabbat peace. *Amen.*
May we be blessed with Shabbat light. *Amen.*

~ ~

Welcoming Shabbat קבלת שבת

One or more of the following passages may be read or chanted

*From Psalm 95*

לְכוּ נְרַנְּנָה לַיהוה, נָרִיעָה לְצוּר יִשְׁעֵנוּ.

נְקַדְּמָה פָנָיו בְּתוֹדָה, בִּזְמִרוֹת נָרִיעַ לוֹ.

כִּי אֵל גָּדוֹל יהוה, וּמֶלֶךְ גָּדוֹל עַל־כָּל־אֱלֹהִים.

אֲשֶׁר בְּיָדוֹ מֶחְקְרֵי־אָרֶץ, וְתוֹעֲפוֹת הָרִים לוֹ.

אֲשֶׁר־לוֹ הַיָּם וְהוּא עָשָׂהוּ, וְיַבֶּשֶׁת יָדָיו יָצָרוּ.

כִּי הוּא אֱלֹהֵינוּ, וַאֲנַחְנוּ עַם מַרְעִיתוֹ וְצֹאן יָדוֹ:

הַיּוֹם אִם־בְּקֹלוֹ תִשְׁמָעוּ!

Come, let us sing to the Eternal One;
*let our song ring out to our sheltering Rock.*

Let us come before God with thanksgiving,
*our voices loud with song.*

For great are You, Eternal One,
*high above the gods that are worshipped.*

In Your hands are the depths of the earth;
*Yours are the mountain–peaks.*

You made the sea; it is Yours;
*the dry land is the work of Your hands.*

You are our God and our Shepherd;
*we are Your people and Your flock:*

If only today we would listen to Your voice!

39

From Psalm 96

שִׁירוּ לַיהוה שִׁיר חָדָשׁ; שִׁירוּ לַיהוה כָּל־הָאָרֶץ!
שִׁירוּ לַיהוה, בָּרְכוּ שְׁמוֹ; בַּשְּׂרוּ מִיּוֹם־לְיוֹם יְשׁוּעָתוֹ.

Sing a new song to God;
*all the earth sing to the Eternal One!*

Sing to the Eternal One, praise God's name,
*tell of God's power from day to day.*

סַפְּרוּ בַגּוֹיִם כְּבוֹדוֹ, בְּכָל־הָעַמִּים נִפְלְאוֹתָיו.
כִּי גָדוֹל יהוה, וּמְהֻלָּל מְאֹד, נוֹרָא הוּא עַל־כָּל־אֱלֹהִים.

Declare God's glory among the nations,
*God's wonders among the peoples.*

For great is the Eternal One, beyond all praise,
*and awesome, far above the gods that are worshipped!*

כִּי כָּל־אֱלֹהֵי הָעַמִּים אֱלִילִים, וַיהוה שָׁמַיִם עָשָׂה.
הוֹד־וְהָדָר לְפָנָיו, עֹז וְתִפְאֶרֶת בְּמִקְדָּשׁוֹ.

Other gods are but idols:
*the Eternal One made the heavens.*

Honor and beauty attend You;
*strength and splendor are in Your presence.*

הָבוּ לַיהוה מִשְׁפְּחוֹת עַמִּים, הָבוּ לַיהוה כָּבוֹד וָעֹז.
הָבוּ לַיהוה כְּבוֹד שְׁמוֹ; הִשְׁתַּחֲווּ לַיהוה בְּהַדְרַת־קֹדֶשׁ.

Honor the Eternal One, all races and peoples;
*acknowledge the Eternal One's glory and might.*

40

Honor the Eternal One's glory;
*worship your God in the beauty of holiness.*

חִילוּ מִפָּנָיו כָּל־הָאָרֶץ. אִמְרוּ בַגּוֹיִם: יהוה מָלָךְ;
אַף־תִּכּוֹן תֵּבֵל, בַּל־תִּמּוֹט: יָדִין עַמִּים בְּמֵישָׁרִים.
יִשְׂמְחוּ הַשָּׁמַיִם וְתָגֵל הָאָרֶץ; יִרְעַם הַיָּם וּמְלֹאוֹ.

Let all the earth tremble at God's presence.
Declare to the nations: God reigns;
*now the world is secure and firmly based;*
*God rules the peoples with justice.*

Let the heavens be glad and the earth rejoice;
*let the sea roar, and all that fills it.*

יַעֲלֹז שָׂדַי וְכָל־אֲשֶׁר־בּוֹ;
אָז יְרַנְּנוּ כָּל־עֲצֵי־יָעַר לִפְנֵי יהוה.
כִּי בָא, כִּי בָא לִשְׁפֹּט הָאָרֶץ:

Let the field and its creatures exult;
*let the trees of the forest sing for joy before God,*
*who comes to rule the earth:*

יִשְׁפֹּט־תֵּבֵל בְּצֶדֶק, וְעַמִּים בֶּאֱמוּנָתוֹ.

to rule the world with justice,
*to rule the peoples with truth.*

*From Psalm 97*

יהוה מָלָךְ: תָּגֵל הָאָרֶץ, יִשְׂמְחוּ אִיִּים רַבִּים.
עָנָן וַעֲרָפֶל סְבִיבָיו; צֶדֶק וּמִשְׁפָּט מְכוֹן כִּסְאוֹ.

The Eternal One reigns: let the earth rejoice;
*let the many isles be glad.*

41

Cloud and mist surround You;
*right and justice are the foundation of Your throne.*

הִגִּידוּ הַשָּׁמַיִם צִדְקוֹ, וְרָאוּ כָל־הָעַמִּים כְּבוֹדוֹ.
שָׁמְעָה וַתִּשְׂמַח צִיּוֹן; וַתָּגֵלְנָה בְּנוֹת יְהוּדָה,
לְמַעַן מִשְׁפָּטֶיךָ, יהוה.

The heavens tell of Your righteousness;
*the peoples witness Your glory.*

Zion hears and is glad;
*the cities of Judah rejoice, Eternal One,*
*over Your judgments.*

כִּי־אַתָּה יהוה עֶלְיוֹן עַל־כָּל־הָאָרֶץ:
מְאֹד נַעֲלֵיתָ עַל־כָּל־אֱלֹהִים.

For You are supreme over all the earth,
*You are exalted far above other gods that are worshipped.*

אוֹר זָרֻעַ לַצַּדִּיק, וּלְיִשְׁרֵי־לֵב שִׂמְחָה.

Light dawns for the righteous,
*gladness for the upright in heart.*

שִׂמְחוּ צַדִּיקִים בַּיהוה, וְהוֹדוּ לְזֵכֶר קָדְשׁוֹ.

Let the righteous rejoice in You,
*and give thanks to Your holy name.*

*From Psalm 98*

מִזְמוֹר. שִׁירוּ לַיהוה שִׁיר חָדָשׁ, כִּי־נִפְלָאוֹת עָשָׂה.
הוֹדִיעַ יהוה יְשׁוּעָתוֹ; לְעֵינֵי הַגּוֹיִם גִּלָּה צִדְקָתוֹ.

42

Sing a new song to the Eternal One,
who has done wonders:

*You have made known Your power,*
*and revealed Your justice for all to see.*

זָכַר חַסְדּוֹ וֶאֱמוּנָתוֹ לְבֵית יִשְׂרָאֵל.

רָאוּ כָל־אַפְסֵי־אָרֶץ אֵת יְשׁוּעַת אֱלֹהֵינוּ.

You have remembered Your love and faithfulness to Israel.
*All the ends of the earth have seen the power of God.*

הָרִיעוּ לַיהוה כָּל־הָאָרֶץ; פִּצְחוּ וְרַנְּנוּ וְזַמֵּרוּ!

בַּחֲצֹצְרוֹת וְקוֹל שׁוֹפָר הָרִיעוּ לִפְנֵי הַמֶּלֶךְ יהוה.

Let the earth ring out in song to God;
break forth, sing aloud, shout praise!

*Sound trumpet and horn*
*before the sovereign God.*

יִרְעַם הַיָּם וּמְלֹאוֹ; תֵּבֵל וְיֹשְׁבֵי בָהּ.

נְהָרוֹת יִמְחֲאוּ־כָף! יַחַד הָרִים יְרַנֵּנוּ לִפְנֵי־יהוה,

כִּי בָא לִשְׁפֹּט הָאָרֶץ:

Let the sea roar, and all that fills it,
*the world, and all who dwell there.*

Let the rivers clap hands!
*Let the mountains sing for joy before God,*
*who comes to rule the earth:*

יִשְׁפֹּט־תֵּבֵל בְּצֶדֶק, וְעַמִּים בְּמֵישָׁרִים.

to rule the world with justice,
*and the peoples with righteousness.*

43

*From Psalm 99*

יהוה מָלָךְ: יִרְגְּזוּ עַמִּים. יֹשֵׁב כְּרוּבִים, תָּנוּט הָאָרֶץ.
יהוה בְּצִיּוֹן גָּדוֹל, וְרָם הוּא עַל־כָּל־הָעַמִּים. יוֹדוּ
שְׁמֶךָ: גָּדוֹל וְנוֹרָא, קָדוֹשׁ הוּא. וְעֹז מֶלֶךְ, מִשְׁפָּט
אָהֵב: אַתָּה כּוֹנַנְתָּ מֵישָׁרִים, מִשְׁפָּט וּצְדָקָה בְּיַעֲקֹב
אַתָּה עָשִׂיתָ. רוֹמְמוּ יהוה אֱלֹהֵינוּ, וְהִשְׁתַּחֲווּ לְהַר
קָדְשׁוֹ, כִּי־קָדוֹשׁ יהוה אֱלֹהֵינוּ.

The Eternal One reigns: let the peoples quake with awe; God sits enthroned, and the earth trembles. You are exalted in Zion, Eternal One, high above the peoples. Let them praise Your name, great and awesome and holy. Your power, O Sovereign God, is in Your love of justice. You make righteousness stand firm; justice and right take root in Jacob. We will exalt You, our Eternal God, and worship at Your holy mountain, for our Eternal God is holy.

*Psalm 29*

מִזְמוֹר לְדָוִד.
הָבוּ לַיהוה, בְּנֵי אֵלִים, הָבוּ לַיהוה כָּבוֹד וָעֹז! הָבוּ
לַיהוה כְּבוֹד שְׁמוֹ, הִשְׁתַּחֲווּ לַיהוה בְּהַדְרַת־קֹדֶשׁ.

A Song of David.
Ascribe glory and strength to the Eternal One, all celestial beings! Praise the Eternal One, whose name is great; worship your God in the beauty of holiness.

קוֹל יהוה עַל־הַמָּיִם! אֵל־הַכָּבוֹד הִרְעִים! יהוה עַל־מַיִם
רַבִּים! קוֹל יהוה בַּכֹּחַ, קוֹל יהוה בֶּהָדָר, קוֹל יהוה שֹׁבֵר
אֲרָזִים, וַיְשַׁבֵּר יהוה אֶת־אַרְזֵי הַלְּבָנוֹן. וַיַּרְקִידֵם כְּמוֹ־עֵגֶל
לְבָנוֹן, וְשִׂרְיֹן כְּמוֹ בֶן־רְאֵמִים.

44

The Eternal One's voice above the waters! The God of glory thunders!
The Eternal One's voice, with power—the Eternal One's voice, majestic—
the Eternal One's voice breaks cedars; God shatters Lebanon's cedars,
making Lebanon skip like a calf, Sirion like a wild young ox.

קוֹל־יהוה חֹצֵב לַהֲבוֹת אֵשׁ; קוֹל יהוה יָחִיל מִדְבָּר;
יָחִיל יהוה מִדְבַּר קָדֵשׁ; קוֹל יהוה יְחוֹלֵל אַיָּלוֹת,
וַיֶּחֱשֹׂף יְעָרוֹת, וּבְהֵיכָלוֹ כֻּלּוֹ אֹמֵר: כָּבוֹד!

Eternal God! Your voice sparks fiery flames; Eternal God! Your voice
makes the desert spin; Eternal God! Your voice shakes the Kadesh desert;
Eternal God! Your voice uproots the oaks, and strips the forests bare,
while in Your temple all cry: 'Glory!'

יהוה לַמַּבּוּל יָשָׁב, וַיֵּשֶׁב יהוה מֶלֶךְ לְעוֹלָם.
יהוה עֹז לְעַמּוֹ יִתֵּן, יהוה יְבָרֵךְ אֶת־עַמּוֹ בַשָּׁלוֹם.

The Eternal One, enthroned above the flood, the Eternal One reigns for
ever. You give strength to Your people, O God; You bless Your people
with peace.

〜〜

לכה דודי

לְכָה דוֹדִי לִקְרַאת כַּלָּה, פְּנֵי שַׁבָּת נְקַבְּלָה.

לְכָה דוֹדִי לִקְרַאת כַּלָּה, פְּנֵי שַׁבָּת נְקַבְּלָה.

L'cha do–di lik–rat ka–la, p'nei Shabbat n'ka–b'la.
L'cha do–di lik–rat ka–la, p'nei Shabbat n'ka–b'la.

שָׁמוֹר וְזָכוֹר, בְּדִבּוּר אֶחָד, הִשְׁמִיעָנוּ אֵל הַמְיֻחָד.

יְיָ אֶחָד וּשְׁמוֹ אֶחָד, לְשֵׁם וּלְתִפְאֶרֶת וְלִתְהִלָּה. לכה ...

Sha-mor v'za-chor b'di-bur eh-chad, hish-mi-anu Eil ha-m'yu-chad;
Adonai Eh-chad u-sh'mo Eh-chad, l'sheim u-l'tif-eh-ret v'li-t'hi-la.
L'cha do-di...

לִקְרַאת שַׁבָּת לְכוּ וְנֵלְכָה, כִּי הִיא מְקוֹר הַבְּרָכָה.

מֵרֹאשׁ מִקֶּדֶם נְסוּכָה, סוֹף מַעֲשֶׂה בְּמַחֲשָׁבָה תְּחִלָּה. לכה ...

Lik-rat Shabbat l'chu v'nei-l'cha, ki hi m'kor ha-b'ra-cha.
Mei-rosh mi-keh-dem n'su-cha, sof ma-a-seh b'ma-cha-sha-va t'chi-la.
L'cha do-di...

הִתְעוֹרְרִי, הִתְעוֹרְרִי, כִּי בָא אוֹרֵךְ! קוּמִי, אוֹרִי,

עוּרִי עוּרִי, שִׁיר דַּבֵּרִי; כְּבוֹד יְיָ עָלַיִךְ נִגְלָה. לכה ...

Hit-o-r'ri, hit-o-r'ri, ki va o-reich! Ku-mi o-ri,
u-ri u-ri, shir da-bei-ri; k'vod Adonai a-la-yich nig-la.
L'cha do-di...

בּוֹאִי בְשָׁלוֹם עֲטֶרֶת בַּעְלָהּ, גַּם בְּשִׂמְחָה וּבְצָהֳלָה,

תּוֹךְ אֱמוּנֵי עַם סְגֻלָּה, בּוֹאִי כַלָּה! בּוֹאִי כַלָּה! לכה ...

Bo-i v'sha-lom a-teh-ret ba-a-lah, gam b'sim-chah u-v'tsa-ho-la,
toch eh-mu-nei am s'gu-la, bo-i cha-la! Bo-i cha-la!
L'cha do-di...

Beloved, come to meet the bride; beloved, come to greet Shabbat.

Keep and Remember: a single command the Only God caused us to hear; the Eternal is One, God's name is One, for honor and glory and praise. Beloved...

Come with me to meet Shabbat, forever a fountain of blessing. Still it flows, as from the start: the last of days, for which the first was made. Beloved…

Awake, awake, your light has come! Arise, shine, awake and sing; the Eternal's glory dawns upon you. Beloved…

Enter in peace, O crown of your husband; enter in gladness, enter in joy. Come to the people that keeps its faith. Enter, O bride! Enter, O bride! Beloved…

Continue with Psalm 92 or 93, or with the Reader's Kaddish on page 49

From *Psalm 92*

A SONG FOR THE SABBATH DAY מִזְמוֹר שִׁיר לְיוֹם הַשַּׁבָּת.

טוֹב לְהֹדוֹת לַיהוה, וּלְזַמֵּר לְשִׁמְךָ, עֶלְיוֹן,
לְהַגִּיד בַּבֹּקֶר חַסְדֶּךָ, וֶאֱמוּנָתְךָ בַּלֵּילוֹת,
עֲלֵי־עָשׂוֹר וַעֲלֵי־נָבֶל, עֲלֵי הִגָּיוֹן בְּכִנּוֹר.

It is good to give thanks to the Eternal One,
to sing hymns to Your name, O Most High!
To tell of Your love in the morning,
Your faithfulness in the night;
to pluck the strings, to sound the lute,
to make the harp vibrate.

כִּי שִׂמַּחְתַּנִי, יהוה, בְּפָעֳלֶךָ, בְּמַעֲשֵׂי יָדֶיךָ אֲרַנֵּן.
מַה־גָּדְלוּ מַעֲשֶׂיךָ, יהוה! מְאֹד עָמְקוּ מַחְשְׁבֹתֶיךָ.

*Your deeds, O God, fill me with gladness,*
*Your work moves me to song.*
*How great are Your works, 0 God!*
*How profound Your design!*

צַדִּיק כַּתָּמָר יִפְרָח, כְּאֶרֶז בַּלְּבָנוֹן יִשְׂגֶּה.
שְׁתוּלִים בְּבֵית יהוה, בְּחַצְרוֹת אֱלֹהֵינוּ יַפְרִיחוּ.

עוֹד יְנוּבוּן בְּשֵׂיבָה, דְּשֵׁנִים וְרַעֲנַנִּים יִהְיוּ,
לְהַגִּיד כִּי־יָשָׁר יהוה, צוּרִי, וְלֹא־עַוְלָתָה בּוֹ.

*The righteous shall flourish like palms,*
*grow tall like cedars in Lebanon.*
*Rooted in the house of their God,*
*they shall be ever fresh and green,*
*proclaiming that God is just,*
*my Rock, in whom no wrong is found.*

Psalm 93

יהוה מָלָךְ, גֵּאוּת לָבֵשׁ; לָבֵשׁ יהוה, עֹז הִתְאַזָּר;
אַף־תִּכּוֹן תֵּבֵל, בַּל־תִּמּוֹט. נָכוֹן כִּסְאֲךָ מֵאָז, מֵעוֹלָם אָתָּה.
נָשְׂאוּ נְהָרוֹת, יהוה, נָשְׂאוּ נְהָרוֹת קוֹלָם, יִשְׂאוּ נְהָרוֹת דָּכְיָם;
מִקֹּלוֹת מַיִם רַבִּים, אַדִּירִים מִשְׁבְּרֵי־יָם, אַדִּיר בַּמָּרוֹם יהוה.
עֵדֹתֶיךָ נֶאֶמְנוּ מְאֹד; לְבֵיתְךָ נַאֲוָה־קֹדֶשׁ, יהוה, לְאֹרֶךְ יָמִים.

The Eternal One is enthroned,
robed in grandeur;
The Eternal One is robed,
girded with strength—
the One who founded the solid earth
to be unmoving.

*Ageless is Your throne,*
*endless Your being.*

The oceans cry out, Eternal God,
the oceans cry out their thunder,
the oceans rage in their fury;
but greater than the thunder of the torrents,
mightier than the breakers of the sea,
is the majesty of God on high!

*Your law stands firm;*

48

*and in Your temple, O Eternal God,*
*holiness abides to the end of time!*

All rise

READER'S KADDISH                                              חצי קדיש

יִתְגַּדַּל וְיִתְקַדַּשׁ שְׁמֵהּ רַבָּא בְּעָלְמָא דִי־בְרָא כִרְעוּתֵהּ,
וְיַמְלִיךְ מַלְכוּתֵהּ בְּחַיֵּיכוֹן וּבְיוֹמֵיכוֹן וּבְחַיֵּי דְכָל־בֵּית
יִשְׂרָאֵל, בַּעֲגָלָא וּבִזְמַן קָרִיב, וְאִמְרוּ: אָמֵן.

יְהֵא שְׁמֵהּ רַבָּא מְבָרַךְ לְעָלַם וּלְעָלְמֵי עָלְמַיָּא.

יִתְבָּרַךְ וְיִשְׁתַּבַּח, וְיִתְפָּאַר וְיִתְרוֹמַם וְיִתְנַשֵּׂא, וְיִתְהַדָּר
וְיִתְעַלֶּה וְיִתְהַלָּל שְׁמֵהּ דְּקֻדְשָׁא, בְּרִיךְ הוּא,
לְעֵלָּא מִן־כָּל־בִּרְכָתָא וְשִׁירָתָא, תֻּשְׁבְּחָתָא וְנֶחֱמָתָא
דַּאֲמִירָן בְּעָלְמָא, וְאִמְרוּ: אָמֵן.

Yit-ga-dal v'yit–ka–dash sh'mei ra-ba b'al-ma di-v'ra chi-r'u'tei, v'yam-lich
mal-chu-tei b'cha-yei-chon u-v'yo-mei-chon u-v'cha-yei d'chol beit Yis-ra-
eil, ba-a-ga-la u-vi-z'man ka-riv, v'i-m' ru: A-mein.

Y'hei sh'mei ra-ba m'va-rach l'a-lam u-l'al-mei al-ma-ya.

Yit-ba-rach v'yish-ta-bach, v'yit-pa-ar v'yit-ro-mam v'yit-na-sei, v'yit-ha-dar
v'yit-a-leh v'yit-ha-lal sh'mei d'kud-sha, b'rich hu,

l'ei-la min kol bir-cha-ta v'shi-ra-ta, tush-b'cha-ta v'neh-cheh-ma-ta da-a-
mi-ran b'al-ma, v'i-m' ru: A-mein.

49

The Sh'ma and its Blessings                    שמע וברכותיה

בָּרְכוּ אֶת־יי הַמְבֹרָךּ!

Praise the One to whom our praise is due!

בָּרוּךְ יי הַמְבֹרָךְ לְעוֹלָם וָעֶד!

*Ba-ruch Adonai ha-m'vo-rach l'o-lam va-ed!*

*Praised be the One to whom our praise is due, now and for ever!*

CREATION                                       מעריב ערבים

בָּרוּךְ אַתָּה יי, אֱלֹהֵינוּ מֶלֶךְ הָעוֹלָם, אֲשֶׁר בִּדְבָרוֹ
מַעֲרִיב עֲרָבִים, בְּחָכְמָה פּוֹתֵחַ שְׁעָרִים, וּבִתְבוּנָה מְשַׁנֶּה
עִתִּים, וּמַחֲלִיף אֶת־הַזְּמַנִּים, וּמְסַדֵּר אֶת־הַכּוֹכָבִים
בְּמִשְׁמְרוֹתֵיהֶם בָּרָקִיעַ כִּרְצוֹנוֹ.
בּוֹרֵא יוֹם וָלַיְלָה, גּוֹלֵל אוֹר מִפְּנֵי חֹשֶׁךְ וְחֹשֶׁךְ מִפְּנֵי אוֹר,
וּמַעֲבִיר יוֹם וּמֵבִיא לָיְלָה, וּמַבְדִּיל בֵּין יוֹם וּבֵין לָיְלָה,
יי צְבָאוֹת שְׁמוֹ.
אֵל חַי וְקַיָּם, תָּמִיד יִמְלוֹךְ עָלֵינוּ לְעוֹלָם וָעֶד.
בָּרוּךְ אַתָּה יי, הַמַּעֲרִיב עֲרָבִים.

We praise You, Eternal God, Sovereign of the universe, whose word brings on the evening. With wisdom You open heaven's gates, and with understanding You make the ages pass and the seasons alternate; Your will controls the stars as they travel through the skies.

*You are Creator of day and night, rolling light away from darkness, and darkness from light; You cause day to pass and bring on the night, separating day from night; You command the hosts of heaven! May the living and eternal God rule us*

50

*always, to the end of time! We praise You, O God, whose word makes evening fall.*

REVELATION                                    אהבת עולם

אַהֲבַת עוֹלָם בֵּית יִשְׂרָאֵל עַמְּךָ אָהָבְתָּ.
תּוֹרָה וּמִצְוֹת, חֻקִּים וּמִשְׁפָּטִים אוֹתָנוּ לִמַּדְתָּ.
עַל־כֵּן, יְיָ אֱלֹהֵינוּ, בְּשָׁכְבֵנוּ וּבְקוּמֵנוּ נָשִׂיחַ בְּחֻקֶּיךָ,
וְנִשְׂמַח בְּדִבְרֵי תוֹרָתֶךָ וּבְמִצְוֹתֶיךָ לְעוֹלָם וָעֶד.
כִּי הֵם חַיֵּינוּ וְאֹרֶךְ יָמֵינוּ, וּבָהֶם נֶהְגֶּה יוֹמָם וָלָיְלָה.
וְאַהֲבָתְךָ אַל־תָּסוּר מִמֶּנּוּ לְעוֹלָמִים!
בָּרוּךְ אַתָּה יְיָ, אוֹהֵב עַמּוֹ יִשְׂרָאֵל.

Unending is Your love for Your people, the House of Israel: Torah and Mitzvot, laws and precepts have You taught us.

*Therefore, O God, when we lie down and when we rise up, we will meditate on Your laws and rejoice in Your Torah and Mitzvot for ever.*

*Day and night we will reflect on them, for they are our life and the length of our days. Then Your love shall never depart from our hearts! We praise You, O God: You love Your people Israel.*

שְׁמַע יִשְׂרָאֵל: יהוה אֱלֹהֵינוּ, יהוה אֶחָד!

Sh'ma Yis-ra-eil: Adonai Eh-lo-hei-nu, Adonai Eh-chad!

*Hear, O Israel: the Eternal One is our God,*
*the Eternal God alone!*

בָּרוּךְ שֵׁם כְּבוֹד מַלְכוּתוֹ לְעוֹלָם וָעֶד!

Ba-ruch shem k'vod mal-chu-to l'o-lam va–ed!

*Blessed is God's glorious majesty for ever and ever!*

## All are seated

51

וְאָהַבְתָּ אֵת יְהוָה אֱלֹהֶיךָ בְּכָל־לְבָבְךָ וּבְכָל־נַפְשְׁךָ וּבְכָל־מְאֹדֶךָ:
וְהָיוּ הַדְּבָרִים הָאֵלֶּה אֲשֶׁר אָנֹכִי מְצַוְּךָ הַיּוֹם עַל־לְבָבֶךָ:
וְשִׁנַּנְתָּם לְבָנֶיךָ וְדִבַּרְתָּ בָּם בְּשִׁבְתְּךָ בְּבֵיתֶךָ וּבְלֶכְתְּךָ בַדֶּרֶךְ
וּבְשָׁכְבְּךָ וּבְקוּמֶךָ: וּקְשַׁרְתָּם לְאוֹת עַל־יָדֶךָ וְהָיוּ לְטֹטָפֹת בֵּין
עֵינֶיךָ: וּכְתַבְתָּם עַל־מְזוּזֹת בֵּיתֶךָ וּבִשְׁעָרֶיךָ:
לְמַעַן תִּזְכְּרוּ וַעֲשִׂיתֶם אֶת־כָּל־מִצְוֹתָי וִהְיִיתֶם קְדֹשִׁים
לֵאלֹהֵיכֶם: אֲנִי יְהוָה אֱלֹהֵיכֶם אֲשֶׁר הוֹצֵאתִי אֶתְכֶם
מֵאֶרֶץ מִצְרַיִם לִהְיוֹת לָכֶם לֵאלֹהִים אֲנִי יְהוָה אֱלֹהֵיכֶם:

V'a–hav–ta et Adonai Eh–lo–heh–cha b'chol l'va–v'cha u–v'chol naf–
sh'cha u–v'chol m'o–deh–cha. V'ha–yu ha–d'va–rim ha–ei–leh a–sher a–
no–chi m'tza–v'cha ha–yom al l'va–veh–cha. V'shi–nan–tam l'va–neh–cha
v'di–bar–ta bam b'shiv–t'cha b'vei–teh–cha u–v'lech–t'cha va–deh–rech u–
v'shoch–b'cha u–v'ku–meh–cha. U–k'shar–tam l'ot al ya–deh–cha v'ha–yu
l'to–ta–fot bein ei–neh–cha; u–ch'tav–tam al m'zu–zot bei–teh–cha u–vi–
sh'a–reh–cha.
L'ma–an tiz–k'ru va–a–si–tem et kol mitz–vo–tai, vi–h'yi–tem  k'do–shim
lei–lo–hei–chem. Ani Adonai Eh–lo–hei–chem a–sher ho–tzei–ti et–chem
mei–eh–retz mitz–ra–yim li–h'yot la–chem lei–lo–him. Ani Adonai Eh–lo–
hei–chem.

*You shall love your Eternal God with all your heart, with all
your mind, with all your being. Set these words, which I
command you this day, upon your heart. Teach them faithfully
to your children; speak of them in your home and on your
way, when you lie down and when you rise up. Bind them as
a sign upon your hand; let them be symbols before your eyes;
inscribe them on the doorposts of your house, and on your
gates.*

*Be mindful of all My Mitzvot, and do them: so shall you
consecrate yourselves to your God. I am your Eternal God who
led you out of Egypt to be your God; I am your Eternal God.*

52

REDEMPTION                                             גְּאוּלָה

אֱמֶת וֶאֱמוּנָה כָּל־זֹאת, וְקַיָּם עָלֵינוּ, כִּי הוּא יְיָ אֱלֹהֵינוּ,
וְאֵין זוּלָתוֹ, וַאֲנַחְנוּ יִשְׂרָאֵל עַמּוֹ. הַפּוֹדֵנוּ מִיַּד מְלָכִים, הַגּוֹאֲלֵנוּ
מִכַּף כָּל־הֶעָרִיצִים, וַיּוֹצֵא אֶת־עַמּוֹ יִשְׂרָאֵל מִמִּצְרַיִם לְחֵרוּת
עוֹלָם. וְרָאוּ בָנָיו גְּבוּרָתוֹ; שִׁבְּחוּ וְהוֹדוּ לִשְׁמוֹ. וּמַלְכוּתוֹ בְּרָצוֹן
קִבְּלוּ עֲלֵיהֶם. לְךָ עָנוּ שִׁירָה בְּשִׂמְחָה רַבָּה, וְאָמְרוּ כֻלָּם:

All this we hold to be true and sure: You alone are God;
there is none else, and we are Israel Your people.
*You are our Sovereign: You deliver us from the hand of*
*oppressors, and save us from the fist of tyrants.*

You do wonders without number,
marvels that pass our understanding.
*You give us our life;*
*by Your help we survive all who seek our destruction.*

You did wonders for us in the land of Egypt,
miracles and marvels in the land of Pharaoh,
*You led Your people Israel out, forever to serve You in freedom.*

When Your children witnessed Your power, they extolled You
and gave You thanks; willingly they enthroned You; and, full of
joy, Moses, Miriam, and all Israel sang this song:

מִי־כָמֹכָה בָּאֵלִם, יהוה? מִי כָּמֹכָה, נֶאְדָּר בַּקֹּדֶשׁ,
נוֹרָא תְהִלֹּת, עֹשֵׂה פֶּלֶא?

מַלְכוּתְךָ רָאוּ בָנֶיךָ, בּוֹקֵעַ יָם לִפְנֵי מֹשֶׁה; זֶה אֵלִי!
עָנוּ וְאָמְרוּ: יהוה יִמְלֹךְ לְעֹלָם וָעֶד!

וְנֶאֱמַר: כִּי פָדָה יהוה אֶת־יַעֲקֹב, וּגְאָלוֹ מִיַּד חָזָק מִמֶּנּוּ.
בָּרוּךְ אַתָּה יי, גָּאַל יִשְׂרָאֵל.

Mi cha–mo–cha ba–ei–lim, Adonai?
Mi ka–mo–cha, neh–dar ba–ko–desh, no–ra t'hi–lot, o–sei feh–leh?
Mal–chu–t'cha ra–u va–neh–cha, bo–kei–a yam li–f'nei Mo–sheh; zeh Ei–li!
  A–nu v'a–m'ru: Adonai yim–loch l'o–lam va–ed!
V'neh–eh–mar: Ki fa–da Adonai et Ya–a–kov, u–g'a–lo mi–yad cha–zak
  mi–meh–nu.
Ba–ruch a–ta Adonai, ga–al Yis–ra–eil.

Who is like You, Eternal One, among the gods that are worshipped?
Who is like You, majestic in holiness, awesome in splendor, doing
  wonders?
In their escape from the sea, Your children saw Your sovereign might
  displayed. "This is my God!" they cried. "The Eternal will reign for
  ever and ever!"
And it has been said: The Eternal One delivered Jacob, and redeemed us
  from the hand of one stronger than ourselves.
We praise You, O God, Redeemer of Israel.

DIVINE PROVIDENCE                                    הַשְׁכִּיבֵנוּ

הַשְׁכִּיבֵנוּ, יי אֱלֹהֵינוּ, לְשָׁלוֹם, וְהַעֲמִידֵנוּ, מַלְכֵּנוּ, לְחַיִּים. וּפְרוֹשׂ
עָלֵינוּ סֻכַּת שְׁלוֹמֶךָ, וְתַקְּנֵנוּ בְּעֵצָה טוֹבָה מִלְּפָנֶיךָ, וְהוֹשִׁיעֵנוּ
לְמַעַן שְׁמֶךָ, וְהָגֵן בַּעֲדֵנוּ. וְהָסֵר מֵעָלֵינוּ אוֹיֵב דֶּבֶר וְחֶרֶב וְרָעָב
וְיָגוֹן; וְהָסֵר שָׂטָן מִלְּפָנֵינוּ וּמֵאַחֲרֵינוּ, וּבְצֵל כְּנָפֶיךָ תַּסְתִּירֵנוּ,
כִּי אֵל שׁוֹמְרֵנוּ וּמַצִּילֵנוּ אָתָּה, כִּי אֵל מֶלֶךְ חַנּוּן וְרַחוּם אָתָּה.
וּשְׁמוֹר צֵאתֵנוּ וּבוֹאֵנוּ לְחַיִּים וּלְשָׁלוֹם מֵעַתָּה וְעַד עוֹלָם.
בָּרוּךְ אַתָּה יי, הַפּוֹרֵשׂ סֻכַּת שָׁלוֹם עָלֵינוּ וְעַל כָּל־עַמּוֹ
יִשְׂרָאֵל, וְעַל יְרוּשָׁלָיִם.

54

Grant that we may lie down in peace, Eternal God, and raise us up, O Sovereign, to life renewed. Spread over us the shelter of Your peace; guide us with Your good counsel; and for Your name's sake, be our Help.

*Shield us from hatred and plague; keep us from war and famine and anguish; subdue our inclination to evil. O God, our Guardian and Helper, our gracious and merciful Sovereign, give us refuge in the shadow of Your wings. O guard our coming and our going, that now and always we have life and peace.*

*We praise You, O God, whose shelter of peace is spread over us, over all Your people Israel, and over Jerusalem.*

THE COVENANT OF SHABBAT                                    ושמרו

וְשָׁמְרוּ בְנֵי־יִשְׂרָאֵל אֶת־הַשַּׁבָּת, לַעֲשׂוֹת אֶת־הַשַּׁבָּת לְדֹרֹתָם

בְּרִית עוֹלָם. בֵּינִי וּבֵין בְּנֵי יִשְׂרָאֵל אוֹת הִיא לְעֹלָם. כִּי־שֵׁשֶׁת

יָמִים עָשָׂה יהוה אֶת־הַשָּׁמַיִם וְאֶת־הָאָרֶץ, וּבַיּוֹם הַשְּׁבִיעִי

שָׁבַת וַיִּנָּפַשׁ.

V'sha-m'ru v'nei Yis-ra-eil et ha-Shabbat, la-a-sot et ha-sha-bat l'do-ro-tam b'rit o-lam. Bei-ni u-vein b'nei Yis-ra-eil ot hi l'o-lam. Ki shei-shet ya-mim a-sa Adonai et ha-sha-ma-yim v'et ha-a-retz, u-va-yom ha-sh'vi-i sha-vat va-yi-na-fash.

The people of Israel shall keep the Sabbath, observing the Sabbath in every generation as a covenant for all time. It is a sign for ever between Me and the people of Israel. For in six days the Eternal One made heaven and earth, but on the seventh day God rested and was refreshed.

## All rise

## T'FILAH    תפלה

אֲדֹנָי, שְׂפָתַי תִּפְתָּח, וּפִי יַגִּיד תְּהִלָּתֶךָ.

Eternal God, open my lips, that my mouth may declare Your glory.

GOD OF ALL GENERATIONS    אבות ואמהות

בָּרוּךְ אַתָּה יי, אֱלֹהֵינוּ וֵאלֹהֵי אֲבוֹתֵינוּ וְאִמּוֹתֵינוּ:
אֱלֹהֵי אַבְרָהָם, אֱלֹהֵי יִצְחָק, וֵאלֹהֵי יַעֲקֹב.
אֱלֹהֵי שָׂרָה, אֱלֹהֵי רִבְקָה, אֱלֹהֵי לֵאָה וֵאלֹהֵי רָחֵל.
הָאֵל הַגָּדוֹל הַגִּבּוֹר וְהַנּוֹרָא, אֵל עֶלְיוֹן, גּוֹמֵל חֲסָדִים
טוֹבִים וְקוֹנֵה הַכֹּל, וְזוֹכֵר חַסְדֵי אָבוֹת וְאִמָּהוֹת,
וּמֵבִיא גְאֻלָּה לִבְנֵי בְנֵיהֶם, לְמַעַן שְׁמוֹ בְּאַהֲבָה.

ON SHABBAT SHUVAH ADD:

זָכְרֵנוּ לְחַיִּים, מֶלֶךְ חָפֵץ בַּחַיִּים,

וְכָתְבֵנוּ בְּסֵפֶר הַחַיִּים, לְמַעַנְךָ אֱלֹהִים חַיִּים.

מֶלֶךְ עוֹזֵר וּמוֹשִׁיעַ וּמָגֵן.

בָּרוּךְ אַתָּה יי, מָגֵן אַבְרָהָם וְעֶזְרַת שָׂרָה.

Ba–ruch a–ta Adonai, Eh–lo–hei–nu vei–lo–hei a–vo–tei–nu v'i–mo–tei–nu:
Eh–lo–hei Av–ra–ham, eh–lo–hei Yitz–chak, vei–lo–hei Ya–a–kov.
Eh–lo–hei Sa–ra, Eh–lo–hei Riv–ka, Eh–lo–hei Lei–a vei–lo–hei Ra–cheil.
Ha–eil ha–ga–dol ha–gi–bor v'ha–no–ra, Eil el–yon, go–meil cha–sa–dim
to–vim, v'ko–nei ha–kol, v'zo–cheir cha–s'dei a–vot v'i–ma–hot,
u–mei–vi g'u–la li–v'nei v'nei–hem, l'ma–an sh'mo, b'a–ha–va.
Meh–lech o–zeir u–mo–shi–a u–ma–gein.
Ba–ruch a–ta Adonai, ma–gein Av–ra–ham v'ez–rat Sa–ra.

Praised be our God, the God of our fathers and our mothers:
God of Abraham, God of Isaac, and God of Jacob; God of Sarah,
God of Rebekah, God of Leah and God of Rachel; great, mighty,
and awesome God, God supreme.

Ruler of all the living, Your ways are ways of love. You remember the faithfulness of our ancestors, and in love bring redemption to their children's children for the sake of Your name.

ON SHABBAT SHUVAH ADD::
> Remember us unto life, Sovereign who delights in life, and inscribe us in the Book of Life, that Your will may prevail, O God of life.

You are our Sovereign and our Help, our Redeemer and our Shield. We praise You, Eternal One, Shield of Abraham, Protector of Sarah.

GOD'S POWER                                                    גבורות

אַתָּה גִּבּוֹר לְעוֹלָם, אֲדֹנָי, מְחַיֵּה הַכֹּל אַתָּה, רַב לְהוֹשִׁיעַ.
מְכַלְכֵּל חַיִּים בְּחֶסֶד, מְחַיֵּה הַכֹּל בְּרַחֲמִים רַבִּים. סוֹמֵךְ
נוֹפְלִים, וְרוֹפֵא חוֹלִים, וּמַתִּיר אֲסוּרִים, וּמְקַיֵּם אֱמוּנָתוֹ
לִישֵׁנֵי עָפָר. מִי כָמוֹךָ בַּעַל גְּבוּרוֹת, וּמִי דּוֹמֶה לָּךְ,
מֶלֶךְ מֵמִית וּמְחַיֶּה וּמַצְמִיחַ יְשׁוּעָה?

ON SHABBAT SHUVAH ADD:

מִי כָמוֹךָ, אַב הָרַחֲמִים, זוֹכֵר יְצוּרָיו לְחַיִּים בְּרַחֲמִים?

וְנֶאֱמָן אַתָּה לְהַחֲיוֹת הַכֹּל. בָּרוּךְ אַתָּה יי, מְחַיֵּה הַכֹּל.

A–ta gi–bor l'o–lam, Adonai, m'cha–yei ha–kol a–ta, rav l'ho–shi–a.
M'chal–keil cha–yim b'cheh–sed, m'cha–yei ha–kol b'ra–cha–mim ra–bim.
So–meich no–f'lim, v'ro–fei cho–lim, u–ma–tir a–su–rim, u–m'ka–yeim eh–
mu–na–to li–shei–nei a–far. Mi cha–mo–cha ba–al g'vu–rot, u–mi do–meh
lach, meh–lech mei–mit u–m'cha–yeh u–matz–mi–ach y'shu–a?

V'neh–eh–man a–ta l'ha–cha–yot ha–kol. Ba–ruch a–ta Adonai, m'cha–yei
ha–kol.

*Eternal is Your might, O God; all life is Your gift; great is Your power to save!*

*With love You sustain the living, with great compassion give life to all. You send help to the falling and healing to the sick; You bring freedom to the captive and keep faith with those who sleep in the dust.*

*Who is like You, Mighty One, Author of life and death, Source of salvation?*

ON SHABBAT SHUVAH ADD:

*Who is like You, Source of mercy? In compassion You sustain the life of Your children.*

*We praise You, O God, the Source of life.*

THE HOLINESS OF GOD                                           קְדוּשַׁת הַשֵּׁם

אַתָּה קָדוֹשׁ וְשִׁמְךָ קָדוֹשׁ, וּקְדוֹשִׁים בְּכָל־יוֹם יְהַלְלוּךָ, סֶּלָה.

\* בָּרוּךְ אַתָּה יי, הָאֵל הַקָּדוֹשׁ.

         \* ON SHABBAT SHUVAH CONCLUDE:

בָּרוּךְ אַתָּה יי, הַמֶּלֶךְ הַקָּדוֹשׁ.

You are holy, Your name is holy, and those who strive to be holy declare Your glory day by day.
\* We praise You, Eternal One, the holy God.

      \* ON SHABBAT SHUVAH CONCLUDE:
We praise You, Eternal One: You rule in holiness.

### All are seated

THE HOLINESS OF SHABBAT                                   קְדוּשַׁת הַיּוֹם

אַתָּה קִדַּשְׁתָּ אֶת־יוֹם הַשְּׁבִיעִי לִשְׁמֶךָ; תַּכְלִית מַעֲשֵׂה שָׁמַיִם וָאָרֶץ, וּבֵרַכְתּוֹ מִכָּל־הַיָּמִים, וְקִדַּשְׁתּוֹ מִכָּל־הַזְּמַנִּים, וְכֵן כָּתוּב בְּתוֹרָתֶךָ:

You set the seventh day apart for Your service; it is the goal of creation, more blessed than other days, more sacred than other times, and so we read in the story of creation:

וַיְכֻלּוּ הַשָּׁמַיִם וְהָאָרֶץ וְכָל־צְבָאָם: וַיְכַל אֱלֹהִים בַּיּוֹם הַשְּׁבִיעִי מְלַאכְתּוֹ אֲשֶׁר עָשָׂה וַיִּשְׁבֹּת בַּיּוֹם הַשְּׁבִיעִי מִכָּל־ מְלַאכְתּוֹ אֲשֶׁר עָשָׂה: וַיְבָרֶךְ אֱלֹהִים אֶת־יוֹם הַשְּׁבִיעִי וַיְקַדֵּשׁ אֹתוֹ כִּי בוֹ שָׁבַת מִכָּל־מְלַאכְתּוֹ אֲשֶׁר־בָּרָא אֱלֹהִים לַעֲשׂוֹת:

Now the whole universe—sky, earth, and all their array—was completed. With the seventh day God ended the work of creation, resting on the seventh day, with all the work completed. Then God blessed the seventh day and sanctified it, this day having completed the work of creation.

אֱלֹהֵינוּ וֵאלֹהֵי אֲבוֹתֵינוּ וְאִמּוֹתֵינוּ, רְצֵה בִמְנוּחָתֵנוּ. קַדְּשֵׁנוּ בְּמִצְוֹתֶיךָ וְתֵן חֶלְקֵנוּ בְּתוֹרָתֶךָ. שַׂבְּעֵנוּ מִטּוּבֶךָ, וְשַׂמְּחֵנוּ בִּישׁוּעָתֶךָ, וְטַהֵר לִבֵּנוּ לְעָבְדְּךָ בֶּאֱמֶת. וְהַנְחִילֵנוּ, יְיָ אֱלֹהֵינוּ, בְּאַהֲבָה וּבְרָצוֹן שַׁבַּת קָדְשֶׁךָ, וְיָנוּחוּ בָהּ יִשְׂרָאֵל מְקַדְּשֵׁי שְׁמֶךָ. בָּרוּךְ אַתָּה יְיָ, מְקַדֵּשׁ הַשַּׁבָּת.

Eh-lo-hei-nu vei-lo-hei a-vo-tei-nu v'i-mo-tei-nu, r'tzei vi-m'nu-cha-tei-nu. Ka-d'shei-nu b'mitz-vo-teh-cha v-tein chel-kei-nu b'to-ra-teh-cha. Sab-ei-nu mi-tu-veh-cha, v'sam-chei-nu bi-shu-a-teh-cha, v'ta-heir li-bei-nu l'ov-d'cha beh-eh-met. V'han-chi-lei-nu, Adonai Eh-lo-hei-nu, b'a-ha-va u-v'ra-tzon Shabbat kod-sheh-cha, v'ya-nu-chu va Yis-ra-eil m'ka-d'shei sh'meh-cha. Ba-ruch a-ta Adonai, m'ka-deish ha-Shabbat.

*Our God, God of our fathers and our mothers, may our rest on this day be pleasing in Your sight. Sanctify us with Your Mitzvot, and let Your Torah be our way of life. Satisfy us with Your goodness, gladden us with Your salvation, and purify our hearts to serve You in truth. In Your gracious love, Eternal God,*

*let Your holy Sabbath remain our heritage, that all Israel, hallowing Your name, may find rest and peace. We praise You, O God, for the Sabbath and its holiness.*

WORSHIP                                                              עבודה

רְצֵה, יְיָ אֱלֹהֵינוּ, בְּעַמְּךָ יִשְׂרָאֵל, וּתְפִלָּתָם בְּאַהֲבָה תְקַבֵּל,
וּתְהִי לְרָצוֹן תָּמִיד עֲבוֹדַת יִשְׂרָאֵל עַמֶּךָ. אֵל קָרוֹב לְכָל־
קֹרְאָיו, פְּנֵה אֶל עֲבָדֶיךָ וְחָנֵּנוּ; שְׁפוֹךְ רוּחֲךָ עָלֵינוּ,
וְתֶחֱזֶינָה עֵינֵינוּ בְּשׁוּבְךָ לְצִיּוֹן בְּרַחֲמִים.
בָּרוּךְ אַתָּה יְיָ, הַמַּחֲזִיר שְׁכִינָתוֹ לְצִיּוֹן.

Be gracious, Eternal God, to Your people Israel, and receive our prayers with love. O may our worship always be acceptable to You.

*Fill us with the knowledge that You are near to all who seek You in truth. Let our eyes behold Your presence in our midst and in the midst of our people in Zion. We praise You, O God, whose presence gives life to Zion and all Israel.*

ON ROSH CHODESH AND CHOL HAMOEID :

אֱלֹהֵינוּ וֵאלֹהֵי אֲבוֹתֵינוּ וְאִמּוֹתֵינוּ, יַעֲלֶה וְיָבֹא וְיִזָּכֵר זִכְרוֹנֵנוּ וְזִכְרוֹן
כָּל־עַמְּךָ בֵּית יִשְׂרָאֵל לְפָנֶיךָ לְטוֹבָה לְחֵן לְחֶסֶד וּלְרַחֲמִים,
לְחַיִּים וּלְשָׁלוֹם בְּיוֹם

• רֹאשׁ הַחֹדֶשׁ הַזֶּה.

• חַג הַמַּצּוֹת הַזֶּה.

• חַג הַסֻּכּוֹת הַזֶּה.

| | |
|---|---|
| אָמֵן. | זָכְרֵנוּ, יְיָ אֱלֹהֵינוּ, בּוֹ לְטוֹבָה. |
| אָמֵן. | וּפָקְדֵנוּ בוֹ לִבְרָכָה. |
| אָמֵן. | וְהוֹשִׁיעֵנוּ בוֹ לְחַיִּים. |

Our God, God of our fathers and our mothers, be mindful of Your people Israel on this

60

- first day of the new month,
- festival of Pesach,
- festival of Sukkot,

and renew in us love and compassion, goodness, life, and peace.

This day remember us for well–being.     *Amen.*

This day bless us with Your nearness.     *Amen.*

This day help us to a fuller life.     *Amen.*

### THANKSGIVING                                          הוֹדָאָה

מוֹדִים אֲנַחְנוּ לָךְ, שָׁאַתָּה הוּא יי אֱלֹהֵינוּ וֵאלֹהֵי אֲבוֹתֵינוּ
וְאִמּוֹתֵינוּ לְעוֹלָם וָעֶד. צוּר חַיֵּינוּ, מָגֵן יִשְׁעֵנוּ, אַתָּה הוּא
לְדוֹר וָדוֹר. נוֹדֶה לְךָ וּנְסַפֵּר תְּהִלָּתֶךָ, עַל־חַיֵּינוּ הַמְּסוּרִים
בְּיָדֶךָ, וְעַל־נִשְׁמוֹתֵינוּ הַפְּקוּדוֹת לָךְ, וְעַל־נִסֶּיךָ שֶׁבְּכָל־יוֹם
עִמָּנוּ, וְעַל־נִפְלְאוֹתֶיךָ וְטוֹבוֹתֶיךָ שֶׁבְּכָל־עֵת, עֶרֶב וָבֹקֶר
וְצָהֳרָיִם. הַטּוֹב: כִּי לֹא־כָלוּ רַחֲמֶיךָ, וְהַמְרַחֵם: כִּי־לֹא תַמּוּ
חֲסָדֶיךָ, מֵעוֹלָם קִוִּינוּ לָךְ.
וְעַל כֻּלָּם יִתְבָּרַךְ וְיִתְרוֹמַם שִׁמְךָ, מַלְכֵּנוּ, תָּמִיד לְעוֹלָם וָעֶד.

ON SHABBAT SHUVAH ADD:

וּכְתוֹב לְחַיִּים טוֹבִים כָּל־בְּנֵי בְרִיתֶךָ.

וְכֹל הַחַיִּים יוֹדוּךָ סֶּלָה, וִיהַלְלוּ אֶת־שִׁמְךָ בֶּאֱמֶת, הָאֵל
יְשׁוּעָתֵנוּ וְעֶזְרָתֵנוּ סֶלָה.

בָּרוּךְ אַתָּה יי, הַטּוֹב שִׁמְךָ וּלְךָ נָאֶה לְהוֹדוֹת.

We gratefully acknowledge that You are our God and the God of our people, the God of all generations. You are the Rock of our life, the Power that shields us in every age.

*We thank You and sing Your praises: for our lives, which are in Your hand; for our souls, which are in Your keeping; for the*

*signs of Your presence we encounter every day; and for Your wondrous gifts at all times, morning, noon, and night. You are Goodness: Your mercies never end; You are Compassion: Your love will never fail. You have always been our hope.*

*For all these things, O Sovereign God, let Your name be for ever exalted and blessed.*

ON SHABBAT SHUVAH ADD:

*Let life abundant be the heritage of all the children of Your covenant.*

*O God our Redeemer and Helper, let all who live affirm You and praise Your name in truth. Eternal God, whose nature is Goodness, we give You thanks and praise.*

ON CHANUKAH ADD:

עַל הַנִּסִּים וְעַל הַפֻּרְקָן, וְעַל הַגְּבוּרוֹת וְעַל הַתְּשׁוּעוֹת, וְעַל הַנֶּחָמוֹת שֶׁעָשִׂיתָ לַאֲבוֹתֵינוּ וּלְאִמּוֹתֵינוּ בַּיָּמִים הָהֵם וּבַזְּמַן הַזֶּה. בִּימֵי מַתִּתְיָהוּ בֶּן־יוֹחָנָן כֹּהֵן גָּדוֹל, חַשְׁמוֹנַאי וּבָנָיו, כְּשֶׁעָמְדָה מַלְכוּת יָוָן הָרְשָׁעָה עַל עַמְּךָ יִשְׂרָאֵל, לְהַשְׁכִּיחָם תּוֹרָתֶךָ וּלְהַעֲבִירָם מֵחֻקֵּי רְצוֹנֶךָ. וְאַתָּה בְּרַחֲמֶיךָ הָרַבִּים עָמַדְתָּ לָהֶם בְּעֵת צָרָתָם. מַסְרְתָּ גִבּוֹרִים בְּיַד חַלָּשִׁים, וְרַבִּים בְּיַד מְעַטִּים, וְזֵדִים בְּיַד עוֹסְקֵי תוֹרָתֶךָ. וּלְךָ עָשִׂיתָ שֵׁם גָּדוֹל וְקָדוֹשׁ בְּעוֹלָמֶךָ, וּלְעַמְּךָ יִשְׂרָאֵל עָשִׂיתָ תְּשׁוּעָה גְדוֹלָה וּפֻרְקָן כְּהַיּוֹם הַזֶּה. וְאַחַר כֵּן בָּאוּ בָנֶיךָ לִדְבִיר בֵּיתֶךָ, וּפִנּוּ אֶת־הֵיכָלֶךָ, וְטִהֲרוּ אֶת־מִקְדָּשֶׁךָ, וְהִדְלִיקוּ נֵרוֹת בְּחַצְרוֹת קָדְשֶׁךָ, וְקָבְעוּ שְׁמוֹנַת יְמֵי חֲנֻכָּה אֵלּוּ, לְהוֹדוֹת וּלְהַלֵּל לְשִׁמְךָ הַגָּדוֹל.

In days of old, at this season, You saved our people by wonders and mighty deeds. In the days of Mattathias the Hasmonean, the tyrannic Empire sought to destroy our people Israel by making them forget their Torah, and by forcing them to abandon their ancient way of life.

Through the power of Your spirit the weak defeated the strong, the few prevailed over the many, and the righteous were victorious. Then Your children returned to Your House to purify the sanctuary and to kindle its lights.

And they dedicated these days to give thanks and praise to Your majestic glory.

PEACE                                        ברכת שלום

שָׁלוֹם רָב עַל־יִשְׂרָאֵל עַמְּךָ תָּשִׂים לְעוֹלָם, כִּי אַתָּה הוּא
מֶלֶךְ אָדוֹן לְכָל־הַשָּׁלוֹם. וְטוֹב בְּעֵינֶיךָ לְבָרֵךְ אֶת־עַמְּךָ
יִשְׂרָאֵל וְאֶת־כָּל־הָעַמִּים בְּכָל־עֵת וּבְכָל־שָׁעָה בִּשְׁלוֹמֶךָ.
* בָּרוּךְ אַתָּה יי, הַמְבָרֵךְ אֶת־עַמּוֹ יִשְׂרָאֵל בַּשָּׁלוֹם.

* ON SHABBAT SHUVAH CONCLUDE:

בְּסֵפֶר חַיִּים וּבְרָכָה נִכָּתֵב לְחַיִּים טוֹבִים וּלְשָׁלוֹם.

בָּרוּךְ אַתָּה יי, עוֹשֵׂה הַשָּׁלוֹם.

O Sovereign Source of peace, let Israel Your people know enduring peace, for it is good in Your sight to bless Israel and all peoples continually with Your peace.

*We praise You, O God, for You bless Israel with peace.*

* ON SHABBAT SHUVAH CONCLUDE:

*Inscribe us in the Book of life, blessing, and peace. We praise You, O God, the Source of peace.*

SILENT PRAYER

אֱלֹהַי, נְצֹר לְשׁוֹנִי מֵרָע, וּשְׂפָתַי מִדַּבֵּר מִרְמָה. וְלִמְקַלְלַי נַפְשִׁי
תִדּוֹם וְנַפְשִׁי כֶּעָפָר לַכֹּל תִּהְיֶה. פְּתַח לִבִּי בְּתוֹרָתֶךָ, וּבְמִצְוֹתֶיךָ
תִּרְדּוֹף נַפְשִׁי. וְכָל־הַחוֹשְׁבִים עָלַי רָעָה, מְהֵרָה הָפֵר עֲצָתָם
וְקַלְקֵל מַחֲשַׁבְתָּם. עֲשֵׂה לְמַעַן שְׁמֶךָ, עֲשֵׂה לְמַעַן יְמִינֶךָ, עֲשֵׂה

לְמַעַן קְדֻשָּׁתֶךָ, עֲשֵׂה לְמַעַן תּוֹרָתֶךָ; לְמַעַן יֵחָלְצוּן יְדִידֶיךָ, הוֹשִׁיעָה יְמִינְךָ וַעֲנֵנִי.

O God, keep my tongue from evil and my lips from deceit. Help me to be silent in the face of derision, humble in the presence of all. Open my heart to Your Torah, that I may hasten to do Your Mitzvot. Save me with Your power; in time of trouble be my answer, that those who love You may rejoice.

〜 〜

יִהְיוּ לְרָצוֹן אִמְרֵי־פִי וְהֶגְיוֹן לִבִּי לְפָנֶיךָ, יהוה, צוּרִי וְגֹאֲלִי.

Yi-h'yu l'ra-tzon i-m'rei fi v'heg-yon li-bi l'fa-neh-cha, Adonai tzu-ri v'go-a-li.

May the words of my mouth and the meditations of my heart be acceptable to You, O God, my Rock and my Redeemer.

〜

עֹשֶׂה שָׁלוֹם בִּמְרוֹמָיו, הוּא יַעֲשֶׂה שָׁלוֹם עָלֵינוּ וְעַל־כָּל־יִשְׂרָאֵל, וְאִמְרוּ: אָמֵן.

O-seh sha-lom bi-m'ro-mav, hu ya-a-seh sha-lom a-lei-nu v'al kol Yis-ra-eil, v'i-m'ru: A-mein.

• May the One who causes peace to reign in the high heavens cause peace to reign among us, all Israel, and all the world.

For the Reading of the Torah, continue on page 141

Aleinu is on page 148 and page 149

64

הדלקת הנרות

As these candles give light to all who behold them, so may we give light to all who behold us.

As their brightness reminds us of the generations of Israel who have kindled light, so may we, in our own day, be among those who kindle light.

~ ~

Ba-ruch a-ta Adonai, Eh-lo-hei-nu meh-lech ha-o-lam, a-sher ki-d'sha-nu b'mitz-vo-tav v'tzi-va-nu l'had-lik ner shel Shabbat.

בָּרוּךְ אַתָּה יי, אֱלֹהֵינוּ מֶלֶךְ הָעוֹלָם, אֲשֶׁר קִדְּשָׁנוּ בְּמִצְוֹתָיו וְצִוָּנוּ לְהַדְלִיק נֵר שֶׁל שַׁבָּת.

We praise You, Eternal God, Sovereign of the universe: You hallow us with Your Mitzvot, and command us to kindle the lights of Shabbat.

~

Let there be joy!
*Let there be light!*
Let there be peace!
*Let there be Shabbat!*

~ ~

לכה דודי

לְכָה דוֹדִי לִקְרַאת כַּלָּה, פְּנֵי שַׁבָּת נְקַבְּלָה.

לְכָה דוֹדִי לִקְרַאת כַּלָּה, פְּנֵי שַׁבָּת נְקַבְּלָה.

L'cha do–di lik–rat ka–la, p'nei Shabbat n'ka–b'la.
L'cha do–di lik–rat ka–la, p'nei Shabbat n'ka–b'la.

שָׁמוֹר וְזָכוֹר, בְּדִבּוּר אֶחָד, הִשְׁמִיעָנוּ אֵל הַמְיֻחָד.

יְיָ אֶחָד וּשְׁמוֹ אֶחָד, לְשֵׁם וּלְתִפְאֶרֶת וְלִתְהִלָּה. לכה ...

Sha-mor v'za-chor b'di-bur eh-chad, hish-mi-anu Eil ha-m'yu-chad;
Adonai Eh-chad u-sh'mo Eh-chad, l'sheim u-l'tif-eh-ret v'li-t'hi-la.
L'cha do-di...

לִקְרַאת שַׁבָּת לְכוּ וְנֵלְכָה, כִּי הִיא מְקוֹר הַבְּרָכָה.

מֵרֹאשׁ מִקֶּדֶם נְסוּכָה, סוֹף מַעֲשֶׂה בְּמַחֲשָׁבָה תְּחִלָּה. לכה ...

Lik-rat Shabbat l'chu v'nei-l'cha, ki hi m'kor ha-b'ra-cha.
Mei-rosh mi-keh-dem n'su-cha, sof ma-a-seh b'ma-cha-sha-va t'chi-la.
L'cha do-di...

הִתְעוֹרְרִי, הִתְעוֹרְרִי, כִּי בָא אוֹרֵךְ! קוּמִי, אוֹרִי,

עוּרִי עוּרִי, שִׁיר דַּבֵּרִי; כְּבוֹד יְיָ עָלַיִךְ נִגְלָה. לכה ...

Hit-o-r'ri, hit-o-r'ri, ki va o-reich! Ku-mi o-ri,
u-ri u-ri, shir da-bei-ri; k'vod Adonai a-la-yich nig-la.
L'cha do-di...

בּוֹאִי בְשָׁלוֹם עֲטֶרֶת בַּעְלָהּ, גַּם בְּשִׂמְחָה וּבְצָהֳלָה,

תּוֹךְ אֱמוּנֵי עַם סְגֻלָּה, בּוֹאִי כַלָּה! בּוֹאִי כַלָּה! לכה ...

Bo-i v'sha-lom a-teh-ret ba-a-lah, gam b'sim-chah u-v'tsa-ho-la,
toch eh-mu-nei  am s'gu-la, bo-i cha-la! Bo-i cha-la!
L'cha do-di...

Beloved, come to meet the bride; beloved, come to greet Shabbat.

Keep and Remember: a single command the Only God caused us to hear; the Eternal is One, God's name is One, for honor and glory and praise. Beloved...

Come with me to meet Shabbat, forever a fountain of blessing. Still it flows, as from the start: the last of days, for which the first was made. Beloved...

Awake, awake, your light has come! Arise, shine, awake and sing; the Eternal's glory dawns upon you. Beloved...

Enter in peace, O crown of your husband; enter in gladness, enter in joy. Come to the people that keeps its faith. Enter, O bride! Enter, O bride! Beloved...

O Source of light and truth, Creator of the eternal law of goodness, and of the impulse within us for justice and mercy, we pray that this hour of worship may be one of vision and inspiration. Help us to find knowledge by which to live; lead us to take the words we shall speak into our hearts and our lives.

*Bless all who enter this sanctuary in search and in need, all who bring to this place the offering of their hearts. May our worship here lead us to fulfill our words and intentions with acts of kindness, peace, and love. Amen.*

We have come together to strengthen our bonds with our people Israel. Like Jews of generations past, we celebrate the grandeur of creation. Like Jews of every age, we echo our people's ancient call for justice.

*Our celebration is a sharing of memory and hope.*

We are Jews, but each of us is unique. We stand apart and alone, with differing feelings and insights. And yet we are not entirely alone and separate, for we are children of one people and one heritage.

*Our celebration unites many separate selves into a single chorus.*

And we are one in search of life's meaning. All of us know despair and exaltation; all bear burdens; all have moments of weakness and times of strength; all sing songs of sorrow and love.

*May our celebration bring us strength along our way.*

In this circle of hope, in the presence of the sacred, may the heart come to know itself and its best, finding a fresh impulse to love the good.

*May our celebration lead us to work for the good; and may this Shabbat give strength to us and to our people Israel.*

~ ~

Hi-nei mah-tov u-mah na-im

sheh-vet a-chim gam ya-chad.

הִנֵּה מַה־טּוֹב וּמַה־נָּעִים
שֶׁבֶת אַחִים גַּם־יָחַד.

How good it is, and how pleasant,
when we dwell together in unity.

~ ~

Many are the generations of Israel, and in every age we have sought the living God through Sabbath rest and worship. This time and place hold the power to increase our joy in the Eternal. O God, even as we seek You in the sanctuary, help us to know that Your glory fills all space; make us understand that You are with us at all times, if we but open our minds to You.

*We feel the presence of Your spirit in our homes and on our ways; we see the beauty of Your creation in mountain, sea, and sky, and in the human form; we hear You in the silence of our own hearts speaking the truths the heart knows.*

May we be Your witness to the world,
Your messenger to all the earth.

*May we show forth Your image within us,
the divine spark that makes us human.*

## All rise

READER'S KADDISH                                    חצי קדיש

יִתְגַּדַּל וְיִתְקַדַּשׁ שְׁמֵהּ רַבָּא בְּעָלְמָא דִּי־בְרָא כִרְעוּתֵהּ,
וְיַמְלִיךְ מַלְכוּתֵהּ בְּחַיֵּיכוֹן וּבְיוֹמֵיכוֹן וּבְחַיֵּי דְכָל־בֵּית
יִשְׂרָאֵל, בַּעֲגָלָא וּבִזְמַן קָרִיב, וְאִמְרוּ: אָמֵן.

יְהֵא שְׁמֵהּ רַבָּא מְבָרַךְ לְעָלַם וּלְעָלְמֵי עָלְמַיָּא.

יִתְבָּרַךְ וְיִשְׁתַּבַּח, וְיִתְפָּאַר וְיִתְרוֹמַם וְיִתְנַשֵּׂא, וְיִתְהַדָּר
וְיִתְעַלֶּה וְיִתְהַלַּל שְׁמֵהּ דְּקוּדְשָׁא, בְּרִיךְ הוּא,
לְעֵלָּא מִן־כָּל־בִּרְכָתָא וְשִׁירָתָא, תֻּשְׁבְּחָתָא וְנֶחֱמָתָא
דַּאֲמִירָן בְּעָלְמָא, וְאִמְרוּ: אָמֵן.

Yit-ga-dal v'yit–ka–dash sh'mei ra-ba b'al-ma di-v'ra chi-r'u'tei, v'yam-lich
mal-chu-tei b'cha-yei-chon u-v'yo-mei-chon u-v'cha-yei d'chol beit Yis-ra-
eil, ba-a-ga-la u-vi-z'man ka-riv, v'i-m' ru: A-mein.

Y'hei sh'mei ra-ba m'va-rach l'a-lam u-l'al-mei al-ma-ya.

Yit-ba-rach v'yish-ta-bach, v'yit-pa-ar v'yit-ro-mam v'yit-na-sei, v'yit-ha-dar
v'yit-a-leh v'yit-ha-lal sh'mei d'kud-sha, b'rich hu,

l'ei-la min kol bir-cha-ta v'shi-ra-ta, tush-b'cha-ta v'neh-cheh-ma-ta da-a-
mi-ran b'al-ma, v'i-m' ru: A-mein.

~ ~

## The Sh'ma and its Blessings

שמע וברכותיה

בָּרְכוּ אֶת־יי הַמְבֹרָך!

Praise the One to whom our praise is due!

בָּרוּךְ יי הַמְבֹרָךְ לְעוֹלָם וָעֶד!

*Ba-ruch Adonai ha-m'vo-rach l'o-lam va-ed!*

*Praised be the One to whom our praise is due, now and for ever!*

CREATION

מעריב ערבים

בָּרוּךְ אַתָּה יי, אֱלֹהֵינוּ מֶלֶךְ הָעוֹלָם, אֲשֶׁר בִּדְבָרוֹ
מַעֲרִיב עֲרָבִים, בְּחָכְמָה פּוֹתֵחַ שְׁעָרִים, וּבִתְבוּנָה מְשַׁנֶּה
עִתִּים, וּמַחֲלִיף אֶת־הַזְּמַנִּים, וּמְסַדֵּר אֶת־הַכּוֹכָבִים
בְּמִשְׁמְרוֹתֵיהֶם בָּרָקִיעַ כִּרְצוֹנוֹ.
בּוֹרֵא יוֹם וָלַיְלָה, גּוֹלֵל אוֹר מִפְּנֵי חֹשֶׁךְ וְחֹשֶׁךְ מִפְּנֵי אוֹר,
וּמַעֲבִיר יוֹם וּמֵבִיא לָיְלָה, וּמַבְדִּיל בֵּין יוֹם וּבֵין לָיְלָה,
יי צְבָאוֹת שְׁמוֹ.
אֵל חַי וְקַיָּם, תָּמִיד יִמְלוֹךְ עָלֵינוּ לְעוֹלָם וָעֶד.
בָּרוּךְ אַתָּה יי, הַמַּעֲרִיב עֲרָבִים.

° As day departs, as the dark of night descends, we lift our eyes
to the heavens. In awe and wonder our hearts cry out:

*Eternal God, how majestic is Your name in all the earth!*

A vast universe: who can know it? What mind can fathom it?
We look out to the endless suns and ask: What are we, what are
our dreams and our hopes? What are we, that You are mindful of
us? What are we, that You should care for us?

*And yet, within us abides a measure of Your spirit. You are
remote, but, oh, how near! Ordering the stars in the vast*

70

*solitudes of the dark, yet whispering in our minds that You are
closer than the air we breathe. For You have made us little less
than divine, and crowned us with glory and honor! With love
and awe we turn to You, and in the dark of evening we seek
the light of Your presence.*

REVELATION　　　　　　　　　　　　　　　　　　　　　אהבת עולם

אֲהֲבַת עוֹלָם בֵּית יִשְׂרָאֵל עַמְּךָ אָהָבְתָּ.

תּוֹרָה וּמִצְוֹת, חֻקִּים וּמִשְׁפָּטִים אוֹתָנוּ לִמַּדְתָּ.

עַל־כֵּן, יי אֱלֹהֵינוּ, בְּשָׁכְבֵּנוּ וּבְקוּמֵנוּ נָשִׂיחַ בְּחֻקֶּיךָ,

וְנִשְׂמַח בְּדִבְרֵי תוֹרָתֶךָ וּבְמִצְוֹתֶיךָ לְעוֹלָם וָעֶד.

כִּי הֵם חַיֵּינוּ וְאֹרֶךְ יָמֵינוּ, וּבָהֶם נֶהְגֶּה יוֹמָם וָלָיְלָה.

וְאַהֲבָתְךָ אַל־תָּסוּר מִמֶּנּוּ לְעוֹלָמִים!

בָּרוּךְ אַתָּה יי, אוֹהֵב עַמּוֹ יִשְׂרָאֵל.

° One and Only God, You have made each of us unique, and
formed us to be united in one family of life. Be with us, Eternal
One, as we seek to unite our lives with Your power and Your love.

*We proclaim now Your Oneness and our own hope for unity;
we acclaim Your creative power in the universe and in
ourselves, the Law that binds world to world and heart to
heart:*

שְׁמַע יִשְׂרָאֵל: יהוה אֱלֹהֵינוּ, יהוה אֶחָד!

Sh'ma Yis-ra-eil: Adonai Eh-lo-hei-nu, Adonai Eh-chad!

*Hear, O Israel: the Eternal One is our God,
the Eternal God alone!*

בָּרוּךְ שֵׁם כְּבוֹד מַלְכוּתוֹ לְעוֹלָם וָעֶד!

Ba-ruch shem k'vod mal-chu-to l'o-lam va–ed!

*Blessed is God's glorious majesty for ever and ever!*

All are seated

71

וְאָהַבְתָּ אֵת יְהֹוָה אֱלֹהֶיךָ בְּכָל־לְבָבְךָ וּבְכָל־נַפְשְׁךָ וּבְכָל־מְאֹדֶךָ:
וְהָיוּ הַדְּבָרִים הָאֵלֶּה אֲשֶׁר אָנֹכִי מְצַוְּךָ הַיּוֹם עַל־לְבָבֶךָ:
וְשִׁנַּנְתָּם לְבָנֶיךָ וְדִבַּרְתָּ בָּם בְּשִׁבְתְּךָ בְּבֵיתֶךָ וּבְלֶכְתְּךָ בַדֶּרֶךְ
וּבְשָׁכְבְּךָ וּבְקוּמֶךָ: וּקְשַׁרְתָּם לְאוֹת עַל־יָדֶךָ וְהָיוּ לְטֹטָפֹת בֵּין
עֵינֶיךָ: וּכְתַבְתָּם עַל־מְזוּזֹת בֵּיתֶךָ וּבִשְׁעָרֶיךָ:

לְמַעַן תִּזְכְּרוּ וַעֲשִׂיתֶם אֶת־כָּל־מִצְוֹתָי וִהְיִיתֶם קְדֹשִׁים
לֵאלֹהֵיכֶם: אֲנִי יְהֹוָה אֱלֹהֵיכֶם אֲשֶׁר הוֹצֵאתִי אֶתְכֶם
מֵאֶרֶץ מִצְרַיִם לִהְיוֹת לָכֶם לֵאלֹהִים אֲנִי יְהֹוָה אֱלֹהֵיכֶם:

V'a–hav–ta et Adonai Eh–lo–heh–cha b'chol l'va–v'cha u–v'chol naf–
sh'cha u–v'chol m'o–deh–cha. V'ha–yu ha–d'va–rim ha–ei–leh a–sher a–
no–chi m'tza–v'cha ha–yom al l'va–veh–cha. V'shi–nan–tam l'va–neh–cha
v'di–bar–ta bam b'shiv–t'cha b'vei–teh–cha u–v'lech–t'cha va–deh–rech u–
v'shoch–b'cha u–v'ku–meh–cha. U–k'shar–tam l'ot al ya–deh–cha v'ha–yu
l'to–ta–fot bein ei–neh–cha; u–ch'tav–tam al m'zu–zot bei–teh–cha u–vi–
sh'a–reh–cha.

L'ma–an tiz–k'ru va–a–si–tem et kol mitz–vo–tai, vi–h'yi–tem  k'do–shim
lei–lo–hei–chem. Ani Adonai Eh–lo–hei–chem a–sher ho–tzei–ti et–chem
mei–eh–retz mitz–ra–yim li–h'yot la–chem lei–lo–him. Ani Adonai Eh–lo–
hei–chem.

*You shall love your Eternal God with all your heart, with all
your mind, with all your being. Set these words, which I
command you this day, upon your heart. Teach them faithfully
to your children; speak of them in your home and on your
way, when you lie down and when you rise up. Bind them as
a sign upon your hand; let them be symbols before your eyes;
inscribe them on the doorposts of your house, and on your
gates.*

*Be mindful of all My Mitzvot, and do them: so shall you
consecrate yourselves to your God. I am your Eternal God who
led you out of Egypt to be your God; I am your Eternal God.*

72

REDEMPTION  גְּאוּלָה

אֱמֶת וֶאֱמוּנָה כָּל־זֹאת, וְקַיָּם עָלֵינוּ, כִּי הוּא יי אֱלֹהֵינוּ,
וְאֵין זוּלָתוֹ, וַאֲנַחְנוּ יִשְׂרָאֵל עַמּוֹ. הַפּוֹדֵנוּ מִיַּד מְלָכִים, הַגּוֹאֲלֵנוּ
מִכַּף כָּל־הֶעָרִיצִים, וַיּוֹצֵא אֶת־עַמּוֹ יִשְׂרָאֵל מִמִּצְרַיִם לְחֵרוּת
עוֹלָם. וְרָאוּ בָנָיו גְּבוּרָתוֹ; שִׁבְּחוּ וְהוֹדוּ לִשְׁמוֹ. וּמַלְכוּתוֹ בְּרָצוֹן
קִבְּלוּ עֲלֵיהֶם. לְךָ עָנוּ שִׁירָה בְּשִׂמְחָה רַבָּה, וְאָמְרוּ כֻלָּם:

° In a world torn by violence and pain, a world far from
wholeness, a world waiting still to be redeemed, give us, O Source
of good, the courage to say: There is one God in heaven and
earth.

*The high heavens declare Your glory; may earth reveal Your
justice and Your love.*

From Egypt, the house of bondage, we were delivered; at Sinai,
amid peals of thunder, we bound ourselves to Your purpose.
Inspired by prophets and instructed by sages, we survived
oppression and exile, time and again overcoming the forces that
would have destroyed us.

*Our failings are many—our faults are great—yet it has been
our glory to bear witness to our God, and to keep alive in dark
ages the vision of a world redeemed.*

May this vision never fade; let us continue to work for the day
when the nations will be one and at peace. Then shall we sing
with one accord, as Moses, Miriam and Israel sang at the shores
of the Sea:

מִי־כָמֹכָה בָּאֵלִם, יהוה? מִי כָּמֹכָה, נֶאְדָּר בַּקֹּדֶשׁ,
נוֹרָא תְהִלֹּת, עֹשֵׂה פֶלֶא?

מַלְכוּתְךָ רָאוּ בָנֶיךָ, בּוֹקֵעַ יָם לִפְנֵי מֹשֶׁה; זֶה אֵלִי!
עָנוּ וְאָמְרוּ: יהוה יִמְלֹךְ לְעֹלָם וָעֶד!

וְנֶאֱמַר: כִּי פָדָה יהוה אֶת־יַעֲקֹב, וּגְאָלוֹ מִיַּד חָזָק מִמֶּנּוּ.
בָּרוּךְ אַתָּה יי, גָּאַל יִשְׂרָאֵל.

Mi cha–mo–cha ba–ei–lim, Adonai?
Mi ka–mo–cha, neh–dar ba–ko–desh, no–ra t'hi–lot, o–sei feh–leh?
Mal–chu–t'cha ra–u va–neh–cha, bo–kei–a yam li–f'nei Mo–sheh; zeh Ei–li!
A–nu v'a–m'ru: Adonai yim–loch l'o–lam va–ed!
V'neh–eh–mar: Ki fa–da Adonai et Ya–a–kov, u–g'a–lo mi–yad cha–zak
mi–meh–nu.
Ba–ruch a–ta Adonai, ga–al Yis–ra–eil.

Who is like You, Eternal One, among the gods that are worshipped?
Who is like You, majestic in holiness, awesome in splendor, doing
wonders?

In their escape from the sea, Your children saw Your sovereign might
displayed. "This is my God!" they cried. "The Eternal will reign for
ever and ever!"

And it has been said: The Eternal One delivered Jacob, and redeemed us
from the hand of one stronger than ourselves.

We praise You, O God, Redeemer of Israel.

DIVINE PROVIDENCE                                             הַשְׁכִּיבֵנוּ

הַשְׁכִּיבֵנוּ, יי אֱלֹהֵינוּ, לְשָׁלוֹם, וְהַעֲמִידֵנוּ, מַלְכֵּנוּ, לְחַיִּים. וּפְרוֹשׂ
עָלֵינוּ סֻכַּת שְׁלוֹמֶךָ, וְתַקְּנֵנוּ בְּעֵצָה טוֹבָה מִלְּפָנֶיךָ, וְהוֹשִׁיעֵנוּ
לְמַעַן שְׁמֶךָ, וְהָגֵן בַּעֲדֵנוּ. וְהָסֵר מֵעָלֵינוּ אוֹיֵב דֶּבֶר וְחֶרֶב וְרָעָב
וְיָגוֹן; וְהָסֵר שָׂטָן מִלְּפָנֵינוּ וּמֵאַחֲרֵינוּ, וּבְצֵל כְּנָפֶיךָ תַּסְתִּירֵנוּ,
כִּי אֵל שׁוֹמְרֵנוּ וּמַצִּילֵנוּ אָתָּה, כִּי אֵל מֶלֶךְ חַנּוּן וְרַחוּם אָתָּה.
וּשְׁמוֹר צֵאתֵנוּ וּבוֹאֵנוּ לְחַיִּים וּלְשָׁלוֹם מֵעַתָּה וְעַד עוֹלָם.
בָּרוּךְ אַתָּה יי, הַפּוֹרֵשׂ סֻכַּת שָׁלוֹם עָלֵינוּ וְעַל כָּל־עַמּוֹ
יִשְׂרָאֵל, וְעַל יְרוּשָׁלָיִם.

° Let there be love and understanding among us; let peace and
friendship be our shelter from life's storms. Eternal God, help us

to walk with good companions, to live with hope in our hearts and eternity in our thoughts, that we may lie down in peace and rise up to find our hearts waiting to do Your will.

*We praise You, Guardian of Israel, whose love gives light to all the world.*

O God of Israel, may our worship on this day help us to grow in loyalty to our covenant with You and to the way of life it demands: the way of gentleness and justice, the path of truth and of peace.

THE COVENANT OF SHABBAT                                             ושמרו

וְשָׁמְרוּ בְנֵי־יִשְׂרָאֵל אֶת־הַשַּׁבָּת, לַעֲשׂוֹת אֶת־הַשַּׁבָּת לְדֹרֹתָם
בְּרִית עוֹלָם. בֵּינִי וּבֵין בְּנֵי יִשְׂרָאֵל אוֹת הִיא לְעֹלָם. כִּי־שֵׁשֶׁת
יָמִים עָשָׂה יהוה אֶת־הַשָּׁמַיִם וְאֶת־הָאָרֶץ, וּבַיּוֹם הַשְּׁבִיעִי
שָׁבַת וַיִּנָּפַשׁ.

V'sha-m'ru v'nei Yis-ra-eil et ha-Shabbat, la-a-sot et ha-sha-bat l'do-ro-tam b'rit o-lam. Bei-ni u-vein b'nei Yis-ra-eil ot hi l'o-lam. Ki shei-shet ya-mim a-sa Adonai et ha-sha-ma-yim v'et ha-a-retz, u-va-yom ha-sh'vi-i sha-vat va-yi-na-fash.

The people of Israel shall keep the Sabbath, observing the Sabbath in every generation as a covenant for all time. It is a sign for ever between Me and the people of Israel. For in six days the Eternal One made heaven and earth, but on the seventh day God rested and was refreshed.

## MEDITATION

Prayer invites God to let the Divine Presence suffuse our spirits, to let the Divine will prevail in our lives. Prayer cannot bring water to parched fields, nor mend a broken bridge, nor rebuild a ruined city; but prayer can water an arid soul, mend a broken heart, and rebuild a weakened will.

## All rise

75

T'FILAH　תפלה

אֲדֹנָי, שְׂפָתַי תִּפְתָּח, וּפִי יַגִּיד תְּהִלָּתֶךָ.

Eternal God, open my lips, that my mouth may declare Your glory.

GOD OF ALL GENERATIONS　אבות ואמהות

בָּרוּךְ אַתָּה יי, אֱלֹהֵינוּ וֵאלֹהֵי אֲבוֹתֵינוּ וְאִמּוֹתֵינוּ:
אֱלֹהֵי אַבְרָהָם, אֱלֹהֵי יִצְחָק, וֵאלֹהֵי יַעֲקֹב.
אֱלֹהֵי שָׂרָה, אֱלֹהֵי רִבְקָה, אֱלֹהֵי לֵאָה וֵאלֹהֵי רָחֵל.
הָאֵל הַגָּדוֹל הַגִּבּוֹר וְהַנּוֹרָא, אֵל עֶלְיוֹן, גּוֹמֵל חֲסָדִים
טוֹבִים וְקוֹנֵה הַכֹּל, וְזוֹכֵר חַסְדֵי אָבוֹת וְאִמָּהוֹת,
וּמֵבִיא גְאֻלָּה לִבְנֵי בְנֵיהֶם, לְמַעַן שְׁמוֹ בְּאַהֲבָה.
מֶלֶךְ עוֹזֵר וּמוֹשִׁיעַ וּמָגֵן.
בָּרוּךְ אַתָּה יי, מָגֵן אַבְרָהָם וְעֶזְרַת שָׂרה.

Ba–ruch a–ta Adonai, Eh–lo–hei–nu vei–lo–hei a–vo–tei–nu v'i–mo–tei–nu:
Eh–lo–hei Av–ra–ham, eh–lo–hei Yitz–chak, vei–lo–hei Ya–a–kov.
Eh–lo–hei Sa–ra, Eh–lo–hei Riv–ka, Eh–lo–hei Lei–a vei–lo–hei Ra–cheil.
Ha–eil ha–ga–dol ha–gi–bor v'ha–no–ra, Eil el–yon, go–meil cha–sa–dim
to–vim, v'ko–nei ha–kol, v'zo–cheir cha-s'dei a–vot v'i–ma–hot,
u–mei–vi g'u–la li–v'nei v'nei–hem, l'ma–an sh'mo, b'a–ha–va.
Meh–lech o–zeir u–mo–shi–a u–ma–gein.
Ba–ruch a–ta Adonai, ma–gein Av–ra–ham v'ez–rat Sa–ra.

° Source of all being, we turn to You as did our people in ancient days. They beheld You in the heavens; they felt You in their hearts; they sought You in their lives.

Now their quest is ours. Help us, O God, to celebrate the wonder of being. Give us the courage to search for truth. Teach us the path to a better life. So shall we, by our lives and our labors, bring nearer to realization the great hope inherited from ages past, for a world transformed by liberty, justice, and peace.

GOD'S POWER                                                        גְּבוּרוֹת

אַתָּה גִּבּוֹר לְעוֹלָם, אֲדֹנָי, מְחַיֵּה הַכֹּל אַתָּה, רַב לְהוֹשִׁיעַ.

מְכַלְכֵּל חַיִּים בְּחֶסֶד, מְחַיֵּה הַכֹּל בְּרַחֲמִים רַבִּים. סוֹמֵךְ

נוֹפְלִים, וְרוֹפֵא חוֹלִים, וּמַתִּיר אֲסוּרִים, וּמְקַיֵּם אֱמוּנָתוֹ

לִישֵׁנֵי עָפָר. מִי כָמְוֹךָ בַּעַל גְּבוּרוֹת, וּמִי דְוֹמֶה לָךְ,

מֶלֶךְ מֵמִית וּמְחַיֶּה וּמַצְמִיחַ יְשׁוּעָה?

וְנֶאֱמָן אַתָּה לְהַחֲיוֹת הַכֹּל. בָּרוּךְ אַתָּה יי, מְחַיֵּה הַכֹּל.

A-ta gi-bor l'o-lam, Adonai, m'cha-yei ha-kol a-ta, rav l'ho-shi-a.
M'chal-keil cha-yim b'cheh-sed, m'cha-yei ha-kol b'ra-cha-mim ra-bim.
So-meich no-f'lim, v'ro-fei cho-lim, u-ma-tir a-su-rim, u-m'ka-yeim eh-
mu-na-to li-shei-nei a-far. Mi cha-mo-cha ba-al g'vu-rot, u-mi do-meh
lach, meh-lech mei-mit u-m'cha-yeh u-matz-mi-ach y'shu-a?
V'neh-eh-man a-ta l'ha-cha-yot ha-kol. Ba-ruch a-ta Adonai, m'cha-yei
ha-kol.

° Your might, O God, is everlasting;
*Help us to use our strength for good.*

You are the Source of life and blessing;
*Help us to choose life for ourselves and our children.*

You are the support of the falling;
*Help us to lift up the fallen.*

You are the Author of freedom;
*Help us to free the captive.*

You are our hope in death as in life.
*Help us to keep faith with those who sleep in the dust.*

Your might, O God, is everlasting;
*Help us to use our strength for good.*

THE HOLINESS OF GOD                                              קְדוּשַׁת הַשֵּׁם

אַתָּה קָדוֹשׁ וְשִׁמְךָ קָדוֹשׁ, וּקְדוֹשִׁים בְּכָל־יוֹם יְהַלְלוּךָ, סֶּלָה.
בָּרוּךְ אַתָּה יי, הָאֵל הַקָּדוֹשׁ.

You are holy, Your name is holy, and those who strive to be
holy declare Your glory day by day.

We praise You, Eternal One, the holy God.

### All are seated

MOST PRECIOUS OF DAYS                                             יִשְׂמְחוּ

יִשְׂמְחוּ בְמַלְכוּתְךָ שׁוֹמְרֵי שַׁבָּת וְקוֹרְאֵי עֹנֶג. עַם מְקַדְּשֵׁי שְׁבִיעִי
כֻּלָּם יִשְׂבְּעוּ וְיִתְעַנְּגוּ מִטּוּבֶךָ. וְהַשְּׁבִיעִי רָצִיתָ בּוֹ וְקִדַּשְׁתּוֹ.
חֶמְדַּת יָמִים אוֹתוֹ קָרָאתָ, זֵכֶר לְמַעֲשֵׂה בְרֵאשִׁית.

Yis–m'chu v'ma–l'chu–t'cha sho–m'rei Shabbat v'ko–r'ei o–neg. Am m'ka–
d'shei sh'vi–i ku–lam yis–b'u v'yit–a–n'gu mi–tu–veh–cha. V'ha–sh'vi–i ra–
tzi–ta bo v'ki–dash–to. Chem–dat ya–mim o–to ka–ra–ta, zei–cher l'ma–a–
sei v'rei–sheet.

Those who keep the Sabbath and call it a delight shall rejoice in Your
deliverance. All who hallow the seventh day shall be gladdened by Your
goodness. This day is Israel's festival of the spirit, sanctified and blessed
by You, the most precious of days, a symbol of the joy of creation.

THE HOLINESS OF SHABBAT                                         קְדוּשַׁת הַיּוֹם

אֱלֹהֵינוּ וֵאלֹהֵי אֲבוֹתֵינוּ וְאִמּוֹתֵינוּ, רְצֵה בִמְנוּחָתֵנוּ. קַדְּשֵׁנוּ
בְּמִצְוֹתֶיךָ וְתֵן חֶלְקֵנוּ בְּתוֹרָתֶךָ. שַׂבְּעֵנוּ מִטּוּבֶךָ, וְשַׂמְּחֵנוּ
בִּישׁוּעָתֶךָ, וְטַהֵר לִבֵּנוּ לְעָבְדְּךָ בֶּאֱמֶת. וְהַנְחִילֵנוּ, יי
אֱלֹהֵינוּ, בְּאַהֲבָה וּבְרָצוֹן שַׁבַּת קָדְשֶׁךָ, וְיָנוּחוּ בָהּ יִשְׂרָאֵל
מְקַדְּשֵׁי שְׁמֶךָ. בָּרוּךְ אַתָּה יי, מְקַדֵּשׁ הַשַּׁבָּת.

78

Eh-lo-hei-nu vei-lo-hei a-vo-tei-nu v'i-mo-tei-nu, r'tzei vi-m'nu-cha-tei-nu. Ka-d'shei-nu b'mitz-vo-teh-cha v-tein chel-kei-nu b'to-ra-teh-cha. Sab-ei-nu mi-tu-veh-cha, v'sam-chei-nu bi-shu-a-teh-cha, v'ta-heir li-bei-nu l'ov-d'cha beh-eh-met. V'han-chi-lei-nu, Adonai Eh-lo-hei-nu, b'a-ha-va u-v'ra-tzon Shabbat kod-sheh-cha, v'ya-nu-chu va Yis-ra-eil m'ka-d'shei sh'meh-cha. Ba-ruch a-ta Adonai, m'ka-deish ha-Shabbat.

° *God of Israel, may our worship on this Sabbath bring us near to all that is high and holy. May it bind the generations in bonds of love and sharing, and unite us with our people in common hope and faith. And through Sabbath rest and worship, may we learn to find fulfillment and joy in the vision of peace for all the world.*

WORSHIP                                                              עבודה

רְצֵה, יי אֱלֹהֵינוּ, בְּעַמְּךָ יִשְׂרָאֵל, וּתְפִלָּתָם בְּאַהֲבָה תְקַבֵּל,
וּתְהִי לְרָצוֹן תָּמִיד עֲבוֹדַת יִשְׂרָאֵל עַמֶּךָ.
בָּרוּךְ אַתָּה יי, שֶׁאוֹתְךָ לְבַדְּךָ בְּיִרְאָה נַעֲבוֹד.

° You are with us in our prayer, in our love and our doubt, in our longing to feel Your presence and do Your will. You are the still, clear voice within us. Therefore, O God, when doubt troubles us, when anxiety makes us tremble, and pain clouds the mind, we look inward for the answer to our prayers. There may we find You, and there find courage, insight, and endurance. And let our worship bring us closer to one another, that all Israel, and all who seek You, may find new strength for Your service.

THANKSGIVING                                                         הודאה

מוֹדִים אֲנַחְנוּ לָךְ שָׁאַתָּה הוּא יי אֱלֹהֵינוּ וֵאלֹהֵי אֲבוֹתֵינוּ
וְאִמּוֹתֵינוּ, אֱלֹהֵי כָל־בָּשָׂר, יוֹצְרֵנוּ יוֹצֵר בְּרֵאשִׁית. בְּרָכוֹת
וְהוֹדָאוֹת לְשִׁמְךָ הַגָּדוֹל וְהַקָּדוֹשׁ עַל־שֶׁהֶחֱיִיתָנוּ וְקִיַּמְתָּנוּ.
כֵּן תְּחַיֵּנוּ וּתְקַיְּמֵנוּ, יי אֱלֹהֵינוּ, וּתְאַמְּצֵנוּ לִשְׁמֹר חֻקֶּיךָ,
לַעֲשׂוֹת רְצוֹנֶךָ, וּלְעָבְדְּךָ בְּלֵבָב שָׁלֵם. בָּרוּךְ אֵל הַהוֹדָאוֹת.

79

° *Eternal Source of good, we give thanks for the numberless gifts and blessings that fill our days: for life itself and its endless variety; for all that sustains body and mind; for love and friendship; for the delights of the senses; and for the excellence of Your Torah, which deepens our life and enriches our days.*

*Teach us, God of wonders, to work for a just and compassionate society, where all may share Your gifts in the joy of freedom.*

PEACE                                                     ברכת שלום

שָׁלוֹם רָב עַל־יִשְׂרָאֵל עַמְּךָ תָּשִׂים לְעוֹלָם, כִּי אַתָּה הוּא
מֶלֶךְ אָדוֹן לְכָל־הַשָּׁלוֹם. וְטוֹב בְּעֵינֶיךָ לְבָרֵךְ אֶת־עַמְּךָ
יִשְׂרָאֵל וְאֶת־כָּל־הָעַמִּים בְּכָל־עֵת וּבְכָל־שָׁעָה בִּשְׁלוֹמֶךָ.
בָּרוּךְ אַתָּה יְיָ, הַמְבָרֵךְ אֶת־עַמּוֹ יִשְׂרָאֵל בַּשָּׁלוֹם.

° Grant us peace, Your most precious gift, O Eternal Source of peace, and give us the will to proclaim its message to all the peoples of the earth.

*Bless our country, that it may always be a stronghold of peace, and its advocate among the nations.*

*May contentment reign within its borders, health and happiness within its homes.*

*Strengthen the bonds of friendship among the inhabitants of all lands, and may the love of Your name hallow every home and every heart. We praise You, O God, the Source of peace.*

SILENT PRAYER

These quiet moments of Shabbat open my soul. Blessed with another week of life, I give thanks to the One who creates and sustains me.

For all the good I have known during the days that have passed, I am very grateful. I know that I have not always responded with

my best effort, but often I did earnestly try. I have tried to give my family and friends love and devotion, and I pray that I may grow more loving as the years pass.

Even as I regret my weaknesses, I rejoice in my accomplishments. Let these achievements, O God, lead to many others. May I be blessed on each Shabbat with the sense of having grown in goodness and compassion.

~ ~

יִהְיוּ לְרָצוֹן אִמְרֵי־פִי וְהֶגְיוֹן לִבִּי לְפָנֶיךָ, יהוה, צוּרִי וְגֹאֲלִי.

Yi-h'yu l'ra-tzon i-m'rei fi v'heg-yon li-bi l'fa-neh-cha, Adonai tzu-ri v'go-a-li.

May the words of my mouth and the meditations of my heart be acceptable to You, O God, my Rock and my Redeemer.

~

עֹשֶׂה שָׁלוֹם בִּמְרוֹמָיו, הוּא יַעֲשֶׂה שָׁלוֹם עָלֵינוּ וְעַל־כָּל־יִשְׂרָאֵל, וְאִמְרוּ: אָמֵן.

O-seh sha-lom bi-m'ro-mav, hu ya-a-seh sha-lom a-lei-nu v'al kol Yis-ra-eil, v'i-m'ru: A-mein.

• May the One who causes peace to reign in the high heavens cause peace to reign among us, all Israel, and all the world.

~ Pray as if everything depended on God;
act as if everything depended on you. ~

~ Who rise from prayer better persons,
their prayer is answered. ~

For the Reading of the Torah, continue on page 141

Aleinu is on page 148 and page 149

הדלקת הנרות

These lights
are only flickering flames,
yet flames
illumine
our uncertain steps.

Flames remind us
of Sabbaths long past,
and of their beauty
that delighted our hearts.

May they inspire us
to work
for the Great Sabbath of peace.

~ ~

Ba-ruch a-ta Adonai, Eh-lo-hei-nu
meh-lech ha-o-lam, a-sher ki-d'sha-
nu b'mitz-vo-tav v'tzi-va-nu l'had-
lik ner shel Shabbat.

בָּרוּךְ אַתָּה יי, אֱלֹהֵינוּ מֶלֶךְ
הָעוֹלָם, אֲשֶׁר קִדְּשָׁנוּ בְּמִצְוֹתָיו
וְצִוָּנוּ לְהַדְלִיק נֵר שֶׁל שַׁבָּת.

We praise You, Eternal God, Sovereign of the universe: You
hallow us with Your Mitzvot, and command us to kindle the
Sabbath lights.

**Welcoming Shabbat** קבלת שבת

*From Psalm 15*

יהוה, מִי־יָגוּר בְּאָהֳלֶךָ, מִי־יִשְׁכֹּן בְּהַר קָדְשֶׁךָ?

הוֹלֵךְ תָּמִים, וּפֹעֵל צֶדֶק, וְדֹבֵר אֱמֶת בִּלְבָבוֹ.

לֹא־רָגַל עַל־לְשֹׁנוֹ, לֹא־עָשָׂה לְרֵעֵהוּ רָעָה,

וְחֶרְפָּה לֹא־נָשָׂא עַל־קְרֹבוֹ.

נִשְׁבַּע לְהָרַע וְלֹא יָמִר.

כַּסְפּוֹ לֹא־נָתַן בְּנֶשֶׁךְ, וְשֹׁחַד עַל־נָקִי לֹא לָקָח.

עֹשֵׂה־אֵלֶּה לֹא יִמּוֹט לְעוֹלָם.

Eternal God:
Who may abide in Your house?
Who may dwell in Your holy mountain?
*Those who are upright; who do justly;*
*all whose hearts are true.*

Who do not slander others,
nor wrong them,
nor bring shame upon their kin.
*Who give their word and, come what may, do not retract.*

Who do not exploit others,
who never take bribes.
*Those who live in this way*
*shall never be shaken.*

There are days
when we seek material things,
and measure failure by what we do not own.
*On Shabbat we wish not to acquire but to share.*

83

There are days
when we exploit nature with reckless greed.
*On Shabbat we stand in wonder before the mystery of creation.*

There are days
when we think only of ourselves.
*On Shabbat*
*we open our hearts to the needs of others.*

Therefore we welcome Shabbat—
*day of rest, day of joy, day of peace.*

SHALOM ALEICHEM                  שלום עליכם

שָׁלוֹם עֲלֵיכֶם, מַלְאֲכֵי הַשָּׁרֵת, מַלְאֲכֵי עֶלְיוֹן,
מִמֶּלֶךְ מַלְכֵי הַמְּלָכִים, הַקָּדוֹשׁ בָּרוּךְ הוּא.

בּוֹאֲכֶם לְשָׁלוֹם, מַלְאֲכֵי הַשָּׁלוֹם, מַלְאֲכֵי עֶלְיוֹן,
מִמֶּלֶךְ מַלְכֵי הַמְּלָכִים, הַקָּדוֹשׁ בָּרוּךְ הוּא.

בָּרְכוּנִי לְשָׁלוֹם, מַלְאֲכֵי הַשָּׁלוֹם, מַלְאֲכֵי עֶלְיוֹן,
מִמֶּלֶךְ מַלְכֵי הַמְּלָכִים, הַקָּדוֹשׁ בָּרוּךְ הוּא.

צֵאתְכֶם לְשָׁלוֹם, מַלְאֲכֵי הַשָּׁלוֹם, מַלְאֲכֵי עֶלְיוֹן,
מִמֶּלֶךְ מַלְכֵי הַמְּלָכִים, הַקָּדוֹשׁ בָּרוּךְ הוּא.

Sha-lom a-lei-chem mal-a-chei ha-sha-reit, mal-a-chei El-yon,
Mi-meh-lech ma-l'chei ha-m'la-chim, ha-ka-dosh ba-ruch hu.

Bo-a-chem l'sha-lom, mal-a-chei ha-sha-lom, mal-a-chei El-yon,
Mi-meh-lech ma-l'chei ha-m'la-chim, ha-ka-dosh ba-ruch hu.

Ba-r'chu-ni l'sha-lom, mal-a-chei ha-sha-lom, mal-a-chei El-yon,
Mi-meh-lech ma-l'chei ha-m'la-chim, ha-ka-dosh ba-ruch hu.

Tzei-t'chem l'sha-lom, mal-a-chei ha-sha-lom, mal-a-chei El-yon,
Mi-meh-lech ma-l'chei ha-m'la-chim, ha-ka-dosh ba-ruch hu.

Peace be to you, ministering angels, messengers of the Most High, of the supreme Sovereign, the Holy One, ever to be praised.

Enter in peace, O messengers of the Most High, of the supreme Sovereign, the Holy One, ever to be praised.

Bless us with peace, O messengers of the Most High, of the supreme Sovereign, the Holy One, ever to be praised.

Depart in peace, O messengers of the Most High, of the supreme Sovereign, the Holy One, ever to be praised.

The synagogue is the sanctuary of Israel. Born of our longing for the living God, it has been to Israel, throughout our wanderings, a visible token of the presence of God in our people's midst. Its beauty is the beauty of holiness; steadfast it has stood as the champion of justice, mercy, and peace.

*Its truths are true for all people. Its love is a love for all people. Its God is the God of all people, as it has been said: "My house shall be called a house of prayer for all peoples."*

Let all the family of Israel, all who hunger for righteousness, all who seek the Eternal, find God here—and here find life!

### All rise

READER'S KADDISH          חֲצִי קַדִּישׁ

יִתְגַּדַּל וְיִתְקַדַּשׁ שְׁמֵהּ רַבָּא בְּעָלְמָא דִי־בְרָא כִרְעוּתֵהּ,
וְיַמְלִיךְ מַלְכוּתֵהּ בְּחַיֵּיכוֹן וּבְיוֹמֵיכוֹן וּבְחַיֵּי דְכָל־בֵּית
יִשְׂרָאֵל, בַּעֲגָלָא וּבִזְמַן קָרִיב, וְאִמְרוּ: אָמֵן.

יְהֵא שְׁמֵהּ רַבָּא מְבָרַךְ לְעָלַם וּלְעָלְמֵי עָלְמַיָּא.

יִתְבָּרַךְ וְיִשְׁתַּבַּח, וְיִתְפָּאַר וְיִתְרוֹמַם וְיִתְנַשֵּׂא, וְיִתְהַדָּר
וְיִתְעַלֶּה וְיִתְהַלָּל שְׁמֵהּ דְּקוּדְשָׁא, בְּרִיךְ הוּא,

לְעֵלָּא מִן־כָּל־בִּרְכָתָא וְשִׁירָתָא, תֻּשְׁבְּחָתָא וְנֶחֱמָתָא
דַּאֲמִירָן בְּעָלְמָא, וְאִמְרוּ: אָמֵן.

Yit-ga-dal v'yit–ka–dash sh'mei ra-ba b'al-ma di-v'ra chi-r'u'tei, v'yam-lich
mal-chu-tei b'cha-yei-chon u-v'yo-mei-chon u-v'cha-yei d'chol beit Yis-ra-
eil, ba-a-ga-la u-vi-z'man ka-riv, v'i-m' ru: A-mein.

Y'hei sh'mei ra-ba m'va-rach l'a-lam u-l'al-mei al-ma-ya.

Yit-ba-rach v'yish-ta-bach, v'yit-pa-ar v'yit-ro-mam v'yit-na-sei, v'yit-ha-dar
v'yit-a-leh v'yit-ha-lal sh'mei d'kud-sha, b'rich hu,

l'ei-la min kol bir-cha-ta v'shi-ra-ta, tush-b'cha-ta v'neh-cheh-ma-ta da-a-
mi-ran b'al-ma, v'i-m' ru: A-mein.

**The Sh'ma and its Blessings**                         שמע וברכותיה

בָּרְכוּ אֶת־יי הַמְבֹרָךְ!

Praise the One to whom our praise is due!

בָּרוּךְ יי הַמְבֹרָךְ לְעוֹלָם וָעֶד!

*Ba-ruch Adonai ha-m'vo-rach l'o-lam va-ed!*

*Praised be the One to whom our praise is due, now and for ever!*

CREATION                                              מעריב ערבים

בָּרוּךְ אַתָּה יי, אֱלֹהֵינוּ מֶלֶךְ הָעוֹלָם, אֲשֶׁר בִּדְבָרוֹ
מַעֲרִיב עֲרָבִים, בְּחָכְמָה פּוֹתֵחַ שְׁעָרִים, וּבִתְבוּנָה מְשַׁנֶּה
עִתִּים, וּמַחֲלִיף אֶת־הַזְּמַנִּים, וּמְסַדֵּר אֶת־הַכּוֹכָבִים
בְּמִשְׁמְרוֹתֵיהֶם בָּרָקִיעַ כִּרְצוֹנוֹ.
בּוֹרֵא יוֹם וָלַיְלָה, גּוֹלֵל אוֹר מִפְּנֵי חֹשֶׁךְ וְחֹשֶׁךְ מִפְּנֵי אוֹר,
וּמַעֲבִיר יוֹם וּמֵבִיא לַיְלָה, וּמַבְדִּיל בֵּין יוֹם וּבֵין לַיְלָה,
יי צְבָאוֹת שְׁמוֹ.

אֵל חַי וְקַיָּם, תָּמִיד יִמְלוֹךְ עָלֵינוּ לְעוֹלָם וָעֶד.
בָּרוּךְ אַתָּה יי, הַמַּעֲרִיב עֲרָבִים.

° O God, how can we know You? Where can we find You? You are as close to us as breathing, yet You are farther than the farthermost star.

You are as mysterious as the vast solitudes of night, yet as familiar to us as the light of the sun. To Moses You said: "You cannot see My face, but I will make all My goodness pass before you."

Even so does Your goodness pass before us: in the realm of nature, and in the joys and sorrows of life.

REVELATION                                                                     אהבת עולם

אַהֲבַת עוֹלָם בֵּית יִשְׂרָאֵל עַמְּךָ אָהָבְתָּ.
תּוֹרָה וּמִצְוֹת, חֻקִּים וּמִשְׁפָּטִים אוֹתָנוּ לִמַּדְתָּ.
עַל־כֵּן, יי אֱלֹהֵינוּ, בְּשָׁכְבֵנוּ וּבְקוּמֵנוּ נָשִׂיחַ בְּחֻקֶּיךָ,
וְנִשְׂמַח בְּדִבְרֵי תוֹרָתֶךָ וּבְמִצְוֹתֶיךָ לְעוֹלָם וָעֶד.
כִּי הֵם חַיֵּינוּ וְאֹרֶךְ יָמֵינוּ, וּבָהֶם נֶהְגֶּה יוֹמָם וָלַיְלָה.
וְאַהֲבָתְךָ אַל־תָּסוּר מִמֶּנּוּ לְעוֹלָמִים!
בָּרוּךְ אַתָּה יי, אוֹהֵב עַמּוֹ יִשְׂרָאֵל.

° When justice burns within us like a flaming fire, when love evokes willing sacrifice from us, when, to the last full measure of selfless devotion, we demonstrate our belief in the ultimate triumph of truth and righteousness, then Your goodness enters our lives and we can begin to change the world; and then You live within our hearts, and we through righteousness behold Your presence.

שְׁמַע יִשְׂרָאֵל: יהוה אֱלֹהֵינוּ, יהוה אֶחָד!

Sh'ma Yis-ra-eil: Adonai Eh-lo-hei-nu, Adonai Eh-chad!

*Hear, O Israel: the Eternal One is our God,*
*the Eternal God alone!*

בָּרוּךְ שֵׁם כְּבוֹד מַלְכוּתוֹ לְעוֹלָם וָעֶד!

Ba-ruch shem k'vod mal-chu-to l'o-lam va–ed!

*Blessed is God's glorious majesty for ever and ever!*

# All are seated

וְאָהַבְתָּ אֵת יְהֹוָה אֱלֹהֶיךָ בְּכָל־לְבָבְךָ וּבְכָל־נַפְשְׁךָ וּבְכָל־מְאֹדֶךָ:
וְהָיוּ הַדְּבָרִים הָאֵלֶּה אֲשֶׁר אָנֹכִי מְצַוְּךָ הַיּוֹם עַל־לְבָבֶךָ:
וְשִׁנַּנְתָּם לְבָנֶיךָ וְדִבַּרְתָּ בָּם בְּשִׁבְתְּךָ בְּבֵיתֶךָ וּבְלֶכְתְּךָ בַדֶּרֶךְ
וּבְשָׁכְבְּךָ וּבְקוּמֶךָ: וּקְשַׁרְתָּם לְאוֹת עַל־יָדֶךָ וְהָיוּ לְטֹטָפֹת בֵּין
עֵינֶיךָ: וּכְתַבְתָּם עַל־מְזוּזֹת בֵּיתֶךָ וּבִשְׁעָרֶיךָ:
לְמַעַן תִּזְכְּרוּ וַעֲשִׂיתֶם אֶת־כָּל־מִצְוֹתָי וִהְיִיתֶם קְדֹשִׁים
לֵאלֹהֵיכֶם: אֲנִי יְהֹוָה אֱלֹהֵיכֶם אֲשֶׁר הוֹצֵאתִי אֶתְכֶם
מֵאֶרֶץ מִצְרַיִם לִהְיוֹת לָכֶם לֵאלֹהִים אֲנִי יְהֹוָה אֱלֹהֵיכֶם:

V'a–hav–ta et Adonai Eh–lo–heh–cha b'chol l'va–v'cha u–v'chol naf–
sh'cha u–v'chol m'o–deh–cha. V'ha–yu ha–d'va–rim ha–ei–leh a–sher a–
no–chi m'tza–v'cha ha–yom al l'va–veh–cha. V'shi–nan–tam l'va–neh–cha
v'di–bar–ta bam b'shiv–t'cha b'vei–teh–cha u–v'lech–t'cha va–deh–rech u–
v'shoch–b'cha u–v'ku–meh–cha. U–k'shar–tam l'ot al ya–deh–cha v'ha–yu
l'to–ta–fot bein ei–neh–cha; u–ch'tav–tam al m'zu–zot bei–teh–cha u–vi–
sh'a–reh–cha.
L'ma–an tiz–k'ru va–a–si–tem et kol mitz–vo–tai, vi–h'yi–tem  k'do–shim
lei–lo–hei–chem. Ani Adonai Eh–lo–hei–chem a–sher ho–tzei–ti et–chem
mei–eh–retz mitz–ra–yim li–h'yot la–chem lei–lo–him.  Ani Adonai Eh–lo–
hei–chem.

*You shall love your Eternal God with all your heart, with all*
*your mind, with all your being. Set these words, which I*
*command you this day, upon your heart. Teach them faithfully*

*to your children; speak of them in your home and on your way, when you lie down and when you rise up. Bind them as a sign upon your hand; let them be symbols before your eyes; inscribe them on the doorposts of your house, and on your gates.*

*Be mindful of all My Mitzvot, and do them: so shall you consecrate yourselves to your God. I am your Eternal God who led you out of Egypt to be your God; I am your Eternal God.*

REDEMPTION                                                גאולה

אֲנִי, יהוה, קְרָאתִיךָ בְצֶדֶק וְאַחְזֵק בְּיָדֶךָ,
וְאֶצָּרְךָ; וְאֶתֶּנְךָ לִבְרִית עָם, לְאוֹר גּוֹיִם.

"I, the Eternal One, have called you to righteousness, and taken you by the hand, and kept you; I have made you a covenant people, a light to the nations."

*We are Israel: witness to the covenant between God and God's children.*

כִּי זֹאת הַבְּרִית אֲשֶׁר אֶכְרֹת אֶת־בֵּית יִשְׂרָאֵל:
נָתַתִּי אֶת־תּוֹרָתִי בְּקִרְבָּם, וְעַל־לִבָּם אֶכְתֲּבֶנָּה.
וְהָיִיתִי לָהֶם לֵאלֹהִים, וְהֵמָּה יִהְיוּ־לִי לְעָם.

"This is the covenant I make with Israel: I will place My Torah in your midst, and write it upon your hearts. I will be your God, and you shall be My people."

*We are Israel: our Torah forbids the worship of race or nation, possessions or power.*

הַמִּתְפַּלְלִים אֶל־אֵל לֹא יוֹשִׁיעַ, שִׁמְעוּ דְּבַר־יהוה:
הֲלוֹא אֲנִי יהוה, וְאֵין־עוֹד אֱלֹהִים מִבַּלְעָדָי!

"You who worship gods that cannot save you, hear the words of the Eternal One: 'I am God, there is none else!'"

*We are Israel: our prophets proclaimed an exalted vision for the world.*

שִׂנְאוּ־רָע וְאֶהֱבוּ טוֹב. וְיִגַּל כַּמַּֽיִם מִשְׁפָּט
וּצְדָקָה כְּנַֽחַל אֵיתָן.

"Hate evil, and love what is good; let justice well up as waters and righteousness as a mighty stream."

*We are Israel, schooled in the suffering of the oppressed.*

לֹא־תַעֲשֹׁק אֶת־רֵעֲךָ וְלֹא תִגְזֹל.
לֹא תַעֲמֹד עַל־דַּם רֵעֶֽךָ.

"You shall not oppress your neighbors nor rob them. You shall not stand idle while your neighbor bleeds."

*We are Israel, taught to beat swords into plowshares, commanded to pursue peace.*

לֹא־יִשָּׁמַע עוֹד חָמָס בְּאַרְצֵךְ, שֹׁד וָשֶֽׁבֶר בִּגְבוּלָֽיִךְ.
וְכָל־בָּנַֽיִךְ לִמּוּדֵי יהוה, וְרַב שְׁלוֹם בָּנָֽיִךְ.

"Violence shall no longer be heard in your land, desolation and destruction within your borders. All your children will be taught of your God, and great shall be the peace of your children."

*We are Israel, O God, when we are witnesses to Your love and messengers of Your truth.*

אַתֶּם עֵדַי, נְאֻם־יהוה, וְעַבְדִּי אֲשֶׁר בָּחָֽרְתִּי;
לְמַֽעַן תֵּדְעוּ וְתַאֲמִֽינוּ לִי.

"You are My witnesses, says the Eternal One, and My servant whom I have chosen; know Me, therefore, and put your trust in Me."

*We are Israel, O God, when we proclaim You God our Redeemer, as did our ancestors on the shores of the Red Sea:*

90

מִי־כָמֹכָה בָּאֵלִם, יהוה? מִי כָּמֹכָה, נֶאְדָּר בַּקֹּדֶשׁ,
נוֹרָא תְהִלֹת, עֹשֵׂה פֶלֶא?

מַלְכוּתְךָ רָאוּ בָנֶיךָ, בּוֹקֵעַ יָם לִפְנֵי מֹשֶׁה; זֶה אֵלִי!
עָנוּ וְאָמְרוּ: יהוה יִמְלֹךְ לְעֹלָם וָעֶד!

וְנֶאֱמַר: כִּי פָדָה יהוה אֶת־יַעֲקֹב, וּגְאָלוֹ מִיַּד חָזָק מִמֶּנּוּ.
בָּרוּךְ אַתָּה יי, גָּאַל יִשְׂרָאֵל.

Mi cha–mo–cha ba–ei–lim, Adonai?
Mi ka–mo–cha, neh–dar ba–ko–desh, no–ra t'hi–lot, o–sei feh–leh?
Mal–chu–t'cha ra–u va–neh–cha, bo–kei–a yam li–f'nei Mo–sheh; zeh Ei–li!
  A–nu v'a–m'ru: Adonai yim–loch l'o–lam va–ed!
V'neh–eh–mar: Ki fa–da Adonai et Ya–a–kov, u–g'a–lo mi–yad cha–zak
  mi–meh–nu.
Ba–ruch a–ta Adonai, ga–al Yis–ra–eil.

Who is like You, Eternal One, among the gods that are worshipped?
  Who is like You, majestic in holiness, awesome in splendor, doing
  wonders?

In their escape from the sea, Your children saw Your sovereign might
  displayed. "This is my God!" they cried. "The Eternal will reign for
  ever and ever!"

And it has been said: The Eternal One delivered Jacob, and redeemed us
  from the hand of one stronger than ourselves.

We praise You, O God, Redeemer of Israel.

DIVINE PROVIDENCE                                        הַשְׁכִּיבֵנוּ

הַשְׁכִּיבֵנוּ, יי אֱלֹהֵינוּ, לְשָׁלוֹם, וְהַעֲמִידֵנוּ, מַלְכֵּנוּ, לְחַיִּים טוֹבִים
וּלְשָׁלוֹם. וּפְרוֹשׂ עָלֵינוּ סֻכַּת שְׁלוֹמֶךָ, וְתַקְּנֵנוּ בְּעֵצָה טוֹבָה
מִלְּפָנֶיךָ, וְהוֹשִׁיעֵנוּ לְמַעַן שְׁמֶךָ, וְהָגֵן בַּעֲדֵנוּ. וּפְרוֹשׂ עָלֵינוּ
סֻכַּת רַחֲמִים וְשָׁלוֹם.

91

° May we lie down this night in peace, and rise up to life renewed. O God, spread over us Your shelter of peace, of quiet and calm, and bless us with rest. And let a time come when morning will bring no word of war or famine or anguish, a time of happiness, of contentment and rest.

בָּרוּךְ אַתָּה יְיָ, הַפּוֹרֵשׂ סֻכַּת שָׁלוֹם עָלֵינוּ וְעַל כָּל־עַמּוֹ יִשְׂרָאֵל, וְעַל יְרוּשָׁלָיִם.

We give thanks for the night and its rest, and the promise of peace for all the world.

THE COVENANT OF SHABBAT                             ושמרו

וְשָׁמְרוּ בְנֵי־יִשְׂרָאֵל אֶת־הַשַּׁבָּת, לַעֲשׂוֹת אֶת־הַשַּׁבָּת לְדֹרֹתָם בְּרִית עוֹלָם. בֵּינִי וּבֵין בְּנֵי יִשְׂרָאֵל אוֹת הִיא לְעֹלָם. כִּי־שֵׁשֶׁת יָמִים עָשָׂה יהוה אֶת־הַשָּׁמַיִם וְאֶת־הָאָרֶץ, וּבַיּוֹם הַשְּׁבִיעִי שָׁבַת וַיִּנָּפַשׁ.

V'sha-m'ru v'nei Yis-ra-eil et ha-Shabbat, la-a-sot et ha-sha-bat l'do-ro-tam b'rit o-lam. Bei-ni u-vein b'nei Yis-ra-eil ot hi l'o-lam. Ki shei-shet ya-mim a-sa Adonai et ha-sha-ma-yim v'et ha-a-retz, u-va-yom ha-sh'vi-i sha-vat va-yi-na-fash.

The people of Israel shall keep the Sabbath, observing the Sabbath in every generation as a covenant for all time. It is a sign for ever between Me and the people of Israel. For in six days the Eternal One made heaven and earth, but on the seventh day God rested and was refreshed.

MEDITATION

"The soul that You have given me is pure!"

Yet I know that within it my yearning for the sacred must struggle with my inclination for the profane. At times the profane seems the winner. Love and truth are debased. The divine gift of compassion is depleted. The anguish of others goes unfelt and unheeded.

How much I need You, O God, at such times! I need the sense of Your presence within me, giving me the strength to elevate my soul beyond the sordid to the sacred.

Your presence is the light that dispels the darkness that would envelop me, the light that shows me the path to a life of honor and truth.

### All rise

T'FILAH    תפלה

אֲדֹנָי, שְׂפָתַי תִּפְתָּח, וּפִי יַגִּיד תְּהִלָּתֶךָ.

Eternal God, open my lips, that my mouth may declare Your glory.

GOD OF ALL GENERATIONS    אבות ואמהות

בָּרוּךְ אַתָּה יי, אֱלֹהֵינוּ וֵאלֹהֵי אֲבוֹתֵינוּ וְאִמּוֹתֵינוּ:
אֱלֹהֵי אַבְרָהָם, אֱלֹהֵי יִצְחָק, וֵאלֹהֵי יַעֲקֹב.
אֱלֹהֵי שָׂרָה, אֱלֹהֵי רִבְקָה, אֱלֹהֵי לֵאָה וֵאלֹהֵי רָחֵל.
הָאֵל הַגָּדוֹל הַגִּבּוֹר וְהַנּוֹרָא, אֵל עֶלְיוֹן, גּוֹמֵל חֲסָדִים
טוֹבִים וְקוֹנֵה הַכֹּל, וְזוֹכֵר חַסְדֵי אָבוֹת וְאִמָּהוֹת,
וּמֵבִיא גְאֻלָּה לִבְנֵי בְנֵיהֶם, לְמַעַן שְׁמוֹ בְּאַהֲבָה.
מֶלֶךְ עוֹזֵר וּמוֹשִׁיעַ וּמָגֵן.
בָּרוּךְ אַתָּה יי, מָגֵן אַבְרָהָם וְעֶזְרַת שָׂרָה.

Ba–ruch a–ta Adonai, Eh–lo–hei–nu vei–lo–hei a–vo–tei–nu v'i–mo–tei–nu:
Eh–lo–hei Av–ra–ham, eh–lo–hei Yitz–chak, vei–lo–hei Ya–a–kov.
Eh–lo–hei Sa–ra, Eh–lo–hei Riv–ka, Eh–lo–hei Lei–a vei–lo–hei Ra–cheil.
Ha–eil ha–ga–dol ha–gi–bor v'ha–no–ra, Eil el–yon, go–meil cha–sa–dim
to–vim, v'ko–nei ha–kol, v'zo–cheir cha–s'dei a–vot v'i–ma–hot,
u–mei–vi g'u–la li–v'nei v'nei–hem, l'ma–an sh'mo, b'a–ha–va.
Meh–lech o–zeir u–mo–shi–a u–ma–gein.
Ba–ruch a–ta Adonai, ma–gein Av–ra–ham v'ez–rat Sa–ra.

GOD'S POWER     גבורות

אַתָּה גִבּוֹר לְעוֹלָם, אֲדֹנָי, מְחַיֵּה הַכֹּל אַתָּה, רַב לְהוֹשִׁיעַ.
מְכַלְכֵּל חַיִּים בְּחֶסֶד, מְחַיֵּה הַכֹּל בְּרַחֲמִים רַבִּים. סוֹמֵךְ
נוֹפְלִים, וְרוֹפֵא חוֹלִים, וּמַתִּיר אֲסוּרִים, וּמְקַיֵּם אֱמוּנָתוֹ
לִישֵׁנֵי עָפָר. מִי כָמוֹךָ בַּעַל גְּבוּרוֹת, וּמִי דוֹמֶה לָּךְ,
מֶלֶךְ מֵמִית וּמְחַיֵּה וּמַצְמִיחַ יְשׁוּעָה?
וְנֶאֱמָן אַתָּה לְהַחֲיוֹת הַכֹּל. בָּרוּךְ אַתָּה יי, מְחַיֵּה הַכֹּל.

A-ta gi–bor l'o–lam, Adonai, m'cha–yei ha–kol a-ta, rav l'ho–shi–a.
M'chal–keil cha–yim b'cheh–sed, m'cha–yei ha–kol b'ra–cha–mim ra–bim.
So–meich no–f'lim, v'ro–fei cho–lim, u–ma–tir a–su–rim, u–m'ka–yeim eh–
mu–na–to li–shei–nei a–far. Mi cha–mo–cha ba–al g'vu–rot, u–mi do–meh
lach, meh–lech mei–mit u–m'cha–yeh u–matz–mi–ach y'shu–a?
V'neh–eh–man a–ta l'ha–cha–yot ha–kol. Ba–ruch a–ta Adonai, m'cha–yei
ha–kol.

° God of all generations, of Abraham and Isaac and Jacob; of
Sarah, Rebekah, Leah and Rachel: be praised! Your wondrous
creative power fills heaven and earth.

*God of life and death, be praised! Through us send help to the
falling, healing to the sick, freedom to the captive; confirm Your
faithfulness to those who sleep in the dust.*

THE HOLINESS OF GOD     קדושת השם

אַתָּה קָדוֹשׁ וְשִׁמְךָ קָדוֹשׁ, וּקְדוֹשִׁים בְּכָל־יוֹם יְהַלְלוּךָ, סֶלָה.
בָּרוּךְ אַתָּה יי, הָאֵל הַקָּדוֹשׁ.

THE HOLINESS OF SHABBAT     קדושת היום

אֱלֹהֵינוּ וֵאלֹהֵי אֲבוֹתֵינוּ וְאִמּוֹתֵינוּ, רְצֵה בִמְנוּחָתֵנוּ. קַדְּשֵׁנוּ
בְּמִצְוֹתֶיךָ וְתֵן חֶלְקֵנוּ בְּתוֹרָתֶךָ. שַׂבְּעֵנוּ מִטּוּבֶךָ, וְשַׂמְּחֵנוּ
בִּישׁוּעָתֶךָ, וְטַהֵר לִבֵּנוּ לְעָבְדְּךָ בֶּאֱמֶת. וְהַנְחִילֵנוּ, יי

אֱלֹהֵינוּ, בְּאַהֲבָה וּבְרָצוֹן שַׁבַּת קָדְשֶׁךָ, וְיָנוּחוּ בָהּ יִשְׂרָאֵל
מְקַדְּשֵׁי שְׁמֶךָ. בָּרוּךְ אַתָּה יְיָ, מְקַדֵּשׁ הַשַּׁבָּת.

Eh-lo-hei-nu vei-lo-hei a-vo-tei-nu v'i-mo-tei-nu, r'tzei vi-m'nu-cha-tei-nu.
Ka-d'shei-nu b'mitz-vo-teh-cha v-tein chel-kei-nu b'to-ra-teh-cha. Sab-ei-
nu mi-tu-veh-cha, v'sam-chei-nu bi-shu-a-teh-cha, v'ta-heir li-bei-nu l'ov-
d'cha beh-eh-met. V'han-chi-lei-nu, Adonai Eh-lo-hei-nu, b'a-ha-va u-v'ra-
tzon Shabbat kod-sheh-cha, v'ya-nu-chu va Yis-ra-eil m'ka-d'shei sh'meh-
cha. Ba-ruch a-ta Adonai, m'ka-deish ha-Shabbat.

° Awesome and Holy God, be praised! With acts of love and
truth we hallow Your name, as it is said: "Be holy, for I, your
Eternal God, am holy."

*God of times and seasons, be praised! Enable us through
Sabbath rest to explore, and learn, and impart the meanings of
Your Torah. Make our hearts ready to serve You, this day and
all days.*

## All are seated

WORSHIP                                                    עבודה

רְצֵה, יְיָ אֱלֹהֵינוּ, בְּעַמְּךָ יִשְׂרָאֵל, וּתְפִלָּתָם בְּאַהֲבָה תְקַבֵּל,
וּתְהִי לְרָצוֹן תָּמִיד עֲבוֹדַת יִשְׂרָאֵל עַמֶּךָ.
בָּרוּךְ אַתָּה יְיָ, שֶׁאוֹתְךָ לְבַדְּךָ בְּיִרְאָה נַעֲבוֹד.

THANKSGIVING                                               הודאה

מוֹדִים אֲנַחְנוּ לָךְ שָׁאַתָּה הוּא יְיָ אֱלֹהֵינוּ וֵאלֹהֵי אֲבוֹתֵינוּ
וְאִמּוֹתֵינוּ, אֱלֹהֵי כָל־בָּשָׂר, יוֹצְרֵנוּ יוֹצֵר בְּרֵאשִׁית. בְּרָכוֹת
וְהוֹדָאוֹת לְשִׁמְךָ הַגָּדוֹל וְהַקָּדוֹשׁ עַל־שֶׁהֶחֱיִיתָנוּ וְקִיַּמְתָּנוּ.
כֵּן תְּחַיֵּנוּ וּתְקַיְּמֵנוּ, יְיָ אֱלֹהֵינוּ, וְתֶאֱמְצֵנוּ לִשְׁמֹר חֻקֶּיךָ,
לַעֲשׂוֹת רְצוֹנֶךָ, וּלְעָבְדְּךָ בְּלֵבָב שָׁלֵם. בָּרוּךְ אֵל הַהוֹדָאוֹת.

95

° God who answers prayer, be praised! May we, Your people Israel, be worthy in our deeds and our prayer. Wherever we live, wherever we seek You—in this land, in Zion restored, in all lands—You are our God.

*Source of life and its wonders, be praised! You are the miracle within all we behold. You are Goodness, You are Compassion: we give thanks to You for ever.*

PEACE                                                     ברכת שלום

שָׁלוֹם רָב עַל־יִשְׂרָאֵל עַמְּךָ תָּשִׂים לְעוֹלָם, כִּי אַתָּה הוּא
מֶלֶךְ אָדוֹן לְכָל־הַשָּׁלוֹם. וְטוֹב בְּעֵינֶיךָ לְבָרֵךְ אֶת־עַמְּךָ
יִשְׂרָאֵל וְאֶת־כָּל־הָעַמִּים בְּכָל־עֵת וּבְכָל־שָׁעָה בִּשְׁלוֹמֶךָ.
בָּרוּךְ אַתָּה יְיָ, עוֹשֵׂה הַשָּׁלוֹם.

° God of peace, of justice, and of love, be praised! Inspire us to banish for ever hatred, war, and bloodshed. Help us to establish for ever one human family united in peace. God of peace, bless us with peace!

SILENT PRAYER

Looking inward, I see that all too often I fail to use time and talent to improve myself and to serve others. And yet there is in me a yearning to use my gifts for the well–being of those around me.

Renew my vision, O God; give meaning to my life and substance to my hopes; help me understand those about me and fill me with the desire to serve them. Let me remember that I depend on them as they depend on me; quicken my heart and hand to lift them up, and teach me to make my words of prayer fruitful by deeds of lovingkindness. Amen.

～～

יִהְיוּ לְרָצוֹן אִמְרֵי־פִי וְהֶגְיוֹן לִבִּי לְפָנֶיךָ, יהוה, צוּרִי וְגֹאֲלִי.

Yi-h'yu l'ra-tzon i-m'rei fi v'heg-yon li-bi l'fa-neh-cha, Adonai tzu-ri v'go-a-li.

May the words of my mouth and the meditations of my heart be acceptable to You, O God, my Rock and my Redeemer.

עֹשֶׂה שָׁלוֹם בִּמְרוֹמָיו, הוּא יַעֲשֶׂה שָׁלוֹם עָלֵינוּ וְעַל־כָּל־יִשְׂרָאֵל, וְאִמְרוּ: אָמֵן.

O-seh sha-lom bi-m'ro-mav, hu ya-a-seh sha-lom a-lei-nu v'al kol Yis-ra-eil, v'i-m'ru: A-mein.

• May the One who causes peace to reign in the high heavens cause peace to reign among us, all Israel, and all the world.

For the Reading of the Torah, continue on page 141
Aleinu is on page 148 and page 149

# Shabbat Morning Service

שחרית לשבת

FOR THOSE WHO WEAR A TALLIT

בָּרְכִי נַפְשִׁי אֶת־יהוה! יהוה אֱלֹהַי, גָּדַלְתָּ מְאֹד!
הוֹד וְהָדָר לָבָשְׁתָּ, עֹטֶה־אוֹר כַּשַּׂלְמָה, נוֹטֶה שָׁמַיִם כַּיְרִיעָה.

Praise the Eternal One, O my soul!
O God, You are very great!
Arrayed in glory and majesty, You wrap Yourself in light as with a
garment, and stretch out the heavens like a curtain.

בָּרוּךְ אַתָּה יי, אֱלֹהֵינוּ מֶלֶךְ הָעוֹלָם,
אֲשֶׁר קִדְּשָׁנוּ בְּמִצְוֹתָיו וְצִוָּנוּ לְהִתְעַטֵּף בַּצִּיצִית.

We praise You, Eternal God, Sovereign of the universe:
You hallow us with Your Mitzvot, and teach us to wrap ourselves
in the fringed Tallit.

~ ~

## Alternative Opening Prayers

### The Service may begin here, or on page 103

I

הִנֵּה מַה־טּוֹב וּמַה־

נָּעִים שֶׁבֶת אַחִים גַּם־יָחַד.

Hi–nei ma–tov u–ma na–im
sheh–vet a–chim gam ya–chad.

How good it is, and how pleasant,
when we dwell together in unity.

Surrounded by the members of the community in which I live, I come before You, Eternal God. I share my happiness with them and it becomes greater. I share my trouble with them and it seem smaller. May I never be too selfish to give, nor too proud to receive, for in giving and receiving I discover You, as I begin to discover the meaning of my life.

Let me not separate myself from the true strength of my community: the experience and wisdom of old people, the hopes of the young, and the examples of care and courage which sustain me. Give me an open heart and an open mind to welcome those who need me, and to receive Your presence in my daily life.

I think of what our community could be and the harmony that could unite us. I think of our loneliness and the friendship that could fill our lives. I think of the good that we could do if we were one in spirit. I know that this is Your will and pray for Your help. May I and those around me find our joy together, and thank You for the power You give us to help each other.

At a morning service, we continue on page 104 or 108

At an afternoon service, we continue on page 125 or page 128

The Service may begin here, or on page 103

## II

כִּי אֶשְׁמְרָה שַׁבָּת, אֵל יִשְׁמְרֵנִי.

אוֹת הִיא לְעוֹלְמֵי עַד, בֵּינוֹ וּבֵינִי.

Ki esh-m'ra Shabbat, Eil yish-m'reini.
Ot hi l'o-l'mei ad, bei-no u–vei-ni.

When we keep Shabbat, God keeps us;
It is a sign between God and Israel for ever...

Speak to the whole community of Israel, and say to them:
"You shall be holy, for I, the Eternal God, am holy."
*As God is merciful and gracious,*
*so shall you be merciful and gracious.*

Let your neighbor's property be as dear to you as your own.
*And let your neighbor's honor be as dear to you as your own.*

You shall not oppress a stranger,
for you were strangers in the land of Egypt.
*The strangers who live among you shall be to you as the*
*home–born, and you shall love them as yourself.*

You shall not rejoice when your enemy falls;
*You shall not exult when your enemy stumbles.*

You shall not hate another in your heart;
*but you shall love your neighbor as yourself.*

At a morning service, we continue on page 104 or 108
At an afternoon service, we continue on page 125 or page 128

～～

100

The Service may begin here, or on page 103

III

מַה־יָּפֶה הַיּוֹם: שַׁבָּת שָׁלוֹם.

Mah ya–feh ha–yom: Shabbat Shalom
How beautiful this day is: Shabbat Shalom.

*May the One whose spirit is with us*
*in every righteous deed,*
*be with all*
*who spend themselves for the good of humanity*
*and bear the burdens of others,*
*who give bread to the hungry,*
*clothe the naked,*
*and take the friendless into their homes.*
*May the work of their hands endure,*
*and may the good seed they are sowing*
*bring forth an abundant harvest.*

At a morning service, we continue on page 104 or 108
At an afternoon service, we continue on page 125 or page 128

~ ~

The Service may begin here, or on page 103

IV

עַל שְׁלֹשָׁה דְבָרִים הָעוֹלָם עוֹמֵד:
עַל הַתּוֹרָה, וְעַל הָעֲבוֹדָה, וְעַל גְּמִילוּת חֲסָדִים.

Al sh'lo–sha d'va–rim ha–o–lam o–meid:
Al ha–Torah, v'al ha–a–vo–da, v'al g'mi–lut cha–sa–dim.

The world depends on three things:
On Torah, worship, and loving deeds.

101

God of dawn and dusk, open my eyes to the beauty of the world and its goodness. Let me be the servant of Your peace which brings all life together: the love of mother and child, the loyalty of friends, and the companionship of animal and human. As I awaken to the world You have made, I know this harmony again and Your presence in it. With all creation I respond with praise, and give thanks to Your name. Amen.

At a morning service, we continue on page 104 or 108

At an afternoon service, we continue on page 125 or page 128

〜 〜

The Service may begin here, or on page 103

V

דָּוִד מֶלֶךְ יִשְׂרָאֵל חַי וְקַיָּם.

Da–vid meh–lech Yis–ra–eil chai v'ka–yam.

David king of Israel lives and endures.

Eternal God, we thank You for Your gift of hope, our strength in times of trouble. Beyond the injustice of our time, its cruelty and its wars, we look forward to a world at peace when men and women deal kindly with each other, and no one is afraid. Every bad deed delays its coming, every good one brings it nearer. May our lives be Your witness, so that future generations bless us. May the time come, as the prophet taught, when the sun of righteousness will rise with healing on its wings. Help us to pray for it, to wait for it, to work for it and to be worthy of it. We praise You, O God, the Hope of Israel.

At a morning service, we continue on page 104 or 108

At an afternoon service, we continue on page 125 or page 128

We thank You, O God, for this time of prayer, when we become conscious of Your presence, and place before You our desires, our hopes, and our gratitude. This consciousness, this inner certainty of Your presence is our greatest blessing. God, bless our worship this day. May the gleams of Your light, the visions of Your truth, which bless us here, abide with us when we go out into the world, keeping us steadfast in loyalty to You and Your commandments. Amen.

## MEDITATION

Each of us enters this sanctuary with a different need.

Some hearts are full of gratitude and joy:
They are overflowing with the happiness of love and the joy of life; they are eager to confront the day, to make the world more fair; they are recovering from illness or have escaped misfortune.
And we rejoice with them.

Some hearts ache with sorrow:
Disappointments weigh heavily upon them, and they have tasted despair; families have been broken; loved ones lie on a bed of pain; death has taken those whom they cherished.
May our presence and sympathy bring them comfort.

Some hearts are embittered:
They have sought answers in vain; ideals are mocked and betrayed; life has lost its meaning and value.
May the knowledge that we too are searching, restore their hope and give them courage to believe that not all is emptiness.

Some spirits hunger:
They long for friendship; they crave understanding; they yearn for warmth.

May we in our common need and striving gain strength from one another, as we share our joys, lighten each other's burdens, and pray for the welfare of our community.

103

FOR THE BLESSING OF WORSHIP                    מה טבו

מַה־טֹּבוּ אֹהָלֶיךָ, יַעֲקֹב, מִשְׁכְּנֹתֶיךָ, יִשְׂרָאֵל!
וַאֲנִי, בְּרֹב חַסְדְּךָ אָבוֹא בֵיתֶךָ,
אֶשְׁתַּחֲוֶה אֶל־הֵיכַל קָדְשְׁךָ בְּיִרְאָתֶךָ.

יהוה, אָהַבְתִּי מְעוֹן בֵּיתֶךָ, וּמְקוֹם מִשְׁכַּן כְּבוֹדֶךָ.
וַאֲנִי אֶשְׁתַּחֲוֶה וְאֶכְרָעָה, אֶבְרְכָה לִפְנֵי־יהוה עֹשִׂי.

וַאֲנִי תְפִלָּתִי־לְךָ, יהוה, עֵת רָצוֹן.
אֱלֹהִים, בְּרָב־חַסְדֶּךָ, עֲנֵנִי בֶּאֱמֶת יִשְׁעֶךָ.

Mah to-vu o-ha-leh-cha, Ya-a-kov, mish-k'no-teh-cha, Yis-ra-eil!
Va-a-ni, b'rov chas-d'cha a-vo vei-teh-cha,
esh-ta-cha-veh el hei-chal kod-sh'cha b'yir-a-teh-cha.

Adonai, a-hav-ti m'on bei-teh-cha u-m'kom mish-kan k'vo-deh-cha.
Va-a-ni esh-ta-cha-veh v'ech-ra-ah, ev-r'cha li-f'nei Adonai o-si.

Va-a-ni t'fi-la-ti l'cha, Adonai, eit ra-tzon.
Eh-lo-him b'rov chas-deh-cha a-nei-ni beh-eh-met yish-eh-cha.

How lovely are your tents, O Jacob, your dwelling-places, O Israel!
As for me, O God abounding in grace,
I enter your house to worship with awe in Your sacred place.

I love Your house, Eternal One, the dwelling-place of Your glory;
humbly I worship You, humbly I seek blessing from God my Maker.

To You, Eternal One, goes my prayer: may this be a time of Your favor.
In Your great love, O God, answer me with Your saving truth.

FOR TORAH                            לעסוק בדברי תורה

בָּרוּךְ אַתָּה יי, אֱלֹהֵינוּ מֶלֶךְ הָעוֹלָם, אֲשֶׁר קִדְּשָׁנוּ בְּמִצְוֹתָיו
וְצִוָּנוּ לַעֲסוֹק בְּדִבְרֵי תוֹרָה.

104

We praise You, Eternal God, Sovereign of the universe: You hallow us with the gift of Torah and command us to immerse ourselves in its words.

*Eternal our God, make the words of Your Torah sweet to us, and to the House of Israel, Your people, that we and our children may be lovers of Your name and students of Your Torah. We praise You, O God, Teacher of Torah to Your people Israel.*

| | |
|---|---|
| These are duties whose worth cannot be measured: | אֵלּוּ דְבָרִים שֶׁאֵין לָהֶם שִׁעוּר: |
| *honoring one's father and mother,* | כִּבּוּד אָב וָאֵם, |
| *acts of love and kindness,* | וּגְמִילוּת חֲסָדִים, |
| *diligent pursuit of knowledge and wisdom,* | וְהַשְׁכָּמַת בֵּית הַמִּדְרָשׁ שַׁחֲרִית וְעַרְבִית, |
| *hospitality to strangers,* | וְהַכְנָסַת אוֹרְחִים, |
| *visiting the sick,* | וּבִקּוּר חוֹלִים, |
| *celebrating with bride and groom,* | וְהַכְנָסַת כַּלָּה, |
| *consoling the bereaved,* | וּלְוָיַת הַמֵּת, |
| *praying with sincerity,* | וְעִיּוּן תְּפִלָּה, |
| *and making peace where there is strife.* | וַהֲבָאַת שָׁלוֹם בֵּין אָדָם לַחֲבֵרוֹ. |
| *And the study of Torah leads to them all.* | וְתַלְמוּד תּוֹרָה כְּנֶגֶד כֻּלָּם. |

FOR THE SOUL

אלהי נשמה

אֱלֹהַי, נְשָׁמָה שֶׁנָּתַתָּ בִּי טְהוֹרָה הִיא! אַתָּה בְרָאתָהּ, אַתָּה יְצַרְתָּהּ, אַתָּה נְפַחְתָּהּ בִּי, וְאַתָּה מְשַׁמְּרָהּ בְּקִרְבִּי. כָּל־זְמַן שֶׁהַנְּשָׁמָה בְקִרְבִּי, מוֹדֶה אֲנִי לְפָנֶיךָ, יְיָ אֱלֹהַי וֵאלֹהֵי אֲבוֹתַי

וְאִמּוֹתַי, רִבּוֹן כָּל־הַמַּעֲשִׂים, אֲדוֹן כָּל־הַנְּשָׁמוֹת.

בָּרוּךְ אַתָּה יְיָ, אֲשֶׁר בְּיָדוֹ נֶפֶשׁ כָּל־חָי וְרוּחַ כָּל־בְּשַׂר־אִישׁ.

The soul that You have given me, O God, is pure! You created and formed it, breathed it into me, and within me You sustain it. So long as I have breath, therefore, I will give thanks to You, my God and the God of all ages, Source of all being, loving Guide of every human spirit.

We praise You, O God, in whose hands are the souls of all the living and the spirits of all flesh.

FOR OUR BLESSINGS                                                  נסים בכל יום

בָּרוּךְ אַתָּה יְיָ, אֱלֹהֵינוּ מֶלֶךְ הָעוֹלָם,

אֲשֶׁר נָתַן לַשֶּׂכְוִי בִינָה לְהַבְחִין בֵּין יוֹם וּבֵין לָיְלָה.

*Praised be the Eternal God, who has implanted mind and instinct within every living being.*

בָּרוּךְ אַתָּה יְיָ, אֱלֹהֵינוּ מֶלֶךְ הָעוֹלָם, שֶׁעָשַׂנִי יִשְׂרָאֵל.

*Praised be the Eternal God, who has made me a Jew.*

בָּרוּךְ אַתָּה יְיָ, אֱלֹהֵינוּ מֶלֶךְ הָעוֹלָם, שֶׁעָשַׂנִי בֶּן חוֹרִין.

*Praised be the Eternal God, who has made me to be free.*

בָּרוּךְ אַתָּה יְיָ, אֱלֹהֵינוּ מֶלֶךְ הָעוֹלָם, פּוֹקֵחַ עִוְרִים.

*Praised be the Eternal God, who helps the blind to see.*

בָּרוּךְ אַתָּה יְיָ, אֱלֹהֵינוּ מֶלֶךְ הָעוֹלָם, מַלְבִּישׁ עֲרֻמִּים.

*Praised be the Eternal God, who clothes the naked.*

בָּרוּךְ אַתָּה יְיָ, אֱלֹהֵינוּ מֶלֶךְ הָעוֹלָם, מַתִּיר אֲסוּרִים.

*Praised be the Eternal God, who frees the captive.*

בָּרוּךְ אַתָּה יְיָ, אֱלֹהֵינוּ מֶלֶךְ הָעוֹלָם, זוֹקֵף כְּפוּפִים.

*Praised be the Eternal God, who lifts up the fallen.*

106

בָּרוּךְ אַתָּה יְיָ, אֱלֹהֵינוּ מֶלֶךְ הָעוֹלָם, הַמֵּכִין מִצְעֲדֵי־גָבֶר.

*Praised be the Eternal God, who makes firm our steps.*

בָּרוּךְ אַתָּה יְיָ, אֱלֹהֵינוּ מֶלֶךְ הָעוֹלָם, אוֹזֵר יִשְׂרָאֵל בִּגְבוּרָה.

*Praised be the Eternal God, who girds our people Israel with strength.*

בָּרוּךְ אַתָּה יְיָ, אֱלֹהֵינוּ מֶלֶךְ הָעוֹלָם, עוֹטֵר יִשְׂרָאֵל בְּתִפְאָרָה.

*Praised be the Eternal God, who crowns Israel with glory.*

בָּרוּךְ אַתָּה יְיָ, אֱלֹהֵינוּ מֶלֶךְ הָעוֹלָם, הַנּוֹתֵן לַיָּעֵף כֹּחַ.

*Praised be the Eternal God, who gives strength to the weary.*

בָּרוּךְ אַתָּה יְיָ, אֱלֹהֵינוּ מֶלֶךְ הָעוֹלָם, הַמַּעֲבִיר שֵׁנָה מֵעֵינַי
וּתְנוּמָה מֵעַפְעַפָּי.

*Praised be the Eternal God, who removes sleep from the eyes, slumber from the eyelids.*

FOR CONSCIENCE                                                תורה ומצוות

יְהִי רָצוֹן מִלְּפָנֶיךָ, יְיָ אֱלֹהֵינוּ וֵאלֹהֵי אֲבוֹתֵינוּ, שֶׁתַּרְגִּילֵנוּ
בְּתוֹרָתֶךָ, וְדַבְּקֵנוּ בְּמִצְוֹתֶיךָ, וְאַל תְּבִיאֵנוּ לֹא לִידֵי חֵטְא,
וְלֹא לִידֵי עֲבֵרָה וְעָוֹן, וְלֹא לִידֵי נִסָּיוֹן, וְלֹא לִידֵי בִזָּיוֹן,
וְאַל תַּשְׁלֶט־בָּנוּ יֵצֶר הָרָע, וְהַרְחִיקֵנוּ מֵאָדָם רָע וּמֵחָבֵר
רָע, וְדַבְּקֵנוּ בְּיֵצֶר הַטּוֹב וּבְמַעֲשִׂים טוֹבִים, וְכֹף אֶת־
יִצְרֵנוּ לְהִשְׁתַּעְבֶּד־לָךְ, וּתְנֵנוּ הַיּוֹם וּבְכָל־יוֹם לְחֵן וּלְחֶסֶד
וּלְרַחֲמִים בְּעֵינֶיךָ וּבְעֵינֵי כָל־רוֹאֵינוּ, וְתִגְמְלֵנוּ חֲסָדִים
טוֹבִים.
בָּרוּךְ אַתָּה יְיָ, גּוֹמֵל חֲסָדִים טוֹבִים לְעַמּוֹ יִשְׂרָאֵל.

Eternal One, our God and God of all ages, school us in Your Torah and bind us to Your Mitzvot.

Help us to keep far from sin, to master temptation, and to avoid falling under its spell. May our darker passions not rule us, nor evil companions lead us astray.

*Strengthen in us the voice of conscience; prompt us to deeds of goodness; and bend our every impulse to Your service, so that this day and always we may know Your love and the good will of all who behold us. We praise You, O God: You bestow love and kindness on Your people Israel.*

~ ~

At all times revere God inwardly as well as outwardly, acknowledge the truth and speak it in your heart.

## All rise

READER'S KADDISH

חֲצִי קַדִּישׁ

יִתְגַּדַּל וְיִתְקַדַּשׁ שְׁמֵהּ רַבָּא בְּעָלְמָא דִי־בְרָא כִרְעוּתֵהּ, וְיַמְלִיךְ מַלְכוּתֵהּ בְּחַיֵּיכוֹן וּבְיוֹמֵיכוֹן וּבְחַיֵּי דְכָל־בֵּית יִשְׂרָאֵל, בַּעֲגָלָא וּבִזְמַן קָרִיב, וְאִמְרוּ: אָמֵן.

יְהֵא שְׁמֵהּ רַבָּא מְבָרַךְ לְעָלַם וּלְעָלְמֵי עָלְמַיָּא.

יִתְבָּרַךְ וְיִשְׁתַּבַּח, וְיִתְפָּאַר וְיִתְרוֹמַם וְיִתְנַשֵּׂא, וְיִתְהַדָּר וְיִתְעַלֶּה וְיִתְהַלָּל שְׁמֵהּ דְּקוּדְשָׁא, בְּרִיךְ הוּא, לְעֵלָּא מִן־כָּל־בִּרְכָתָא וְשִׁירָתָא, תֻּשְׁבְּחָתָא וְנֶחֱמָתָא דַּאֲמִירָן בְּעָלְמָא, וְאִמְרוּ: אָמֵן.

Yit-ga-dal v'yit–ka–dash sh'mei ra-ba b'al-ma di-v'ra chi-r'u'tei, v'yam-lich mal-chu-tei b'cha-yei-chon u-v'yo-mei-chon u-v'cha-yei d'chol beit Yis-ra-eil, ba-a-ga-la u-vi-z'man ka-riv, v'i-m' ru: A-mein.

Y'hei sh'mei ra-ba m'va-rach l'a-lam u-l'al-mei al-ma-ya.

Yit-ba-rach v'yish-ta-bach, v'yit-pa-ar v'yit-ro-mam v'yit-na-sei, v'yit-ha-dar v'yit-a-leh v'yit-ha-lal sh'mei d'kud-sha, b'rich hu,

l'ei-la min kol bir-cha-ta v'shi-ra-ta, tush-b'cha-ta v'neh-cheh-ma-ta da-a-mi-ran b'al-ma, v'i-m' ru: A-mein.

~ ~

**The Sh'ma and its Blessings**　　　　　　שמע וברכותיה

בָּרְכוּ אֶת־יי הַמְבֹרָךּ!

Praise the One to whom our praise is due!

בָּרוּךְ יי הַמְבֹרָךְ לְעוֹלָם וָעֶד!

*Ba-ruch Adonai ha-m'vo-rach l'o-lam va-ed!*

*Praised be the One to whom our praise is due, now and for ever!*

CREATION　　　　　　　　　　　　　　　　　　יוצר

בָּרוּךְ אַתָּה יי, אֱלֹהֵינוּ מֶלֶךְ הָעוֹלָם, יוֹצֵר אוֹר וּבוֹרֵא חֹשֶׁךְ, עֹשֶׂה שָׁלוֹם וּבוֹרֵא אֶת־הַכֹּל. הַמֵּאִיר לָאָרֶץ וְלַדָּרִים עָלֶיהָ בְּרַחֲמִים, וּבְטוּבוֹ מְחַדֵּשׁ בְּכָל־יוֹם תָּמִיד מַעֲשֵׂה בְרֵאשִׁית. מָה רַבּוּ מַעֲשֶׂיךָ, ייִ! כֻּלָּם בְּחָכְמָה עָשִׂיתָ, מָלְאָה הָאָרֶץ קִנְיָנֶךָ. תִּתְבָּרַךְ, יי אֱלֹהֵינוּ, עַל־שֶׁבַח מַעֲשֵׂה יָדֶיךָ, וְעַל־מְאוֹרֵי־אוֹר שֶׁעָשִׂיתָ: יְפָאֲרוּךָ. סֶלָה בָּרוּךְ אַתָּה יי, יוֹצֵר הַמְּאוֹרוֹת.

• We praise You, Eternal God, Sovereign of the universe. Your mercy makes light to shine over the earth and all its inhabitants, and Your goodness renews day by day the work of creation.

*How manifold are Your works, O God! In wisdom You have made them all. The heavens declare Your glory. The earth*

*reveals Your creative power. You form light and darkness, bring harmony into nature, and peace to the human heart.*

*We praise You, O God, Creator of light.*

REVELATION                                              אהבה רבה

אַהֲבָה רַבָּה אֲהַבְתָּנוּ, יי אֱלֹהֵינוּ, חֶמְלָה גְדוֹלָה וִיתֵרָה חָמַלְתָּ
עָלֵינוּ. אָבִינוּ מַלְכֵּנוּ, בַּעֲבוּר אֲבוֹתֵינוּ וְאִמּוֹתֵינוּ שֶׁבָּטְחוּ בְךָ
וַתְּלַמְּדֵם חֻקֵּי חַיִּים, כֵּן תְּחָנֵּנוּ וּתְלַמְּדֵנוּ. אָבִינוּ, הָאָב הָרַחֲמָן,
הַמְרַחֵם, רַחֵם עָלֵינוּ וְתֵן בְּלִבֵּנוּ לְהָבִין וּלְהַשְׂכִּיל, לִשְׁמֹעַ,
לִלְמֹד וּלְלַמֵּד, לִשְׁמֹר וְלַעֲשׂוֹת וּלְקַיֵּם אֶת־כָּל־דִּבְרֵי תַלְמוּד
תּוֹרָתֶךָ בְּאַהֲבָה. וְהָאֵר עֵינֵינוּ בְּתוֹרָתֶךָ, וְדַבֵּק לִבֵּנוּ בְּמִצְוֹתֶיךָ,
וְיַחֵד לְבָבֵנוּ לְאַהֲבָה וּלְיִרְאָה אֶת־שְׁמֶךָ. וְלֹא־נֵבוֹשׁ לְעוֹלָם וָעֶד,
כִּי בְשֵׁם קָדְשְׁךָ הַגָּדוֹל וְהַנּוֹרָא בָּטָחְנוּ. נָגִילָה וְנִשְׂמְחָה
בִּישׁוּעָתֶךָ, כִּי אֵל פּוֹעֵל יְשׁוּעוֹת אָתָּה, וּבָנוּ בָחַרְתָּ וְקֵרַבְתָּנוּ
לְשִׁמְךָ הַגָּדוֹל סֶלָה בֶּאֱמֶת, לְהוֹדוֹת לְךָ וּלְיַחֶדְךָ בְּאַהֲבָה.
בָּרוּךְ אַתָּה יי, הַבּוֹחֵר בְּעַמּוֹ יִשְׂרָאֵל בְּאַהֲבָה.

• Deep is Your love for us, abiding Your compassion. From of old we have put our trust in You, and You have taught us the laws of life. Be gracious now to us, that we may understand and fulfill the teachings of Your word.

*Enlighten our eyes in Your Torah, that we may cling to Your Mitzvot. Unite our hearts to love and revere Your name.*

*We trust in You and rejoice in Your saving power, for You are the Source of our help. You have called us and drawn us near to You in faithfulness.*

*Joyfully we lift up our voices and proclaim Your unity, O God. In love, You have called us to Your service.*

שְׁמַע יִשְׂרָאֵל: יהוה אֱלֹהֵינוּ, יהוה אֶחָד!

Sh'ma Yis-ra-el: Adonai Eh-lo-hei-nu, Adonai Eh-chad!

*Hear, O Israel: the Eternal One is our God,
the Eternal God alone!*

בָּרוּךְ שֵׁם כְּבוֹד מַלְכוּתוֹ לְעוֹלָם וָעֶד!

Ba-ruch shem k'vod mal-chu-to l'o-lam va–ed!

*Blessed is God's glorious majesty for ever and ever!*

## All are seated

וְאָהַבְתָּ אֵת יהוה אֱלֹהֶיךָ בְּכָל־לְבָבְךָ וּבְכָל־נַפְשְׁךָ וּבְכָל־מְאֹדֶךָ:
וְהָיוּ הַדְּבָרִים הָאֵלֶּה אֲשֶׁר אָנֹכִי מְצַוְּךָ הַיּוֹם עַל־לְבָבֶךָ:
וְשִׁנַּנְתָּם לְבָנֶיךָ וְדִבַּרְתָּ בָּם בְּשִׁבְתְּךָ בְּבֵיתֶךָ וּבְלֶכְתְּךָ בַדֶּרֶךְ
וּבְשָׁכְבְּךָ וּבְקוּמֶךָ: וּקְשַׁרְתָּם לְאוֹת עַל־יָדֶךָ וְהָיוּ לְטֹטָפֹת בֵּין
עֵינֶיךָ: וּכְתַבְתָּם עַל־מְזוּזֹת בֵּיתֶךָ וּבִשְׁעָרֶיךָ:
לְמַעַן תִּזְכְּרוּ וַעֲשִׂיתֶם אֶת־כָּל־מִצְוֺתָי וִהְיִיתֶם קְדֹשִׁים
לֵאלֹהֵיכֶם: אֲנִי יהוה אֱלֹהֵיכֶם אֲשֶׁר הוֹצֵאתִי אֶתְכֶם
מֵאֶרֶץ מִצְרַיִם לִהְיוֹת לָכֶם לֵאלֹהִים אֲנִי יהוה אֱלֹהֵיכֶם:

V'a–hav–ta et Adonai Eh–lo–heh–cha b'chol l'va–v'cha u–v'chol naf–
sh'cha u–v'chol m'o–deh–cha. V'ha–yu ha–d'va–rim ha–ei–leh a–sher a–
no–chi m'tza–v'cha ha–yom al l'va–veh–cha. V'shi–nan–tam l'va–neh–cha
v'di–bar–ta bam b'shiv–t'cha b'vei–teh–cha u–v'lech–t'cha va–deh–rech u–
v'shoch–b'cha u–v'ku–meh–cha. U–k'shar–tam l'ot al ya–deh–cha v'ha–yu
l'to–ta–fot bein ei–neh–cha; u–ch'tav–tam al m'zu–zot bei–teh–cha u–vi–
sh'a–reh–cha.

L'ma–an tiz–k'ru va–a–si–tem et kol mitz–vo–tai, vi–h'yi–tem k'do–shim
lei–lo–hei–chem. Ani Adonai Eh–lo–hei–chem a–sher ho–tzei–ti et–chem
mei–eh–retz mitz–ra–yim li–h'yot la–chem lei–lo–him. Ani Adonai Eh–lo–
hei–chem.

111

*You shall love your Eternal God with all your heart, with all your mind, with all your being. Set these words, which I command you this day, upon your heart. Teach them faithfully to your children; speak of them in your home and on your way, when you lie down and when you rise up. Bind them as a sign upon your hand; let them be symbols before your eyes; inscribe them on the doorposts of your house, and on your gates.*

*Be mindful of all My Mitzvot, and do them: so shall you consecrate yourselves to your God. I am your Eternal God who led you out of Egypt to be your God; I am your Eternal God.*

REDEMPTION                                                        גאולה

אֱמֶת וְיַצִּיב וְיָשָׁר וְקַיָּם וְטוֹב וְיָפֶה הַדָּבָר הַזֶּה עָלֵינוּ לְעוֹלָם
וָעֶד. אֱמֶת שָׁאַתָּה הוּא יי אֱלֹהֵינוּ וֵאלֹהֵי אֲבוֹתֵינוּ וְאִמּוֹתֵינוּ,
יוֹצְרֵנוּ צוּר יְשׁוּעָתֵנוּ, פּוֹדֵנוּ וּמַצִּילֵנוּ מֵעוֹלָם הוּא שְׁמֶךָ, אֵין
אֱלֹהִים זוּלָתֶךָ. אֱמֶת אַתָּה הוּא רִאשׁוֹן וְאַתָּה הוּא אַחֲרוֹן,
וּמִבַּלְעָדֶיךָ אֵין לָנוּ מוֹשִׁיעַ. מִמִּצְרַיִם גְּאַלְתָּנוּ, יי אֱלֹהֵינוּ,
וּמִבֵּית עֲבָדִים פְּדִיתָנוּ. מֹשֶׁה וּמִרְיָם וּבְנֵי יִשְׂרָאֵל לְךָ עָנוּ
שִׁירָה בְּשִׂמְחָה רַבָּה, וְאָמְרוּ כֻלָּם:

- Eternal truth it is that You alone are God,
and there is none else.
*May all the world rejoice in Your love
and exult in Your justice.*

Let them beat their swords into plowshares;
*let them beat their spears into pruning–hooks.*

Let nation not lift up sword against nation;
let them study war no more.
*You shall not hate another in your heart;
you shall love your neighbor as yourself.*

112

Let the stranger in your midst be to you as the native;
for you were strangers in the land of Egypt.

*From the house of bondage we went forth to freedom;*
*so let all be free to sing with joy:*

מִי־כָמְכָה בָּאֵלִם, יהוה? מִי כָּמְכָה, נֶאְדָּר בַּקֹּדֶשׁ,
נוֹרָא תְהִלֹּת, עֹשֵׂה פֶלֶא?
שִׁירָה חֲדָשָׁה שִׁבְּחוּ גְאוּלִים לְשִׁמְךָ עַל־שְׂפַת הַיָּם;
יַחַד כֻּלָּם הוֹדוּ וְהִמְלְיכוּ וְאָמְרוּ:
יהוה יִמְלֹךְ לְעֹלָם וָעֶד.

Mi cha–mo–cha ba–ei–lim, Adonai? Mi ka–mo–cha, neh–dar ba–ko–desh,
no–ra t'hi–lot, o–sei feh–leh?
Shi–ra cha–da–sha shi–b'chu g'u–lim l'shi–m'cha al s'fat ha–yam; ya–chad
ku–lam ho–du v'him–li–chu v'a–m'ru: Adonai Yim–loch l'o–lam va–ed!

צוּר יִשְׂרָאֵל, קוּמָה בְּעֶזְרַת יִשְׂרָאֵל,
וּפְדֵה כִנְאֻמֶךָ יְהוּדָה וְיִשְׂרָאֵל.
גֹּאֲלֵנוּ, יי צְבָאוֹת שְׁמוֹ, קְדוֹשׁ יִשְׂרָאֵל.
בָּרוּךְ אַתָּה יי, גָּאַל יִשְׂרָאֵל.

Tzur Yis–ra–eil, ku–mah b'ez–rat Yis–ra–eil,
u–f'dei ki–n'u–meh–cha Y'hu–da v'yis–ra–eil.
Go–a–lei–nu, Adonai Tz'va–ot sh'mo, k'dosh Yis–ra–eil.
Ba–ruch a–ta Adonai, ga–al Yis–ra–eil.

Who is like You, Eternal One, among the gods that are worshipped?
Who is like You, majestic in holiness, awesome in splendor, doing
wonders? A new song the redeemed sang to Your name. At the shore of
the sea, saved from destruction, they proclaimed Your sovereign power:
"The Eternal One will reign for ever and ever!"

O Rock of Israel, come to Israel's help. Our Redeemer is God Most
High, the Holy One of Israel. We praise You, O God, Redeemer of Israel.

## All rise

113

T'FILAH תפלה

אֲדֹנָי, שְׂפָתַי תִּפְתָּח, וּפִי יַגִּיד תְּהִלָּתֶךָ.

Eternal God, open my lips, that my mouth may declare Your glory.

GOD OF ALL GENERATIONS אבות ואמהות

בָּרוּךְ אַתָּה יְיָ, אֱלֹהֵינוּ וֵאלֹהֵי אֲבוֹתֵינוּ וְאִמּוֹתֵינוּ:
אֱלֹהֵי אַבְרָהָם, אֱלֹהֵי יִצְחָק, וֵאלֹהֵי יַעֲקֹב.
אֱלֹהֵי שָׂרָה, אֱלֹהֵי רִבְקָה, אֱלֹהֵי לֵאָה וֵאלֹהֵי רָחֵל.
הָאֵל הַגָּדוֹל הַגִּבּוֹר וְהַנּוֹרָא, אֵל עֶלְיוֹן, גּוֹמֵל חֲסָדִים
טוֹבִים וְקוֹנֵה הַכֹּל, וְזוֹכֵר חַסְדֵי אָבוֹת וְאִמָּהוֹת,
וּמֵבִיא גְאֻלָּה לִבְנֵי בְנֵיהֶם, לְמַעַן שְׁמוֹ בְּאַהֲבָה.

ON SHABBAT SHUVAH ADD:

זָכְרֵנוּ לְחַיִּים, מֶלֶךְ חָפֵץ בַּחַיִּים,
וְכָתְבֵנוּ בְּסֵפֶר הַחַיִּים, לְמַעַנְךָ אֱלֹהִים חַיִּים.

מֶלֶךְ עוֹזֵר וּמוֹשִׁיעַ וּמָגֵן.
בָּרוּךְ אַתָּה יְיָ, מָגֵן אַבְרָהָם וְעֶזְרַת שָׂרָה.

Ba–ruch a–ta Adonai, Eh–lo–hei–nu vei–lo–hei a–vo–tei–nu v'i–mo–tei–nu:
Eh–lo–hei Av–ra–ham, eh–lo–hei Yitz–chak, vei–lo–hei Ya–a–kov.
Eh–lo–hei Sa–ra, Eh–lo–hei Riv–ka, Eh–lo–hei Lei–a vei–lo–hei Ra–cheil.
Ha–eil ha–ga–dol ha–gi–bor v'ha–no–ra, Eil el–yon, go–meil cha–sa–dim
to–vim, v'ko–nei ha–kol, v'zo–cheir cha–s'dei a–vot v'i–ma–hot,
u–mei–vi g'u–la li–v'nei v'nei–hem, l'ma–an sh'mo, b'a–ha–va.
Meh–lech o–zeir u–mo–shi–a u–ma–gein.
Ba–ruch a–ta Adonai, ma–gein Av–ra–ham v'ez–rat Sa–ra.

Praised be our God, the God of our fathers and our mothers:
God of Abraham, God of Isaac, and God of Jacob; God of Sarah,
God of Rebekah, God of Leah and God of Rachel; great, mighty,
and awesome, God supreme.

114

Ruler of all the living, Your ways are ways of love. You remember the faithfulness of our ancestors, and in love bring redemption to their children's children for the sake of Your name.

ON SHABBAT SHUVAH ADD::

Remember us unto life, Sovereign who delights in life, and inscribe us in the Book of Life, that Your will may prevail, O God of life.

You are our Sovereign and our Help, our Redeemer and our Shield. We praise You, Eternal One, Shield of Abraham, Protector of Sarah.

GOD'S POWER                                                         גבורות

אַתָּה גִּבּוֹר לְעוֹלָם, אֲדֹנָי, מְחַיֵּה הַכֹּל אַתָּה, רַב לְהוֹשִׁיעַ.
מְכַלְכֵּל חַיִּים בְּחֶסֶד, מְחַיֵּה הַכֹּל בְּרַחֲמִים רַבִּים. סוֹמֵךְ
נוֹפְלִים, וְרוֹפֵא חוֹלִים, וּמַתִּיר אֲסוּרִים, וּמְקַיֵּם אֱמוּנָתוֹ
לִישֵׁנֵי עָפָר. מִי כָמְוֹךָ בַּעַל גְּבוּרוֹת, וּמִי דּוֹמֶה לָּךְ,
מֶלֶךְ מֵמִית וּמְחַיֵּה וּמַצְמִיחַ יְשׁוּעָה?

ON SHABBAT SHUVAH ADD:

מִי כָמְוֹךָ, אַב הָרַחֲמִים, זוֹכֵר יְצוּרָיו לְחַיִּים בְּרַחֲמִים?

וְנֶאֱמָן אַתָּה לְהַחֲיוֹת הַכֹּל. בָּרוּךְ אַתָּה יי, מְחַיֵּה הַכֹּל.

A–ta gi–bor l'o–lam, Adonai, m'cha–yei ha–kol a–ta, rav l'ho–shi–a.
M'chal–keil cha–yim b'cheh–sed, m'cha–yei ha–kol b'ra–cha–mim ra–bim.
So–meich no–f'lim, v'ro–fei cho–lim, u–ma–tir a–su–rim, u–m'ka–yeim eh–
mu–na–to li–shei–nei a–far. Mi cha–mo–cha ba–al g'vu–rot, u–mi do–meh
lach, meh–lech mei–mit u–m'cha–yeh u–matz–mi–ach y'shu–a?
V'neh–eh–man a–ta l'ha–cha–yot ha–kol. Ba–ruch a–ta Adonai, m'cha–yei
ha–kol.

*Eternal is Your might, O God; all life is Your gift; great is Your power to save!*

115

*With love You sustain the living, with great compassion give life to all. You send help to the falling and healing to the sick; You bring freedom to the captive and keep faith with those who sleep in the dust.*

*Who is like You, Mighty One, Author of life and death, Source of salvation?*

ON SHABBAT SHUVAH ADD:

*Who is like You, Source of mercy? In compassion You sustain the life of Your children.*

*We praise You, O God, the Source of life.*

SANCTIFICATION            קדושה

נְקַדֵּשׁ אֶת־שִׁמְךָ בָּעוֹלָם, כְּשֵׁם שֶׁמַּקְדִּישִׁים אוֹתוֹ בִּשְׁמֵי מָרוֹם,

כַּכָּתוּב עַל־יַד נְבִיאֶךָ: וְקָרָא זֶה אֶל־זֶה וְאָמַר:

We sanctify Your name on earth, even as all things, to the ends of time and space, proclaim Your holiness, and in the words of the prophet we say:

קָדוֹשׁ, קָדוֹשׁ, קָדוֹשׁ יהוה צְבָאוֹת, מְלֹא כָל־הָאָרֶץ כְּבוֹדוֹ.

Ka–dosh, Ka–dosh, Ka–dosh Adonai tz'va–ot, m'lo chol ha–a–retz k'vo–do.

*Holy, Holy, Holy is the God of all being! The whole earth is filled with Your glory!*

אַדִּיר אַדִּירֵנוּ, יהוה אֲדֹנֵינוּ, מָה־אַדִּיר שִׁמְךָ בְּכָל־הָאָרֶץ!

Source of our strength, Sovereign God, how majestic is Your name in all the earth!

בָּרוּךְ כְּבוֹד־יהוה מִמְּקוֹמוֹ.

Ba–ruch k'vod Adonai mi–m'ko–mo.

*Praised be the glory of God in heaven and earth.*

116

אֶחָד הוּא אֱלֹהֵינוּ, הוּא אָבִינוּ, הוּא מַלְכֵּנוּ, הוּא מוֹשִׁיעֵנוּ;
וְהוּא יַשְׁמִיעֵנוּ בְּרַחֲמָיו לְעֵינֵי כָּל־חָי:

You alone are our God and our Creator; You are our Ruler and
our Helper; and in Your mercy You reveal Yourself in the sight of
all the living:

"אֲנִי יהוה אֱלֹהֵיכֶם!"

I AM YOUR ETERNAL GOD!

יִמְלֹךְ יהוה לְעוֹלָם, אֱלֹהַיִךְ צִיּוֹן, לְדֹר וָדֹר. הַלְלוּיָהּ!
Yim–loch Adonai l'o–lam, Eh–lo–ha–yich Tzi–yon, l'dor va–dor.
Halleluyah!

*The Eternal One shall reign for ever; your God, O Zion, from
generation to generation. Halleluyah!*

לְדוֹר וָדוֹר נַגִּיד גָּדְלֶךָ, וּלְנֵצַח נְצָחִים קְדֻשָּׁתְךָ נַקְדִּישׁ.
וְשִׁבְחֲךָ, אֱלֹהֵינוּ, מִפִּינוּ לֹא יָמוּשׁ לְעוֹלָם וָעֶד.
* בָּרוּךְ אַתָּה יְיָ, הָאֵל הַקָּדוֹשׁ.

* ON SHABBAT SHUVAH CONCLUDE:

בָּרוּךְ אַתָּה יְיָ, הַמֶּלֶךְ הַקָּדוֹשׁ.

To all generations we will make known Your greatness, and to
all eternity proclaim Your holiness. Your praise, O God, shall
never depart from our lips.

* We praise You, Eternal One, the holy God.

* ON SHABBAT SHUVAH CONCLUDE:

We praise You, Eternal One: You rule in holiness.

All are seated

117

## MOST PRECIOUS OF DAYS

יִשְׂמְחוּ

יִשְׂמְחוּ בְמַלְכוּתְךָ שׁוֹמְרֵי שַׁבָּת וְקוֹרְאֵי עֹנֶג. עַם מְקַדְּשֵׁי שְׁבִיעִי
כֻּלָּם יִשְׂבְּעוּ וְיִתְעַנְּגוּ מִטּוּבֶךָ. וְהַשְּׁבִיעִי רָצִיתָ בּוֹ וְקִדַּשְׁתּוֹ.
חֶמְדַּת יָמִים אוֹתוֹ קָרֵאתָ, זֵכֶר לְמַעֲשֵׂה בְרֵאשִׁית.

Yis–m'chu v'ma–l'chu–t'cha sho–m'rei Shabbat v'ko–r'ei o–neg. Am m'ka–
d'shei sh'vi–i ku–lam yis–b'u v'yit–a–n'gu mi–tu–veh–cha. V'ha–sh'vi–i ra–
tzi–ta bo v'ki–dash–to. Chem–dat ya–mim o–to ka–ra–ta, zei–cher l'ma–a–
sei v'rei–sheet.

Those who keep the Sabbath and call it a delight shall rejoice in Your
deliverance. All who hallow the seventh day shall be gladdened by Your
goodness. This day is Israel's festival of the spirit, sanctified and blessed
by You, the most precious of days, a symbol of the joy of creation.

## THE HOLINESS OF SHABBAT

קְדֻשַּׁת הַיּוֹם

אֱלֹהֵינוּ וֵאלֹהֵי אֲבוֹתֵינוּ וְאִמּוֹתֵינוּ, רְצֵה בִמְנוּחָתֵנוּ. קַדְּשֵׁנוּ
בְּמִצְוֹתֶיךָ וְתֵן חֶלְקֵנוּ בְּתוֹרָתֶךָ. שַׂבְּעֵנוּ מִטּוּבֶךָ, וְשַׂמְּחֵנוּ
בִּישׁוּעָתֶךָ, וְטַהֵר לִבֵּנוּ לְעָבְדְּךָ בֶּאֱמֶת. וְהַנְחִילֵנוּ, יְיָ
אֱלֹהֵינוּ, בְּאַהֲבָה וּבְרָצוֹן שַׁבַּת קָדְשֶׁךָ, וְיָנוּחוּ בָהּ יִשְׂרָאֵל
מְקַדְּשֵׁי שְׁמֶךָ. בָּרוּךְ אַתָּה יְיָ, מְקַדֵּשׁ הַשַּׁבָּת.

Eh–lo–hei–nu vei–lo–hei a–vo–tei–nu v'i–mo–tei–nu, r'tzei vi–m'nu–cha–tei–nu.
Ka–d'shei–nu b'mitz–vo–teh–cha v–tein chel–kei–nu b'to–ra–teh–cha. Sab–ei–
nu mi–tu–veh–cha, v'sam–chei–nu bi–shu–a–teh–cha, v'ta–heir li–bei–nu l'ov–
d'cha beh–eh–met. V'han–chi–lei–nu, Adonai Eh–lo–hei–nu, b'a–ha–va u–v'ra–
tzon Shabbat kod–sheh–cha, v'ya–nu–chu va Yis–ra–eil m'ka–d'shei sh'meh–
cha. Ba–ruch a–ta Adonai, m'ka–deish ha–Shabbat.

*Our God, God of our fathers and our mothers, may our rest on
this day be pleasing in Your sight. Sanctify us with Your
Mitzvot, and let Your Torah be our way of life. Satisfy us with
Your goodness, gladden us with Your salvation, and purify our
hearts to serve You in truth. In Your gracious love, Eternal God,*

*let Your holy Sabbath remain our heritage, that all Israel, hallowing Your name, may find rest and peace. We praise You, O God, for the Sabbath and its holiness.*

～⁓

Eternal God, establish this sanctuary, dedicated to Your holy name, so that the worship offered within its walls may be worthy of Your greatness and Your love. May every heart which seeks Your presence here find it, as did our people in the Temple on Zion, that this house may be a house of prayer for all peoples.

*God our Creator, hear our prayer and bless us.*

Have compassion upon all the house of Israel. Preserve us from sickness, from war, from strife. Keep us from hatred and uncharitableness toward our neighbors. And grant that, dwelling in safety and walking in uprightness, we may enjoy the fruit of our labors in peace.

*God our Teacher, hear our prayer and bless us.*

Be with all who spend themselves for the good of humanity and bear the burdens of others; who give bread to the hungry, clothe the naked, and provide shelter for the homeless. Establish, O God, the work of their hands, and grant them an abundant harvest of the good seed they are sowing.

*God our Redeemer, hear our prayer and bless us.*

Bless our children, O God, and help us so to fashion their souls by precept and example that they may ever love the good and turn from evil, revere Your Teaching and bring honor to their people. May they guard for future ages the truths revealed to our ancestors.

*God our Friend, hear our prayer and bless us.*

～⁓

WORSHIP · עבודה

רְצֵה, יי אֱלֹהֵינוּ, בְּעַמְּךָ יִשְׂרָאֵל, וּתְפִלָּתָם בְּאַהֲבָה תְקַבֵּל, וּתְהִי לְרָצוֹן תָּמִיד עֲבוֹדַת יִשְׂרָאֵל עַמֶּךָ. בָּרוּךְ אַתָּה יי, שֶׁאוֹתְךָ לְבַדְּךָ בְּיִרְאָה נַעֲבוֹד.

MEDITATION

° We give thanks for the freedom that is ours, and we pray for those in other lands who are persecuted and oppressed. Help them to bear their burdens and keep alive in them the love of freedom and the hope of deliverance. Uphold also the hands of our brothers and sisters in the land of Israel. Cause a new light to shine upon Zion and upon us all, that the time may come when Your Torah will go forth from the house of Israel, Your word from the tents of Jacob. We praise You, our God, whose presence gives life to our people Israel.

THANKSGIVING · הודאה

מוֹדִים אֲנַחְנוּ לָךְ, שָׁאַתָּה הוּא יי אֱלֹהֵינוּ וֵאלֹהֵי אֲבוֹתֵינוּ וְאִמּוֹתֵינוּ לְעוֹלָם וָעֶד. צוּר חַיֵּינוּ, מָגֵן יִשְׁעֵנוּ, אַתָּה הוּא לְדוֹר וָדוֹר. נוֹדֶה לְךָ וּנְסַפֵּר תְּהִלָּתֶךָ, עַל־חַיֵּינוּ הַמְּסוּרִים בְּיָדֶךָ, וְעַל־נִשְׁמוֹתֵינוּ הַפְּקוּדוֹת לָךְ, וְעַל־נִסֶּיךָ שֶׁבְּכָל־יוֹם עִמָּנוּ, וְעַל־נִפְלְאוֹתֶיךָ וְטוֹבוֹתֶיךָ שֶׁבְּכָל־עֵת, עֶרֶב וָבֹקֶר וְצָהֳרָיִם. הַטּוֹב: כִּי לֹא־כָלוּ רַחֲמֶיךָ, וְהַמְרַחֵם: כִּי־לֹא תַמּוּ חֲסָדֶיךָ, מֵעוֹלָם קִוִּינוּ לָךְ.

וְעַל כֻּלָּם יִתְבָּרַךְ וְיִתְרוֹמַם שִׁמְךָ, מַלְכֵּנוּ, תָּמִיד לְעוֹלָם וָעֶד.

ON SHABBAT SHUVAH ADD:

וּכְתוֹב לְחַיִּים טוֹבִים כָּל־בְּנֵי בְרִיתֶךָ.

וְכֹל הַחַיִּים יוֹדוּךָ סֶּלָה, וִיהַלְלוּ אֶת־שִׁמְךָ בֶּאֱמֶת, הָאֵל

120

יְשׁוּעָתֵֽנוּ וְעֶזְרָתֵֽנוּ סֶֽלָה.

בָּרוּךְ אַתָּה יי, הַטּוֹב שִׁמְךָ וּלְךָ נָאֶה לְהוֹדוֹת.

We gratefully acknowledge that You are our God and the God of our people, the God of all generations. You are the Rock of our life, the Power that shields us in every age.

*We thank You and sing Your praises: for our lives, which are in Your hand; for our souls, which are in Your keeping; for the signs of Your presence we encounter every day; and for Your wondrous gifts at all times, morning, noon, and night. You are Goodness: Your mercies never end; You are Compassion: Your love will never fail. You have always been our hope.*

ON SHABBAT SHUVAH ADD:

*Let life abundant be the heritage of all the children of Your covenant.*

*Praised be the Eternal God, to whom our thanks are due.*

ON CHANUKAH ADD:

עַל הַנִּסִּים וְעַל הַפֻּרְקָן, וְעַל הַגְּבוּרוֹת וְעַל הַתְּשׁוּעוֹת, וְעַל הַנִּחָמוֹת שֶׁעָשִֽׂיתָ לַאֲבוֹתֵֽינוּ וּלְאִמּוֹתֵֽינוּ בַּיָּמִים הָהֵם וּבַזְּמַן הַזֶּה. בִּימֵי מַתִּתְיָֽהוּ בֶּן־יוֹחָנָן כֹּהֵן גָּדוֹל, חַשְׁמוֹנַאי וּבָנָיו, כְּשֶׁעָמְדָה מַלְכוּת יָוָן הָרְשָׁעָה עַל עַמְּךָ יִשְׂרָאֵל, לְהַשְׁכִּיחָם תּוֹרָתֶֽךָ וּלְהַעֲבִירָם מֵחֻקֵּי רְצוֹנֶֽךָ. וְאַתָּה בְּרַחֲמֶֽיךָ הָרַבִּים עָמַֽדְתָּ לָהֶם בְּעֵת צָרָתָם. מַֽסַרְתָּ גִבּוֹרִים בְּיַד חַלָּשִׁים, וְרַבִּים בְּיַד מְעַטִּים, וְזֵדִים בְּיַד עוֹסְקֵי תוֹרָתֶֽךָ. וּלְךָ עָשִֽׂיתָ שֵׁם גָּדוֹל וְקָדוֹשׁ בְּעוֹלָמֶֽךָ, וּלְעַמְּךָ יִשְׂרָאֵל עָשִֽׂיתָ תְּשׁוּעָה גְדוֹלָה וּפֻרְקָן כְּהַיּוֹם הַזֶּה. וְאַחַר כֵּן בָּֽאוּ בָנֶֽיךָ לִדְבִיר בֵּיתֶֽךָ, וּפִנּוּ אֶת־הֵיכָלֶֽךָ, וְטִהֲרוּ אֶת־מִקְדָּשֶֽׁךָ, וְהִדְלִֽיקוּ נֵרוֹת בְּחַצְרוֹת קָדְשֶֽׁךָ, וְקָבְעוּ שְׁמוֹנַת יְמֵי חֲנֻכָּה אֵֽלוּ, לְהוֹדוֹת וּלְהַלֵּל לְשִׁמְךָ הַגָּדוֹל.

In days of old, at this season, You saved our people by wonders and mighty deeds. In the days of Mattathias the Hasmonean, the tyrannic Empire sought to destroy our people Israel by making them forget their Torah, and by forcing them to abandon their ancient way of life.

Through the power of Your spirit the weak defeated the strong, the few prevailed over the many, and the righteous were victorious. Then Your children returned to Your House to purify the sanctuary and to kindle its lights.

And they dedicated these days to give thanks and praise to Your majestic glory.

PEACE        ברכת שלום

שִׂים שָׁלוֹם, טוֹבָה וּבְרָכָה, חֵן וָחֶסֶד וְרַחֲמִים, עָלֵינוּ וְעַל
כָּל־יִשְׂרָאֵל עַמֶּךָ . בָּרְכֵנוּ, אָבִינוּ, כֻּלָּנוּ כְּאֶחָד בְּאוֹר פָּנֶיךָ,
כִּי בְאוֹר פָּנֶיךָ נָתַתָּ לָּנוּ, יי אֱלֹהֵינוּ, תּוֹרַת חַיִּים, וְאַהֲבַת
חֶסֶד, וּצְדָקָה וּבְרָכָה וְרַחֲמִים וְחַיִּים וְשָׁלוֹם. וְטוֹב בְּעֵינֶיךָ
לְבָרֵךְ אֶת־עַמְּךָ יִשְׂרָאֵל וְאֶת־כָּל־הָעַמִּים בְּכָל־עֵת
וּבְכָל־שָׁעָה בִּשְׁלוֹמֶךָ .

* בָּרוּךְ אַתָּה יי, הַמְבָרֵךְ אֶת־עַמּוֹ יִשְׂרָאֵל בַּשָּׁלוֹם.

* ON SHABBAT SHUVAH CONCLUDE:

בְּסֵפֶר חַיִּים וּבְרָכָה נִכָּתֵב לְחַיִּים טוֹבִים וּלְשָׁלוֹם.
בָּרוּךְ אַתָּה יי, עוֹשֶׂה הַשָּׁלוֹם.

Sim sha-lom, to-va u-v'ra-cha, chein va-cheh-sed v'ra-cha-mim, a-lei-nu v'al kol Yis-ra-eil a-meh-cha.

Ba-r'chei-nu, a-vi-nu, ku-la-nu k'eh-chad b'or pa-neh-cha, ki v'or pa-neh-cha na-ta-ta la-nu Adonai Eh-lo-hei-nu, To-rat cha-yim v'a-ha-vat cheh-sed u-tz'da-ka u-v'ra-cha v'ra-cha-mim v'cha-yim v'sha-lom. V'tov b'ei-neh-cha l'va-reich et a-m'cha Yis-ra-eil v'et kol ha-a-mim b'chol eit u-v'chol sha-ah bi-sh'lo-me-cha. Ba-ruch a-ta Adonai, ha-m'va-reich et a-mo Yis-ra-eil ba-sha-lom.

° Grant us peace, Your most precious gift, O Eternal Source of peace, and give us the will to proclaim its message to all the peoples of the earth.

Bless our country, that it may always be a stronghold of peace, and its advocate among the nations.

May contentment reign within its borders, health and happiness within its homes.

Strengthen the bonds of friendship among the inhabitants of all lands, and may the love of Your name hallow every home and every heart. *We praise You, O God, the Source of peace.

* BETWEEN ROSH HASHANAH AND YOM KIPPUR CONCLUDE:

Inscribe us in the Book of life, blessing, and peace.
We praise You, O God, the Source of peace.

### SILENT PRAYER

אֱלֹהַי, נְצֹר לְשׁוֹנִי מֵרָע, וּשְׂפָתַי מִדַּבֵּר מִרְמָה. וְלִמְקַלְלַי נַפְשִׁי
תִדּוֹם וְנַפְשִׁי כֶּעָפָר לַכֹּל תִּהְיֶה. פְּתַח לִבִּי בְּתוֹרָתֶךָ, וּבְמִצְוֹתֶיךָ
תִּרְדֹּף נַפְשִׁי. וְכָל־הַחוֹשְׁבִים עָלַי רָעָה, מְהֵרָה הָפֵר עֲצָתָם
וְקַלְקֵל מַחֲשַׁבְתָּם. עֲשֵׂה לְמַעַן שְׁמֶךָ, עֲשֵׂה לְמַעַן יְמִינֶךָ, עֲשֵׂה
לְמַעַן קְדֻשָּׁתֶךָ, עֲשֵׂה לְמַעַן תּוֹרָתֶךָ; לְמַעַן יֵחָלְצוּן יְדִידֶיךָ,
הוֹשִׁיעָה יְמִינְךָ וַעֲנֵנִי.

O God, keep my tongue from evil and my lips from deceit. Help me to be silent in the face of derision, humble in the presence of all. Open my heart to Your Torah, that I may hasten to do Your Mitzvot. Save me with Your power; in time of trouble be my answer, that those who love You may rejoice.

~ ~

יִהְיוּ לְרָצוֹן אִמְרֵי־פִי וְהֶגְיוֹן לִבִּי לְפָנֶיךָ, יהוה, צוּרִי וְגֹאֲלִי.

Yi-h'yu l'ra-tzon i-m'rei fi v'heg-yon li-bi l'fa-neh-cha, Adonai tzu-ri v'go-a-li.

May the words of my mouth and the meditations of my heart be acceptable to You, O God, my Rock and my Redeemer.

עֹשֶׂה שָׁלוֹם בִּמְרוֹמָיו, הוּא יַעֲשֶׂה שָׁלוֹם עָלֵינוּ וְעַל־כָּל־יִשְׂרָאֵל, וְאִמְרוּ: אָמֵן.

O-seh sha-lom bi-m'ro-mav, hu ya-a-seh sha-lom a-lei-nu v'al kol Yis-ra-eil, v'i-m'ru: A-mein.

• May the One who causes peace to reign in the high heavens cause peace to reign among us, all Israel, and all the world.

For the Reading of the Torah, continue on page 141

Aleinu is on page 148 and page 149

## אשרי

אַשְׁרֵי יוֹשְׁבֵי בֵיתֶךָ; עוֹד יְהַלְלוּךָ סֶּלָה.

אַשְׁרֵי הָעָם שֶׁכָּכָה לּוֹ; אַשְׁרֵי הָעָם שֶׁיהוה אֱלֹהָיו.

Happy are those who dwell in Your house; they will sing your praise for ever.

*Happy the people to whom such blessing falls, happy the people of the Eternal God.*

*Psalm 145*

תְּהִלָּה לְדָוִד.

אֲרוֹמִמְךָ, אֱלוֹהַי הַמֶּלֶךְ, וַאֲבָרְכָה שִׁמְךָ לְעוֹלָם וָעֶד.

בְּכָל־יוֹם אֲבָרְכֶךָּ, וַאֲהַלְלָה שִׁמְךָ לְעוֹלָם וָעֶד.

I will exalt You, my Sovereign God; I will praise Your name for ever.

*Every day I will praise You; I will extol Your name for ever.*

גָּדוֹל יהוה וּמְהֻלָּל מְאֹד, וְלִגְדֻלָּתוֹ אֵין חֵקֶר.

דּוֹר לְדוֹר יְשַׁבַּח מַעֲשֶׂיךָ, וּגְבוּרֹתֶיךָ יַגִּידוּ.

Great are You, Eternal One, and worthy of praise, and infinite is Your greatness.

*One generation shall acclaim Your work to the next; they shall tell of Your mighty acts.*

הֲדַר כְּבוֹד הוֹדֶךָ, וְדִבְרֵי נִפְלְאֹתֶיךָ אָשִׂיחָה.

וֶעֱזוּז נוֹרְאֹתֶיךָ יֹאמֵרוּ, וּגְדוּלָּתְךָ אֲסַפְּרֶנָה.

They shall bring word of Your radiant glory, and bear witness to
Your wondrous works.

*They shall speak of Your awesome might, and make known
Your greatness.*

זֵכֶר רַב־טוּבְךָ יַבִּיעוּ, וְצִדְקָתְךָ יְרַנֵּנוּ.

חַנּוּן וְרַחוּם יהוה, אֶרֶךְ אַפַּיִם וּגְדָל־חָסֶד.

טוֹב־יהוה לַכֹּל, וְרַחֲמָיו עַל־כָּל־מַעֲשָׂיו.

They shall tell the world of Your goodness, and sing of Your
righteousness.

"God is gracious and compassionate, endlessly patient,
overflowing with love."

*"You are good to all; Your compassion shelters all Your
creatures."*

יוֹדוּךָ יהוה כָּל־מַעֲשֶׂיךָ, וַחֲסִידֶיךָ יְבָרְכוּכָה.

כְּבוֹד מַלְכוּתְךָ יֹאמֵרוּ, וּגְבוּרָתְךָ יְדַבֵּרוּ.

All Your works shall glorify You; Your steadfast friends shall
praise You.

*They shall proclaim Your majestic glory, they shall tell of Your
might:*

לְהוֹדִיעַ לִבְנֵי הָאָדָם גְּבוּרֹתָיו, וּכְבוֹד הֲדַר מַלְכוּתוֹ.

מַלְכוּתְךָ מַלְכוּת כָּל־עֹלָמִים, וּמֶמְשַׁלְתְּךָ בְּכָל־דֹּור וָדֹור.

to reveal Your power to the world, and the glorious splendor of
Your rule.

*You are sovereign to the end of time; You reign through all
generations.*

סוֹמֵךְ יהוה לְכָל־הַנֹּפְלִים, וְזוֹקֵף לְכָל־הַכְּפוּפִים.

עֵינֵי־כֹל אֵלֶיךָ יְשַׂבֵּרוּ, וְאַתָּה נוֹתֵן־לָהֶם אֶת־אָכְלָם בְּעִתּוֹ.

You support the falling, Eternal One; You raise up all who are bowed down.

*The eyes of all are turned to You; You sustain them in time of need.*

פּוֹתֵחַ אֶת־יָדֶךָ, וּמַשְׂבִּיעַ לְכָל־חַי רָצוֹן.

צַדִּיק יהוה בְּכָל־דְּרָכָיו, וְחָסִיד בְּכָל־מַעֲשָׂיו.

You open Your hand, to fulfill the needs of all the living.

*You are just in all Your ways, loving in all Your deeds.*

קָרוֹב יהוה לְכָל־קֹרְאָיו, לְכֹל אֲשֶׁר יִקְרָאֻהוּ בֶאֱמֶת.

רְצוֹן־יְרֵאָיו יַעֲשֶׂה, וְאֶת־שַׁוְעָתָם יִשְׁמַע וְיוֹשִׁיעֵם.

שׁוֹמֵר יהוה אֶת־כָּל־אֹהֲבָיו, וְאֵת כָּל־הָרְשָׁעִים יַשְׁמִיד.

You are near to all who call upon You, to all who call upon You in truth:

*You fulfill the hope of all who revere You; You hear their cry and help them.*

תְּהִלַּת יהוה יְדַבֶּר־פִּי; וִיבָרֵךְ כָּל־בָּשָׂר שֵׁם קָדְשׁוֹ לְעוֹלָם וָעֶד.

וַאֲנַחְנוּ נְבָרֵךְ יָהּ מֵעַתָּה וְעַד־עוֹלָם. הַלְלוּיָהּ.

My lips shall declare the glory of God; let all flesh praise Your holy name for ever and ever.

*We will praise Your name now and always. Halleluyah!*

The Reader's Kaddish is on page 132

127

# Additional Readings

## I

פִּתְחוּ־לִי שַׁעֲרֵי־צֶדֶק;
אָבֹא־בָם, אוֹדֶה יָהּ:

Pi-t'chu li  sha-a-rei tzeh-dek;
a-vo vam, o-deh Yah.

Open for me the gates of righteousness;
I will enter them and praise the Eternal One.

And now, O Israel, what is it that your Eternal God asks of you?

*"Walk in My ways, love and serve Me with all your heart and soul."*

Help me to know Your ways, O God; teach me Your paths. Lead me in Your truth, and guide me.

*"I desire love, and not sacrifices; the knowledge of God rather than burnt–offerings."*

With what shall I come before the Eternal God?

*Depart from evil and do good: so shall you abide forever, for God loves justice.*

It is taught: "Do justly, love goodness, and walk humbly with your God."

*It is taught: "Keep justice and righteousness."*

It is taught: "Seek Me and live."

*It is taught: "The righteous shall live by their faith."*

And it has been taught: "It shall come to pass, that God's spirit will be poured out on all flesh; your sons and daughters shall

prophesy; the old shall dream dreams, the young shall see visions."

*Purify my heart to serve You in truth. Consecrate my heart to revere Your name. Create in me a pure heart, O God, and renew a willing spirit within me.*

I am a Jew because the faith of Israel demands of me no abdication of the mind.

*I am a Jew because the faith of Israel requires of me all the devotion of my heart*

I am a Jew because at every time of despair, the Jew hopes.

*I am a Jew because the word of Israel is the oldest and the newest..*

I am a Jew because, for Israel, the world is not completed: we are completing it..

*I am a Jew because, for Israel, humanity is not created: we are creating it.*

I am a Jew because Israel places humanity and its unity above the nations and above Israel itself.

*I am a Jew because, above humanity, image of the divine unity, Israel places the unity which is divine.*

The Reader's Kaddish is on page 132

## II

אַשְׁרֵי תְמִימֵי־דָרֶךְ, הַהֹלְכִים בְּתוֹרַת יהוה. אַשְׁרֵי נֹצְרֵי עֵדֹתָיו,
בְּכָל־לֵב יִדְרְשׁוּהוּ. לְעוֹלָם, יהוה, דְּבָרְךָ נִצָּב בַּשָּׁמָיִם. לְדֹר
וָדֹר אֱמוּנָתֶךָ.

Happy is the one whose way is true,
who walks in the path of Torah,
who seeks You with a whole heart.

*Your word endures forever;*

129

*It is firm as the heavens.*
*Your truth abides through all generations.*

Happy is the one whose help is Israel's God,
whose hope is the Eternal One,

*Who secures justice for the oppressed*
*and gives food to the hungry;*
*who sets free the captive*
*and raises up the fallen;*
*who protects the stranger*
*and sustains the orphan.*

It has been told you what is good,
and what the Eternal God requires of you:

*Only to do justly, to love mercy,*
*to walk humbly with your God.*

It is written: Speak to the whole community of Israel, and say to
them: "You shall be holy, for I, the Eternal God, am holy."

*As God is merciful and gracious,*
*so shall you be merciful and gracious.*

Let your neighbor's property
be as dear to you as your own.

*And let your neighbor's honor*
*be as dear to you as your own.*

You shall not oppress a stranger,
for you were strangers in the land of Egypt.

*The strangers who live among you*
*shall be to you as the home–born,*
*and you shall love them as yourself.*

You shall not rejoice when your enemy falls;
you shall not exult when your enemy stumbles.

*You shall not hate another in your heart;*
*but you shall love your neighbor as yourself.*

130

## III

O God, where can I find You? Your glory fills the world.
Behold, I find You in the mind free to sail by its own star,
In words that spring from the depth of truth,
Where the scientist toils to unravel Your world's secrets,
Where the artist makes beauty in Your world,
Where men and women struggle for freedom in Your world,
Among the lonely and poor, the lowly and lost,
Wherever noble deeds are done.

*Behold, I find You*
*In the merry shouts of children at play,*
*In the mother's lullaby, as she rocks her baby to sleep,*
*In the sleep that falls on an infant's eyes,*
*And in the smile that plays on sleeping lips,*
*And in the child as she grows to embrace a world of wonders,*
*A world of sun and light, of food and drink, laughter,*
*And dream, and the mystery of love.*
*Behold, I find You*
*In the life that dances in my blood,*
*In death knocking on the doors of life,*
*And in birth, as the generations ever renew themselves.*
*O God, where can I find You? Your glory fills the world!*
*I find You here where I am, O God. I find You here.*

O God, You are the fountain of life;
In Your light shall we see light.

*Send forth Your light and Your truth;*
*Let them lead us on our way.*
*Grant that our worship on this Shabbat may*
*bring us nearer to You and to one another.*

## All rise

READER'S KADDISH                                                   חֲצִי קַדִּישׁ

יִתְגַּדַּל וְיִתְקַדַּשׁ שְׁמֵהּ רַבָּא בְּעָלְמָא דִי־בְרָא כִרְעוּתֵהּ,
וְיַמְלִיךְ מַלְכוּתֵהּ בְּחַיֵּיכוֹן וּבְיוֹמֵיכוֹן וּבְחַיֵּי דְכָל־בֵּית
יִשְׂרָאֵל, בַּעֲגָלָא וּבִזְמַן קָרִיב, וְאִמְרוּ: אָמֵן.

יְהֵא שְׁמֵהּ רַבָּא מְבָרַךְ לְעָלַם וּלְעָלְמֵי עָלְמַיָּא.

יִתְבָּרַךְ וְיִשְׁתַּבַּח, וְיִתְפָּאַר וְיִתְרוֹמַם וְיִתְנַשֵּׂא, וְיִתְהַדָּר
וְיִתְעַלֶּה וְיִתְהַלָּל שְׁמֵהּ דְּקוּדְשָׁא, בְּרִיךְ הוּא,
לְעֵלָּא מִן־כָּל־בִּרְכָתָא וְשִׁירָתָא, תֻּשְׁבְּחָתָא וְנֶחֱמָתָא
דַּאֲמִירָן בְּעָלְמָא, וְאִמְרוּ: אָמֵן.

Yit-ga-dal v'yit–ka–dash sh'mei ra-ba b'al-ma di-v'ra chi-r'u'tei, v'yam-lich mal-chu-tei b'cha-yei-chon u-v'yo-mei-chon u-v'cha-yei d'chol beit Yis-ra-eil, ba-a-ga-la u-vi-z'man ka-riv, v'i-m' ru: A-mein.

Y'hei sh'mei ra-ba m'va-rach l'a-lam u-l'al-mei al-ma-ya.

Yit-ba-rach v'yish-ta-bach, v'yit-pa-ar v'yit-ro-mam v'yit-na-sei, v'yit-ha-dar v'yit-a-leh v'yit-ha-lal sh'mei d'kud-sha, b'rich hu,

l'ei-la min kol bir-cha-ta v'shi-ra-ta, tush-b'cha-ta v'neh-cheh-ma-ta da-a-mi-ran b'al-ma, v'i-m' ru: A-mein.

The Weekday T'filah is on page 22

The Shabbat T'filah is on the next page

132

## T'FILAH תפלה

אֲדֹנָי, שְׂפָתַי תִּפְתָּח, וּפִי יַגִּיד תְּהִלָּתֶךָ.

Eternal God, open my lips, that my mouth may declare Your glory.

GOD OF ALL GENERATIONS        אבות ואמהות

בָּרוּךְ אַתָּה יי, אֱלֹהֵינוּ וֵאלֹהֵי אֲבוֹתֵינוּ וְאִמּוֹתֵינוּ:
אֱלֹהֵי אַבְרָהָם, אֱלֹהֵי יִצְחָק, וֵאלֹהֵי יַעֲקֹב.
אֱלֹהֵי שָׂרָה, אֱלֹהֵי רִבְקָה, אֱלֹהֵי לֵאָה וֵאלֹהֵי רָחֵל.
הָאֵל הַגָּדוֹל הַגִּבּוֹר וְהַנּוֹרָא, אֵל עֶלְיוֹן, גּוֹמֵל חֲסָדִים
טוֹבִים וְקוֹנֵה הַכֹּל, וְזוֹכֵר חַסְדֵי אָבוֹת וְאִמָּהוֹת,
וּמֵבִיא גְאֻלָּה לִבְנֵי בְנֵיהֶם, לְמַעַן שְׁמוֹ בְּאַהֲבָה.
מֶלֶךְ עוֹזֵר וּמוֹשִׁיעַ וּמָגֵן.
בָּרוּךְ אַתָּה יי, מָגֵן אַבְרָהָם וְעֶזְרַת שָׂרָה.

Ba–ruch a–ta Adonai, Eh–lo–hei–nu vei–lo–hei a–vo–tei–nu v'i–mo–tei–nu:
Eh–lo–hei Av–ra–ham, eh–lo–hei Yitz–chak, vei–lo–hei Ya–a–kov.
Eh–lo–hei Sa–ra, Eh–lo–hei Riv–ka, Eh–lo–hei Lei–a vei–lo–hei Ra–cheil.
Ha–eil ha–ga–dol ha–gi–bor v'ha–no–ra, Eil el–yon, go–meil cha–sa–dim
to–vim, v'ko–nei ha–kol, v'zo–cheir cha–s'dei a–vot v'i–ma–hot,
u–mei–vi g'u–la li–v'nei v'nei–hem, l'ma–an sh'mo, b'a–ha–va.
Meh–lech o–zeir u–mo–shi–a u–ma–gein.
Ba–ruch a–ta Adonai, ma–gein Av–ra–ham v'ez–rat Sa–ra.

° *God of Israel, You are the hope of all the generations:*
*the ones that are past, and those yet to be. You are our God.*
*You are the first; You are the last; You are the Only One.*
*You made the earth and brought us forth to dwell in it.*
*You called Abraham and Sarah to Your service,*
*their children to bear witness to Your glory.*
*You formed us to be a covenant people,*
*enduring as the stars in heaven.*

133

*Eternal God, You are the Shield of our people,*
*our everlasting Light!*

GOD'S POWER                                          גְּבוּרוֹת

אַתָּה גִּבּוֹר לְעוֹלָם, אֲדֹנָי, מְחַיֵּה הַכֹּל אַתָּה, רַב לְהוֹשִׁיעַ.
מְכַלְכֵּל חַיִּים בְּחֶסֶד, מְחַיֵּה הַכֹּל בְּרַחֲמִים רַבִּים. סוֹמֵךְ
נוֹפְלִים, וְרוֹפֵא חוֹלִים, וּמַתִּיר אֲסוּרִים, וּמְקַיֵּם אֱמוּנָתוֹ
לִישֵׁנֵי עָפָר. מִי כָמוֹךְ בַּעַל גְּבוּרוֹת, וּמִי דּוֹמֶה לָּךְ,
מֶלֶךְ מֵמִית וּמְחַיֵּה וּמַצְמִיחַ יְשׁוּעָה?

וְנֶאֱמָן אַתָּה לְהַחֲיוֹת הַכֹּל. בָּרוּךְ אַתָּה יְיָ, מְחַיֵּה הַכֹּל.

A-ta gi-bor l'o-lam, Adonai, m'cha-yei ha-kol a-ta, rav l'ho-shi-a.
M'chal-keil cha-yim b'cheh-sed, m'cha-yei ha-kol b'ra-cha-mim ra-bim.
So-meich no-f'lim, v'ro-fei cho-lim, u-ma-tir a-su-rim, u-m'ka-yeim eh-
mu-na-to li-shei-nei a-far. Mi cha-mo-cha ba-al g'vu-rot, u-mi do-meh
lach, meh-lech mei-mit u-m'cha-yeh u-matz-mi-ach y'shu-a?
V'neh-eh-man a-ta l'ha-cha-yot ha-kol. Ba-ruch a-ta Adonai, m'cha-yei
ha-kol.

° Your strength is with us always, O God,
Your compassion does not fail.
Winter winds are Your messengers,
summer dew a sign of Your grace.
You reach out to the fallen
and comfort the afflicted;
You give heart to the captive,
and breathe hope into those who lie in the dust.
Praised be the One whose breath is our life.

SANCTIFICATION קדושה

נְקַדֵּשׁ אֶת־שִׁמְךָ בָּעוֹלָם, כְּשֵׁם שֶׁמַּקְדִּישִׁים אוֹתוֹ בִּשְׁמֵי מָרוֹם,
כַּכָּתוּב עַל־יַד נְבִיאֶךָ: וְקָרָא זֶה אֶל־זֶה וְאָמַר:

We sanctify Your name on earth, even as all things, to the ends
of time and space, proclaim Your holiness, and in the words of
the prophet we say:

קָדוֹשׁ, קָדוֹשׁ, קָדוֹשׁ יהוה צְבָאוֹת, מְלֹא כָל־הָאָרֶץ כְּבוֹדוֹ.

Ka–dosh, Ka–dosh, Ka–dosh Adonai tz'va–ot, m'lo chol ha–a–retz k'vo–do.

*Holy, Holy, Holy is the God of all being! The whole earth is
filled with Your glory!*

אַדִּיר אַדִּירֵנוּ, יהוה אֲדֹנֵינוּ, מָה־אַדִּיר שִׁמְךָ בְּכָל־הָאָרֶץ!

Source of our strength, Sovereign God, how majestic is Your
name in all the earth!

בָּרוּךְ כְּבוֹד־יהוה מִמְּקוֹמוֹ.

Ba–ruch  k'vod Adonai mi–m'ko–mo.

*Praised be the glory of God in heaven and earth.*

אֶחָד הוּא אֱלֹהֵינוּ, הוּא אָבִינוּ, הוּא מַלְכֵּנוּ, הוּא מוֹשִׁיעֵנוּ;
וְהוּא יַשְׁמִיעֵנוּ בְּרַחֲמָיו לְעֵינֵי כָּל־חָי:

You alone are our God and our Creator; You are our Ruler and
our Helper; and in Your mercy You reveal Yourself in the sight of
all the living:

"אֲנִי יהוה אֱלֹהֵיכֶם!"

I AM YOUR ETERNAL GOD!

יִמְלֹךְ יהוה לְעוֹלָם, אֱלֹהַיִךְ צִיּוֹן, לְדֹר וָדֹר. הַלְלוּיָהּ!

135

Yim–loch Adonai l'o–lam, Eh–lo–ha–yich Tzi–yon, l'dor va–dor. Halleluyah!

*The Eternal One shall reign for ever; your God, O Zion, from generation to generation. Halleluyah!*

לְדוֹר וָדוֹר נַגִּיד גָּדְלֶךָ, וּלְנֵצַח נְצָחִים קְדֻשָּׁתְךָ נַקְדִּישׁ.
וְשִׁבְחֲךָ, אֱלֹהֵינוּ, מִפִּינוּ לֹא יָמוּשׁ לְעוֹלָם וָעֶד.
בָּרוּךְ אַתָּה יְיָ, הָאֵל הַקָּדוֹשׁ.

To all generations we will make known Your greatness, and to all eternity proclaim Your holiness. Your praise, O God, shall never depart from our lips.

We praise You, Eternal One, the holy God.

## All are seated

YOU ARE ONE                                              אתה אחד

You are One, Your name is One, and who is like Your people Israel, a people unique on the earth? A garland of glory have You given us, a crown of salvation: a day of rest and holiness. May our rest on this day be one of love and devotion, sincerity and faithfulness, peace and tranquility, quietness and confidence: the perfect rest that You desire. Let Your children know and understand that their rest comes from You, and that by it they sanctify Your name.

אַתָּה אֶחָד וְשִׁמְךָ אֶחָד, וּמִי
כְעַמְּךָ יִשְׂרָאֵל, גּוֹי אֶחָד בָּאָרֶץ?
תִּפְאֶרֶת גְּדֻלָּה וַעֲטֶרֶת יְשׁוּעָה,
יוֹם מְנוּחָה וּקְדֻשָּׁה לְעַמְּךָ נָתָתָ.
מְנוּחַת אַהֲבָה וּנְדָבָה, מְנוּחַת
אֱמֶת וֶאֱמוּנָה, מְנוּחַת שָׁלוֹם
וְשַׁלְוָה וְהַשְׁקֵט וָבֶטַח, מְנוּחָה
שְׁלֵמָה שָׁאַתָּה רוֹצֶה בָּהּ. יַכִּירוּ
בָנֶיךָ וְיֵדְעוּ כִּי מֵאִתְּךָ הִיא
מְנוּחָתָם, וְעַל־מְנוּחָתָם יַקְדִּישׁוּ
אֶת־שְׁמֶךָ.

or

## MOST PRECIOUS OF DAYS

ישמחו

יִשְׂמְחוּ בְמַלְכוּתְךָ שׁוֹמְרֵי שַׁבָּת וְקוֹרְאֵי עֹנֶג. עַם מְקַדְּשֵׁי שְׁבִיעִי כֻּלָּם יִשְׂבְּעוּ וְיִתְעַנְּגוּ מִטּוּבֶךָ. וְהַשְּׁבִיעִי רָצִיתָ בּוֹ וְקִדַּשְׁתּוֹ. חֶמְדַּת יָמִים אוֹתוֹ קָרָאתָ, זֵכֶר לְמַעֲשֵׂה בְרֵאשִׁית.

Yis–m'chu v'ma–l'chu–t'cha sho–m'rei Shabbat v'ko–r'ei o–neg. Am m'ka–d'shei sh'vi–i ku–lam yis–b'u v'yit–a–n'gu mi–tu–veh–cha. V'ha–sh'vi–i ra–tzi–ta bo v'ki–dash–to. Chem–dat ya–mim o–to ka–ra–ta, zei–cher l'ma–a–sei v'rei–sheet.

Those who keep the Sabbath and call it a delight shall rejoice in Your deliverance. All who hallow the seventh day shall be gladdened by Your goodness. This day is Israel's festival of the spirit, sanctified and blessed by You, the most precious of days, a symbol of the joy of creation.

## THE HOLINESS OF SHABBAT

קדושת היום

אֱלֹהֵינוּ וֵאלֹהֵי אֲבוֹתֵינוּ וְאִמּוֹתֵינוּ, רְצֵה בִמְנוּחָתֵנוּ. קַדְּשֵׁנוּ בְּמִצְוֹתֶיךָ וְתֵן חֶלְקֵנוּ בְּתוֹרָתֶךָ. שַׂבְּעֵנוּ מִטּוּבֶךָ, וְשַׂמְּחֵנוּ בִּישׁוּעָתֶךָ, וְטַהֵר לִבֵּנוּ לְעָבְדְּךָ בֶּאֱמֶת. וְהַנְחִילֵנוּ, יְיָ אֱלֹהֵינוּ, בְּאַהֲבָה וּבְרָצוֹן שַׁבַּת קָדְשֶׁךָ, וְיָנוּחוּ בָהּ יִשְׂרָאֵל מְקַדְּשֵׁי שְׁמֶךָ. בָּרוּךְ אַתָּה יְיָ, מְקַדֵּשׁ הַשַּׁבָּת.

Eh-lo-hei-nu vei-lo-hei a-vo-tei-nu v'i-mo-tei-nu, r'tzei vi-m'nu-cha-tei-nu. Ka-d'shei-nu b'mitz-vo-teh-cha v-tein chel-kei-nu b'to-ra-teh-cha. Sab-ei-nu mi-tu-veh-cha, v'sam-chei-nu bi-shu-a-teh-cha, v'ta-heir li-bei-nu l'ov-d'cha beh-eh-met. V'han-chi-lei-nu, Adonai Eh-lo-hei-nu, b'a-ha-va u-v'ra-tzon Shabbat kod-sheh-cha, v'ya-nu-chu va Yis-ra-eil m'ka-d'shei sh'meh-cha. Ba-ruch a-ta Adonai, m'ka-deish ha-Shabbat.

• *Our God and God of all ages, may our worship on this Sabbath bring us closer to You.*

*Make us steadfast in spirit, our intention pure, truly to serve You.*

*Enable us to keep this day as a day of peace and joy, a day of rest and learning.*

*We praise You, O God, for the Sabbath and its holiness.*

WORSHIP                                                          עבודה

רְצֵה, יי אֱלֹהֵינוּ, בְּעַמְּךָ יִשְׂרָאֵל, וּתְפִלָּתָם בְּאַהֲבָה תְקַבֵּל,
וּתְהִי לְרָצוֹן תָּמִיד עֲבוֹדַת יִשְׂרָאֵל עַמֶּךָ.
בָּרוּךְ אַתָּה יי, שֶׁאוֹתְךָ לְבַדְּךָ בְּיִרְאָה נַעֲבוֹד.

O God, look with favor upon us, and may our service be acceptable to You. We praise You, Eternal One, whom alone we serve with reverence.

THANKSGIVING                                                     הודאה

מוֹדִים אֲנַחְנוּ לָךְ שָׁאַתָּה הוּא יי אֱלֹהֵינוּ וֵאלֹהֵי אֲבוֹתֵינוּ
וְאִמּוֹתֵינוּ, אֱלֹהֵי כָל־בָּשָׂר, יוֹצְרֵנוּ יוֹצֵר בְּרֵאשִׁית. בְּרָכוֹת
וְהוֹדָאוֹת לְשִׁמְךָ הַגָּדוֹל וְהַקָּדוֹשׁ עַל־שֶׁהֶחֱיִיתָנוּ וְקִיַּמְתָּנוּ.
כֵּן תְּחַיֵּנוּ וּתְקַיְּמֵנוּ, יי אֱלֹהֵינוּ, וּתְאַמְּצֵנוּ לִשְׁמֹר חֻקֶּיךָ,
לַעֲשׂוֹת רְצוֹנֶךָ, וּלְעָבְדְּךָ בְּלֵבָב שָׁלֵם. בָּרוּךְ אֵל הַהוֹדָאוֹת.

We gratefully acknowledge that You, the God of our ancestors, are our God, and that You, the God of all flesh, are our Creator. As you have given us life and sustained us to this day, so may you continue to bless us with life and strength to observe Your statutes, to do Your will, to serve You with a whole heart.

Praised be God, to whom our thanks are due.

PEACE                                                      ברכת שלום

שָׁלוֹם רָב עַל־יִשְׂרָאֵל עַמְּךָ תָּשִׂים לְעוֹלָם, כִּי אַתָּה הוּא
מֶלֶךְ אָדוֹן לְכָל־הַשָּׁלוֹם. וְטוֹב בְּעֵינֶיךָ לְבָרֵךְ אֶת־עַמְּךָ

138

יִשְׂרָאֵל וְאֶת־כָּל־הָעַמִּים בְּכָל־עֵת וּבְכָל־שָׁעָה בִּשְׁלוֹמֶךָ.
בָּרוּךְ אַתָּה יי, הַמְבָרֵךְ אֶת־עַמּוֹ יִשְׂרָאֵל בַּשָּׁלוֹם.

° *Grant us peace, Your most precious gift, O Eternal Source of peace, and give us the will to proclaim its message to all the peoples of the earth.*

*Bless our country, that it may always be a stronghold of peace, and its advocate among the nations.*

*May contentment reign within its borders, health and happiness within its homes.*

*Strengthen the bonds of friendship among the inhabitants of all lands, and may the love of Your name hallow every home and every heart. We praise You, O God, the Source of peace.*

SILENT PRAYER

*From Psalm 15*

Eternal God:
Who may abide in Your house?
Who may dwell in Your holy mountain?
Those who are upright; who do justly;
all whose hearts are true.
Who do not slander others,
nor wrong them,
nor bring shame upon their kin.
Who give their word and, come what may, do not retract.
Who do not exploit others,
who never take bribes.
Those who live in this way
shall never be shaken.

~ ~

139

יִהְיוּ לְרָצוֹן אִמְרֵי־פִי וְהֶגְיוֹן לִבִּי לְפָנֶיךָ, יהוה, צוּרִי וְגֹאֲלִי.

Yi-h'yu l'ra-tzon i-m'rei fi v'heg-yon li-bi l'fa-neh-cha, Adonai tzu-ri v'go-a-li.

May the words of my mouth and the meditations of my heart be acceptable to You, O God, my Rock and my Redeemer.

עֹשֶׂה שָׁלוֹם בִּמְרוֹמָיו, הוּא יַעֲשֶׂה שָׁלוֹם עָלֵינוּ וְעַל־כָּל־יִשְׂרָאֵל, וְאִמְרוּ: אָמֵן.

O-seh sha-lom bi-m'ro-mav, hu ya-a-seh sha-lom a-lei-nu v'al kol Yis-ra-eil, v'i-m'ru: A-mein.

• May the One who causes peace to reign in the high heavens cause peace to reign among us, all Israel, and all the world.

For the Reading of the Torah, continue on page 141

Aleinu is on page 148 and page 149

# For the Reading of the Torah    סדר קריאת התורה

Begin here, or on the next page

Assembled at a mountain,
our people,
still bent from oppression,
found You,
found Your Torah,
found Your truth
and embraced the destiny
that has shaped worlds.
*Help us still to shape the world*
*according to Your will;*
*help us to teach and to learn,*
*to hear Your word anew,*
*and to find in it our path to goodness and truth.*

All rise

THE ARK IS OPENED

עַל שְׁלֹשָׁה דְבָרִים הָעוֹלָם עוֹמֵד:
עַל הַתּוֹרָה, וְעַל הָעֲבוֹדָה, וְעַל גְּמִילוּת חֲסָדִים.

Al sh'lo–sha d'va–rim ha–o–lam o–meid:
Al ha–Torah, v'al ha–a–vo–da, v'al g'mi–lut cha–sa–dim.

The world depends on three things:
On Torah, worship, and loving deeds.

Continue with the opening of the Ark on the next page

141

Begin here, or on the previous page

אֵין־כָּמוֹךָ בָאֱלֹהִים, אֲדֹנָי, וְאֵין כְּמַעֲשֶׂיךָ.

מַלְכוּתְךָ מַלְכוּת כָּל־עוֹלָמִים, וּמֶמְשַׁלְתְּךָ בְּכָל־דּוֹר וָדוֹר.

יהוה מֶלֶךְ, יהוה מָלָךְ, יהוה יִמְלוֹךְ לְעוֹלָם וָעֶד.

יהוה עֹז לְעַמּוֹ יִתֵּן, יהוה יְבָרֵךְ אֶת־עַמּוֹ בַשָּׁלוֹם.

There is none like You, Eternal One, among the gods that are worshipped, and there are no deeds like Yours. Your sovereignty is everlasting; You reign through all generations.

God rules; God will reign for ever and ever. Eternal God, give strength to Your people; Eternal God, bless Your people with peace.

## All rise

אֵל הָרַחֲמִים, הֵיטִיבָה בִרְצוֹנְךָ אֶת־צִיּוֹן; תִּבְנֶה חוֹמוֹת יְרוּשָׁלָיִם.

כִּי בְךָ לְבַד בָּטָחְנוּ, מֶלֶךְ אֵל רָם וְנִשָּׂא, אֲדוֹן עוֹלָמִים.

Source of mercy, let Your goodness be a blessing to Zion; let Jerusalem be rebuilt. In You alone do we trust, O Sovereign God, high and exalted, Ruler of all the worlds.

## ON ALL OCCASIONS:

### The Ark is opened

הָבוּ גֹדֶל לֵאלֹהֵינוּ, וּתְנוּ כָבוֹד לַתּוֹרָה.

Let us declare the greatness of our God,
and give honor to the Torah.

כִּי מִצִּיּוֹן תֵּצֵא תוֹרָה, וּדְבַר־יהוה מִירוּשָׁלָיִם.

בָּרוּךְ שֶׁנָּתַן תּוֹרָה לְעַמּוֹ יִשְׂרָאֵל בִּקְדֻשָּׁתוֹ.

142

For out of Zion shall go forth Torah,
and the word of God from Jerusalem.
Praised be the One who in holiness gives Torah to our people Israel.

בֵּית יַעֲקֹב, לְכוּ וְנֵלְכָה בְּאוֹר יהוה.

O House of Jacob, come, let us walk by the light of our God.

~ ~

שְׁמַע יִשְׂרָאֵל: יהוה אֱלֹהֵינוּ, יהוה אֶחָד!

Sh'ma Yisrael, Adonai Eh–lo–hei–nu, Adonai Echad!
Hear, O Israel: the Eternal One is our God,
the Eternal God alone!

אֶחָד אֱלֹהֵינוּ, גָּדוֹל אֲדֹנֵינוּ, קָדוֹשׁ שְׁמוֹ!

Eh-chad Eh–lo–hei–nu, ga-dol A-do-nei-nu, ka-dosh sh'mo.

Our God is One; great and holy is the Eternal One.

~ ~

גַּדְּלוּ לַיהוה אִתִּי, וּנְרוֹמְמָה שְׁמוֹ יַחְדָּו.

O magnify the Eternal One with me,
and together let us exalt God's name.

MANY CONGREGATIONS CONTINUE WITH A PROCESSION (HAKAFAH)

לְךָ, יהוה, הַגְּדֻלָּה וְהַגְּבוּרָה וְהַתִּפְאֶרֶת וְהַנֵּצַח וְהַהוֹד, כִּי כֹל
בַּשָּׁמַיִם וּבָאָרֶץ. לְךָ, יהוה, הַמַּמְלָכָה וְהַמִּתְנַשֵּׂא לְכֹל לְרֹאשׁ.

Yours, O God, is the greatness, the power, the glory, the victory, and the
majesty; for all that is in heaven and earth is Yours. You, O God, are
sovereign; You are supreme over all.

All are seated

143

## READING OF THE TORAH

### Before the reading

בָּרְכוּ אֶת־יְיָ הַמְבֹרָךְ!

בָּרוּךְ יְיָ הַמְבֹרָךְ לְעוֹלָם וָעֶד!

בָּרוּךְ יְיָ הַמְבֹרָךְ לְעוֹלָם וָעֶד!

בָּרוּךְ אַתָּה יְיָ, אֱלֹהֵינוּ מֶלֶךְ הָעוֹלָם,

אֲשֶׁר בָּחַר־בָּנוּ מִכָּל־הָעַמִּים, וְנָתַן־לָנוּ אֶת־תּוֹרָתוֹ.

בָּרוּךְ אַתָּה יְיָ, נוֹתֵן הַתּוֹרָה.

READER: Ba-r'chu et Adonai ha-m'vo-rach!
CONGREGATION: Ba-ruch Adonai ha-m'vo-rach l'o-lam va-ed!
READER: Ba-ruch Adonai ha-m'vo-rach l'o-lam va-ed!
Ba-ruch a-ta Adonai, Eh–lo–hei–nu meh–lech ha-o-lam, a-sher ba-char ba-nu mi-kol ha-a-mim, v'na-tan la-nu et Torah-to. Ba-ruch a-ta Adonai, no-tein ha-Torah.

Praise the One to whom our praise is due!
Praised be the One to whom our praise is due, now and for ever!
We praise You, Eternal God, Sovereign of the universe: You have called us to Your service by giving us the Torah. We praise You, O God, Giver of the Torah.

### After the reading

בָּרוּךְ אַתָּה יְיָ, אֱלֹהֵינוּ מֶלֶךְ הָעוֹלָם,

אֲשֶׁר נָתַן־לָנוּ תּוֹרַת אֱמֶת, וְחַיֵּי עוֹלָם נָטַע בְּתוֹכֵנוּ.

בָּרוּךְ אַתָּה יְיָ, נוֹתֵן הַתּוֹרָה.

READER: Ba-ruch a-ta Adonai, Eh–lo–hei–nu meh–lech ha-o-lam, a-sher na-tan la-nu To-rat eh-met, v'cha-yei o-lam na-ta b'to-chei-nu. Ba-ruch a-ta Adonai, no-tein ha-Torah.

We praise You, Eternal God, Sovereign  of the universe: You have given us a Torah of truth, implanting within us eternal life. We praise You, O God, Giver of the Torah.

## הגבהה—HAGBAHA—LIFTING THE TORAH

וְזֹאת הַתּוֹרָה אֲשֶׁר־שָׂם מֹשֶׁה לִפְנֵי בְּנֵי יִשְׂרָאֵל,

עַל־פִּי יי בְּיַד־מֹשֶׁה.

• This is the Torah that Moses placed before the people of Israel.

Some congregations continue with Haftarah at an Afternoon Service

## READING OF THE HAFTARAH

### Before the Reading

בָּרוּךְ אַתָּה יי, אֱלֹהֵינוּ מֶלֶךְ הָעוֹלָם, אֲשֶׁר בָּחַר בִּנְבִיאִים

טוֹבִים, וְרָצָה בְדִבְרֵיהֶם הַנֶּאֱמָרִים בֶּאֱמֶת.

בָּרוּךְ אַתָּה יי, הַבּוֹחֵר בַּתּוֹרָה, וּבְמֹשֶׁה עַבְדּוֹ, וּבְיִשְׂרָאֵל עַמּוֹ

וּבִנְבִיאֵי הָאֱמֶת וָצֶדֶק.

We praise You, Eternal God, Sovereign  of the universe: You have called faithful prophets to speak words of truth. We praise You, O God, for the revelation of Torah, for Moses Your servant and Israel Your people, and for the prophets of truth and righteousness.

### After the Reading

בָּרוּךְ אַתָּה יי, אֱלֹהֵינוּ מֶלֶךְ הָעוֹלָם, צוּר כָּל־הָעוֹלָמִים,

צַדִּיק בְּכָל־הַדּוֹרוֹת, הָאֵל הַנֶּאֱמָן, הָאוֹמֵר וְעוֹשֶׂה, הַמְדַבֵּר

וּמְקַיֵּם, שֶׁכָּל־דְּבָרָיו אֱמֶת וָצֶדֶק.

עַל־הַתּוֹרָה וְעַל־הָעֲבוֹדָה וְעַל־הַנְּבִיאִים וְעַל־יוֹם הַשַּׁבָּת הַזֶּה,

שֶׁנָּתַתָּ־לָּנוּ, יי אֱלֹהֵינוּ, לִקְדֻשָּׁה וְלִמְנוּחָה, לְכָבוֹד וּלְתִפְאֶרֶת,

עַל־הַכֹּל, יי אֱלֹהֵינוּ, אֲנַחְנוּ מוֹדִים לָךְ וּמְבָרְכִים אוֹתָךְ.

145

יִתְבָּרַךְ שִׁמְךָ בְּפִי כָּל־חַי תָּמִיד לְעוֹלָם וָעֶד.

בָּרוּךְ אַתָּה יי, מְקַדֵּשׁ הַשַּׁבָּת.

We praise You, Eternal God, Sovereign of the universe, the Rock of all creation, the Righteous One of all generations, the faithful God whose word is deed, whose every command is just and true.

For the Torah, for the privilege of worship, for the prophets, and for this Sabbath day that You, our Eternal God, have given us for holiness and rest, for honor and glory, we thank and praise You. May Your name be praised for ever by every living being. We praise You, O God, for the Sabbath and its holiness.

## RETURNING THE TORAH TO THE ARK

### All rise

יְהַלְלוּ אֶת־שֵׁם יהוה, כִּי־נִשְׂגָּב שְׁמוֹ לְבַדּוֹ.

Let us praise the Eternal God, whose name alone is exalted.

~ ~

הוֹדוֹ עַל־אֶרֶץ וְשָׁמָיִם, וַיָּרֶם קֶרֶן לְעַמּוֹ, תְּהִלָּה

לְכָל־חֲסִידָיו, לִבְנֵי יִשְׂרָאֵל, עַם־קְרֹבוֹ, הַלְלוּיָהּ!

Your splendor covers heaven and earth; You are the strength of Your people, making glorious Your faithful ones, Israel, a people close to You. Halleluyah!

~ ~

תּוֹרַת יהוה תְּמִימָה, מְשִׁיבַת נָפֶשׁ;

עֵדוּת יהוה נֶאֱמָנָה, מַחְכִּימַת פֶּתִי.

God's Teaching is perfect, reviving the soul;
*God's word is unfailing, making wise the simple.*

146

פִּקּוּדֵי יהוה יְשָׁרִים, מְשַׂמְּחֵי־לֵב;
מִצְוַת יהוה בָּרָה, מְאִירַת עֵינָיִם.

God's precepts are right, delighting the mind;
*God's Mitzvah is clear, giving light to the eyes.*

יִרְאַת יהוה טְהוֹרָה, עוֹמֶדֶת לָעַד;
מִשְׁפְּטֵי־יהוה אֱמֶת, צָדְקוּ יַחְדָּו.

God's doctrine is pure, enduring for ever;
*God's guidance is true, and altogether just.*

~ ~

Behold, a good doctrine has been given you, My Torah; do not forsake it. It is a tree of life to those who hold it fast, and all who cling to it find happiness. Its ways are ways of pleasantness, and all its paths are peace.

כִּי לֶקַח טוֹב נָתַתִּי לָכֶם, תּוֹרָתִי אַל־תַּעֲזֹבוּ.
עֵץ־חַיִּים הִיא לַמַּחֲזִיקִים בָּהּ, וְתֹמְכֶיהָ מְאֻשָּׁר.
דְּרָכֶיהָ דַרְכֵי־נֹעַם, וְכָל־נְתִיבוֹתֶיהָ שָׁלוֹם.

Help us to return to You, O God; then truly shall we return. Renew our days as in the past.

הֲשִׁיבֵנוּ יהוה אֵלֶיךָ, וְנָשׁוּבָה. חַדֵּשׁ יָמֵינוּ כְּקֶדֶם.

The Ark is closed

All are seated

147

### All rise

עָלֵֽינוּ לְשַׁבֵּֽחַ לַאֲדוֹן הַכֹּל, לָתֵת גְּדֻלָּה לְיוֹצֵר בְּרֵאשִׁית,
שֶׁלֹּא עָשָֽׂנוּ כְּגוֹיֵי הָאֲרָצוֹת, וְלֹא שָׂמָֽנוּ כְּמִשְׁפְּחוֹת הָאֲדָמָה;
שֶׁלֹּא שָׂם חֶלְקֵֽנוּ כָּהֶם, וְגוֹרָלֵֽנוּ כְּכָל־הֲמוֹנָם.

וַאֲנַֽחְנוּ כּוֹרְעִים וּמִשְׁתַּחֲוִים וּמוֹדִים לִפְנֵי
מֶֽלֶךְ מַלְכֵי הַמְּלָכִים, הַקָּדוֹשׁ בָּרוּךְ הוּא.

A-lei-nu l'sha-bei-ach la-a-don ha-kol, la-teit g'du-la l'yo-tzeir b'rei-sheet,
sheh-lo a-sa-nu k'go-yei ha-a-ra-tzot, v'lo sa-ma-nu k'mish-p'chot ha-a-da-
ma; sheh-lo sam chel-kei-nu ka-hem, v'go-ra-lei-nu k'chol ha-mo-nam.
Va-a-nach-nu ko-r'im u-mish-ta-cha-vim u-mo-dim li-f'nei meh-lech ma-
l'chei ha-m'la-chim, ha-ka-dosh ba-ruch hu.

We must praise the God of all, the Maker of heaven and earth, who has
set us apart from the other families of earth, giving us a destiny unique
among the nations.

Therefore we bow in awe and thanksgiving before the One who is
sovereign over all, the Holy and Blessed One.

~ ~

שֶׁהוּא נוֹטֶה שָׁמַֽיִם וְיוֹסֵד אָֽרֶץ, וּמוֹשַׁב יְקָרוֹ בַּשָּׁמַֽיִם
מִמַּֽעַל, וּשְׁכִינַת עֻזּוֹ בְּגָבְהֵי מְרוֹמִים. הוּא אֱלֹהֵֽינוּ, אֵין עוֹד.
אֱמֶת מַלְכֵּֽנוּ, אֶֽפֶס זוּלָתוֹ, כַּכָּתוּב בְּתוֹרָתוֹ: וְיָדַעְתָּ הַיּוֹם
וַהֲשֵׁבֹתָ אֶל־לְבָבֶֽךָ, כִּי יְיָ הוּא הָאֱלֹהִים בַּשָּׁמַֽיִם מִמַּֽעַל
וְעַל הָאָֽרֶץ מִתַּֽחַת, אֵין עוֹד.

Sheh-hu no-teh sha-ma-yim v'yo-seid a-retz, u-mo-shav y'ka-ro ba-sha-ma-
yim mi-ma-al, u-sh'chi-nat u-zo b'gov-hei m'ro-mim. Hu Eh-lo-hei-nu, ein
od. Eh-met mal-kei-nu, eh-fes zu-la-to , ka-ka-tuv b'to-ra-to: V'ya-da-ta ha-

yom va-ha-shei-vo-ta el l'va-veh-cha, ki Adonai hu ha-eh-lo-him ba-sha-ma-yim mi-ma-al v'al ha-a-retz mi-ta-chat, ein od.

You spread out the heavens and established the earth; You are our God; there is none else. In truth You alone are our Sovereign God, as it is written: "Know then this day and take it to heart: the Eternal One is God in the heavens above and on the earth below; there is none else."

*Eternal God, we face the morrow with hope made stronger by the vision of Your deliverance, a world where poverty and war are banished, where injustice and hate are gone.*

*Teach us more and more to respond to the pain of others, to heed Your call for justice, that we may bring nearer the day when all the world shall be one.*

*On that day the age–old dream shall come true. On that day, O God, You shall be One and Your Name shall be One.*

וְנֶאֱמַר: וְהָיָה יהוה לְמֶלֶךְ עַל־כָּל־הָאָרֶץ;

בַּיּוֹם הַהוּא יִהְיֶה יהוה אֶחָד וּשְׁמוֹ אֶחָד.

V'neh-eh-mar: V'ha-yah Adonai l'meh-lech al kol ha-a-retz;

ba-yom ha-hu yi-h'yeh Adonai Eh-chad, u-sh'mo Eh-chad.

## II ב

ALEINU          עָלֵינוּ

עָלֵינוּ לְשַׁבֵּחַ לַאֲדוֹן הַכֹּל, לָתֵת גְּדֻלָּה לְיוֹצֵר בְּרֵאשִׁית,

אֲשֶׁר שָׂם חֶלְקֵנוּ לְיַחֵד אֶת־שְׁמוֹ, וְגוֹרָלֵנוּ לְהַמְלִיךְ מַלְכוּתוֹ.

A-lei-nu l'sha-bei-ach la-a-don ha-kol, la-teit g'du-la l'yo-tzeir b'rei-sheet, a-sher sam chel-kei-nu l'ya-cheid et sh'mo, v'go-ra-lei-nu l'ham-lich mal-chu-to.

149

Let us adore the ever–living God! We render praise unto You, who spread out the heavens and established the earth, whose glory is revealed in the heavens above, and whose greatness is manifest throughout the world. You are our God; there is none else.

וַאֲנַחְנוּ כּוֹרְעִים וּמִשְׁתַּחֲוִים וּמוֹדִים לִפְנֵי
מֶלֶךְ מַלְכֵי הַמְּלָכִים, הַקָּדוֹשׁ בָּרוּךְ הוּא.

Va-a-nach-nu ko-r'im u-mish-ta-cha-vim u-mo-dim li-f'nei meh-lech ma-l'chei ha-m'la-chim, ha-ka-dosh ba-ruch hu.

We therefore bow in awe and thanksgiving before the One who is Sovereign over all, the Holy and Blessed One.

The day will come when all shall turn with trust to You, O God, hearkening to Your voice, bearing witness to Your truth.

We pray with all our hearts: let violence be gone; let the day come soon when evil shall give way to goodness, when war shall be forgotten, and all at last shall live in freedom.

O Source of life, may we, created in Your image, embrace one another in friendship and in joy. Then shall we be one family, and then shall Your sovereignty be established on earth, and the word of Your prophet fulfilled: "The Eternal God will reign for ever and ever."

*On that day, O God, You shall be One and Your Name shall be One.*

בַּיּוֹם הַהוּא יִהְיֶה יְהוה אֶחָד וּשְׁמוֹ אֶחָד.

Ba-yom ha-hu yi-h'yeh Adonai Eh-chad, u-sh'mo Eh-chad!

150

## Before the Kaddish

Our thoughts turn to those who have departed this earth: our own loved ones, those whom our friends and neighbors have lost, the martyrs of our people, and those of every race and nation whose lives have been a blessing to humanity. As we remember them, let us meditate on the meaning of love and loss, of life and death.

### MEDITATIONS

1.   Facing Death

The contemplation of death should plant within the soul elevation and peace. Above all, it should make us see things in their true light. For all things which seem foolish in the light of death are really foolish in themselves. To be annoyed because someone has slighted us or has been somewhat more successful in social distinctions, pulled himself somehow one rung higher up the ladder than ourselves—how ridiculous all this seems when we couple it with the thought of death!

To pass each day simply and solely in the eager pursuit of money or fame, this also seems like living with shadows when one might take one's part with realities. Surely when death is at hand we should desire to say, "I have contributed my grain to the great store of the eternal. I have borne my part in the struggle for goodness." And let no man or woman suppose that the smallest social act of goodness is wasted for society at large. All our help, whatever it be, is needed; and though we know not the manner, the fruit of every faithful service is gathered in. Let the true and noble words of a great teacher ring in conclusion upon our ears: "The growing good of the world is partly dependent on unhistoric acts; and that things are not so ill with you and me as they might have been, is half owing to the number who lived faithfully a hidden life and rest in unvisited tombs."

2.     In Recent Grief

When cherished ties are broken, and the chain of love is shattered, only trust and the strength of faith can lighten the heaviness of the heart. At times, the pain of separation seems more than we can bear; but love and understanding can help us pass through the darkness toward the light.

Out of affliction the Psalmist learned the law of God. And in truth, grief is a great teacher, when it sends us back to serve and bless the living. We learn how to counsel and comfort those who, like ourselves, are bowed with sorrow. We learn when to keep silence in their presence, and when a word will assure them of our love and concern.

Thus, even when they are gone, the departed are with us, moving us to live as, in their higher moments, they themselves wished to live. We remember them now; they live in our hearts; they are an abiding blessing.

3.     The Blessing of Memory

It is hard to sing of oneness when our world is not complete, when those who once brought wholeness to our life have gone, and naught but memory can fill the emptiness their passing leaves behind.

But memory can tell us only what we were, in company with those we loved; it cannot help us find what each of us, alone, must now become. Yet no one is really alone; those who live no more, echo still within our thoughts and words, and what they did is part of what we have become.

We do best homage to our dead when we live our lives most fully, even in the shadow of our loss. For each of our lives is worth the life of the whole world; in each one is the breath of the Ultimate One. In affirming the One, we affirm the worth of each

one whose life, now ended, brought us closer to the Source of life, in whose unity no one is alone and every life finds purpose.

4.    The Life of Eternity

Life is finite. Like a candle, it burns, it glows, it is radiant with warmth and beauty; then it fades; its substance is consumed, and it is no more.

In light we see; in light we are seen. The flames dance and our lives are full. But as night follows day, the candle of our life burns down and gutters. There is an end to the flames. We see no more and are no more seen. Yet we do not despair, for we are more than a memory slowly fading into the darkness. With our lives we give life. Something of us can never die: we move in the eternal cycle of darkness and death, of light and life.

5.    Strength for Those Who Mourn

In nature's ebb and flow, Your eternal law abides. As You are our support in the struggles of life, so, also, are You our hope in death. In Your care, O God, are the souls of all the living and the spirits of all flesh. Your power gives us strength; Your love comforts us. O Life of our life, Soul of our soul, cause Your light to shine into our hearts. Fill us with trust in You, and turn us again to the tasks of life. And may the memory of our loved ones inspire us to continue their work for the coming of Your sovereign rule.

~ ~

However brief may be our time on earth, O God, You endow our fleeting days with abiding worth. We now recall the loved ones whom death has recently taken from us ... And as we remember those who died at this season in years past, we take them into our hearts with our own ... In this moment of memory,

our griefs and sympathies are mingled. Loving God, we praise
Your name.

MOURNER'S KADDISH                                           קדיש יתום

יִתְגַּדַּל וְיִתְקַדַּשׁ שְׁמֵהּ רַבָּא בְּעָלְמָא דִי־בְרָא כִרְעוּתֵהּ,
וְיַמְלִיךְ מַלְכוּתֵהּ בְּחַיֵּיכוֹן וּבְיוֹמֵיכוֹן וּבְחַיֵּי דְכָל־בֵּית
יִשְׂרָאֵל, בַּעֲגָלָא וּבִזְמַן קָרִיב, וְאִמְרוּ: אָמֵן.

Yit-ga-dal v'yit–ka–dash sh'mei ra-ba b'al-ma di-v'ra chi-r'u'tei, v'yam-lich
mal-chu-tei b'cha-yei-chon u-v'yo-mei-chon u-v'cha-yei d'chol beit Yis-ra-
eil, ba-a-ga-la u-vi-z'man ka-riv, v'i-m' ru: A-mein.

יְהֵא שְׁמֵהּ רַבָּא מְבָרַךְ לְעָלַם וּלְעָלְמֵי עָלְמַיָּא.

Y'hei sh'mei ra-ba m'va-rach l'a-lam u-l'al-mei al-ma-ya.

יִתְבָּרַךְ וְיִשְׁתַּבַּח, וְיִתְפָּאַר וְיִתְרוֹמַם וְיִתְנַשֵּׂא, וְיִתְהַדַּר
וְיִתְעַלֶּה וְיִתְהַלָּל שְׁמֵהּ דְּקֻדְשָׁא, בְּרִיךְ הוּא,

Yit-ba-rach v'yish-ta-bach, v'yit-pa-ar v'yit-ro-mam v'yit-na-sei, v'yit-ha-dar
v'yit-a-leh v'yit-ha-lal sh'mei d'kud-sha, b'rich hu,

לְעֵלָּא מִן־כָּל־בִּרְכָתָא וְשִׁירָתָא, תֻּשְׁבְּחָתָא וְנֶחֱמָתָא
דַּאֲמִירָן בְּעָלְמָא, וְאִמְרוּ: אָמֵן.

l'ei-la min kol bir-cha-ta v'shi-ra-ta, tush-b'cha-ta v'neh-cheh-ma-ta da-a-
mi-ran b'al-ma, v'i-m' ru: A-mein.

יְהֵא שְׁלָמָא רַבָּא מִן־שְׁמַיָּא וְחַיִּים עָלֵינוּ וְעַל־כָּל־יִשְׂרָאֵל,
וְאִמְרוּ: אָמֵן.

Y'hei sh'la-ma ra-ba min sh'ma-ya v'cha-yim, a-lei-nu v'al kol Yis-ra-el,
v'im-ru: A-mein.

154

עֹשֶׂה שָׁלוֹם בִּמְרוֹמָיו, הוּא יַעֲשֶׂה שָׁלוֹם עָלֵינוּ וְעַל
כָּל־יִשְׂרָאֵל, וְאִמְרוּ: אָמֵן.

O-seh sha-lom bi-m'ro-mav, hu ya-a-seh sha-lom a-lei-nu v'al kol Yis-ra-eil, v'i-m-'u: A-mein.

～～

Let the glory of God be extolled, and God's great name be hallowed in the world whose creation God willed. May God rule in our own day, in our own lives, and in the life of all Israel, and let us say: Amen.

Let God's great name be blessed for ever and ever.

Beyond all the praises, songs, and adorations that we can utter is the Holy One, the Blessed One, whom yet we glorify, honor, and exalt. And let us say: Amen.

For us and for all Israel, may the blessing of peace and the promise of life come true, and let us say: Amen.

• May the One who causes peace to reign in the high heavens, cause peace to reign among us, all Israel, and all the world, and let us say: Amen.

May the Source of peace send peace to all who mourn, and comfort to all who are bereaved. Amen.

～～

155

# Songs

אדון עולם

אֲדוֹן עוֹלָם אֲשֶׁר מָלַךְ, בְּטֶרֶם כָּל יְצִיר נִבְרָא;
לְעֵת נַעֲשָׂה בְחֶפְצוֹ כֹּל, אֲזַי מֶלֶךְ שְׁמוֹ נִקְרָא.

A-don o-lam, a-sher ma-lach, b'teh-rem kol y'tzir niv-ra;
L'eit na-a-sa v'chef-tzo kol, a-zai meh-lech sh'mo nik-ra.

וְאַחֲרֵי כִּכְלוֹת הַכֹּל, לְבַדּוֹ יִמְלֹךְ נוֹרָא;
וְהוּא הָיָה וְהוּא הֹוֶה, וְהוּא יִהְיֶה בְּתִפְאָרָה.

V'a-cha-rei kich-lot ha-kol, l'va-do yim-loch no-ra;
V'hu ha-ya, v'hu ho-veh, v'hu yi-h'yeh b'tif-a-ra.

וְהוּא אֶחָד, וְאֵין שֵׁנִי, לְהַמְשִׁיל לוֹ, לְהַחְבִּירָה;
בְּלִי רֵאשִׁית, בְּלִי תַכְלִית, וְלוֹ הָעֹז וְהַמִּשְׂרָה.

V'hu Eh-chad, v'ein shei-ni l'ham-shil lo, l'hach-bi-ra;
B'li rei-sheet, b'li tach-lit, v'lo ha-oz v'ha-mis-ra.

וְהוּא אֵלִי, וְחַי גֹּאֲלִי, וְצוּר חֶבְלִי בְּעֵת צָרָה;
וְהוּא נִסִּי וּמָנוֹס לִי, מְנָת כּוֹסִי בְּיוֹם אֶקְרָא.

V'hu  Ei-li, v'chai go-a-li, v'tzur chev-li b'eit tza-ra;
V'hu ni-si u-ma-nos li, m'nat ko-si b'yom ek-ra.

בְּיָדוֹ אַפְקִיד רוּחִי, בְּעֵת אִישַׁן וְאָעִירָה;
וְעִם רוּחִי גְּוִיָּתִי, יְיָ לִי, וְלֹא אִירָא.

B'ya-do af-kid ru-chi, b'eit i-shan v'a-i-ra;
V'im ru-chi g'vi-ya-ti; Adonai li, v'lo i-ra.

You are the Eternal God, who reigned before any being had been created; when all was done according to Your will, already then you were
Sovereign. And after all has ceased to be, still will You reign in solitary
majesty; You were, You are, You will be in glory. And You are One; none

other can compare to You, or consort with You; You are without beginning, without end; Yours alone are power and dominion. And You are my God, my living Redeemer, my Rock in time of trouble and distress; You are my banner and my refuge, my benefactor when I call on You. Into Your hands I entrust my spirit, when I sleep and when I wake; and with my spirit, my body also: You are with me, I shall not fear.

יגדל

1 יִגְדַּל אֱלֹהִים חַי וְיִשְׁתַּבַּח, נִמְצָא וְאֵין עֵת אֶל־מְצִיאוּתוֹ.
אֶחָד וְאֵין יָחִיד כְּיִחוּדוֹ, נֶעְלָם וְגַם אֵין סוֹף לְאַחְדּוּתוֹ.

Yigdal Eh-lo-him chai v'yish–ta–bach, nim–tza v'ein eit el m'tzi–u–to.
Eh-chad, v'ein ya-chid, k'yi-chu-do, neh-lam v'gam ein sof l'ach-du-to.

2 אֵין לוֹ דְמוּת הַגּוּף וְאֵינוֹ גוּף, לֹא נַעֲרוֹךְ אֵלָיו קְדֻשָּׁתוֹ.
קַדְמוֹן לְכָל־דָּבָר אֲשֶׁר נִבְרָא, רִאשׁוֹן וְאֵין רֵאשִׁית לְרֵאשִׁיתוֹ.

Ein lo d'mut ha-guf, v'ei-no guf, lo na-a-roch ei-lav k'du-sha-to.
Kad-mon l'chol da-var a-sher niv-ra, ri-shon v'ein rei-sheet l'rei-shi-to.

3 הִנּוֹ אֲדוֹן עוֹלָם. לְכָל־נוֹצָר יוֹרֶה גְדֻלָּתוֹ וּמַלְכוּתוֹ.
שֶׁפַע נְבוּאָתוֹ נְתָנוֹ, אֶל־אַנְשֵׁי סְגֻלָּתוֹ וְתִפְאַרְתּוֹ.

Hi-no a-don o-lam. L'chol no-tzar yo-reh g'du-la-toh u-mal-chu-toh.
Sheh-fa n'vu-a-to n'ta'no, el an-shei s'gu-la-to v'tif-ar-to.

4 לֹא קָם בְּיִשְׂרָאֵל כְּמֹשֶׁה עוֹד, נָבִיא וּמַבִּיט אֶת־תְּמוּנָתוֹ.
תּוֹרַת אֱמֶת נָתַן לְעַמּוֹ אֵל, עַל יַד נְבִיאוֹ נֶאֱמַן בֵּיתוֹ.

Lo kam b'yis-ra-eil k'mo-sheh od, na-vi u-ma-bit et t'mu-na-to,
To-rat eh-met na-tan l'a-mo Eil, al yad n'vi-o neh-man bei-to.

5 לֹא יַחֲלִיף הָאֵל, וְלֹא יָמִיר דָּתוֹ, לְעוֹלָמִים לְזוּלָתוֹ.

צוֹפֶה וְיוֹדֵעַ סְתָרֵינוּ, מַבִּיט לְסוֹף דָּבָר בְּקַדְמָתוֹ.

Lo ya-cha-lif ha-eil, v'lo ya-mir da-to, l'o-la-mim l'zu-la-to.
Tzo-feh v'yo-dei-a s'ta-rei-nu, ma-bit l'sof da-var b'kad-ma-to.

6 גּוֹמֵל לְאִישׁ חֶסֶד כְּמִפְעָלוֹ, נוֹתֵן לְרָשָׁע רַע כְּרִשְׁעָתוֹ.

יִשְׁלַח לְקֵץ יָמִין פְּדוּת עוֹלָם, כָּל־חַי וְיֵשׁ יַכִּיר יְשׁוּעָתוֹ.

Go-meil l'ish cheh-sed k'mif-a-lo, no–tein l'ra–sha ra k'rish–a–to.
Yish-lach l'keitz ya-min p'dut o–lam, kol chai v'yeish ya–kir y'shu-a-to.

7 חַיֵּי עוֹלָם נָטַע בְּתוֹכֵנוּ, בָּרוּךְ עֲדֵי עַד שֵׁם תְּהִלָּתוֹ.

Cha–yei o–lam na–ta b'to–chei–nu, ba-ruch a-dei ad sheim t'hi-la-to.

Magnified be the living God, praised, whose existence is eternal, One and Unique in that unity, the unfathomable One whose Oneness is infinite.

A God with no bodily form, incorporeal, whose holiness is beyond compare, who preceded all creation, the Beginning who has no beginning.

You are Eternal Might, who teach every creature Your greatness and sovereignty, with the gift of prophecy inspiring those whom You chose to make Your glory known.

Never has there been a prophet like Moses, whose closeness to You is unmatched. A Torah of truth You gave Your people through Your prophet, Your faithful servant.

A changeless God, ever the same, whose teaching will stand, who watches us and knows our inmost thoughts, who knows all outcomes before events begin.

You give us each what we deserve, the good and bad alike. In the end of days You will send an everlasting redemption; all that lives and has being shall witness Your deliverance.

You have implanted eternal life within us; praised be Your glory to all eternity!

אין כאלהינו

אֵין כֵּאלֹהֵינוּ, אֵין כַּאדוֹנֵינוּ,
אֵין כְּמַלְכֵּנוּ, אֵין כְּמוֹשִׁיעֵנוּ.

Ein kei–lo–hei–nu, ein ka–do–nei–nu,
ein k'mal–kei–nu, ein k'mo–shi–ein–u.

מִי כֵאלֹהֵינוּ? מִי כַאדוֹנֵינוּ?
מִי כְמַלְכֵּנוּ? מִי כְמוֹשִׁיעֵנוּ?

Mi chei–lo–hei–nu? Mi cha–do–nei–nu?
mi ch'mal–kei–nu? Mi ch'mo–shi–ei–nu?

נוֹדֶה לֵאלֹהֵינוּ, נוֹדֶה לַאדוֹנֵינוּ,
נוֹדֶה לְמַלְכֵּנוּ, נוֹדֶה לְמוֹשִׁיעֵנוּ.

No–deh lei–lo–hei–nu, no–deh la–do–nei–nu,
No–deh l'mal–kei–nu, no–deh l'mo–shi–ei–nu.

בָּרוּךְ אֱלֹהֵינוּ, בָּרוּךְ אֲדוֹנֵינוּ,
בָּרוּךְ מַלְכֵּנוּ, בָּרוּךְ מוֹשִׁיעֵנוּ.

Ba–ruch Eh–lo–hei–nu, ba–ruch A–do–nei–nu,
ba–ruch Mal–kei–nu, ba–ruch Mo–shi–ei–nu.

אַתָּה הוּא אֱלֹהֵינוּ, אַתָּה הוּא אֲדוֹנֵינוּ,
אַתָּה הוּא מַלְכֵּנוּ, אַתָּה הוּא מוֹשִׁיעֵנוּ.

A–ta hu Eh–lo–hei–nu, a–ta hu A–do–nei–nu,
a–ta hu Mal–kei–nu, a–ta hu Mo–shi–ei–nu.

There is none like our God, our Sovereign, our Redeemer.
Who is like our God, our Sovereign, our Redeemer?
We give thanks to our God, our Sovereign, our Redeemer.
Praised be our God, our Sovereign, our Redeemer.
You are our God, our Sovereign, our Redeemer.

שבת המלכה

הַחַמָּה מֵרֹאשׁ הָאִילָנוֹת נִסְתַּלְּקָה,
בֹּאוּ וְנֵצֵא לִקְרַאת שַׁבָּת הַמַּלְכָּה.
הִנֵּה הִיא יוֹרֶדֶת, הַקְּדוֹשָׁה הַבְּרוּכָה,
וְעִמָּהּ מַלְאָכִים, צְבָא שָׁלוֹם וּמְנוּחָה.
בֹּאִי בֹּאִי הַמַּלְכָּה!
בֹּאִי בֹּאִי הַכַּלָּה!
שָׁלוֹם עֲלֵיכֶם, מַלְאֲכֵי הַשָּׁלוֹם.

The sun on the treetops no longer is seen,
Come gather to welcome the Sabbath, our queen.
Behold her descending, the holy, the blessed,
And with her the angels of peace and of rest.
Draw near, draw near, and here abide,
Draw near, draw near, O Sabbath bride.
Peace also to you, you angels of peace.

כי אשמרה שבת

כִּי אֶשְׁמְרָה שַׁבָּת, אֵל יִשְׁמְרֵנִי.
אוֹת הִיא לְעוֹלְמֵי עַד, בֵּינוֹ וּבֵינִי.

Ki esh-m'ra Shabbat, Eil yish-m'reini.

Ot hi l'o-l'mei ad, bei-no u–vei-ni.

When we keep Shabbat, God keeps us;
It it a sign between God and Israel for ever...

## אשא עיני

אֶשָּׂא עֵינַי אֶל־הֶהָרִים,    Eh-sa ei-nai el heh–ha-rim,

מֵאַיִן יָבֹא עֶזְרִי?    mei-a-yin ya-vo ez-ri?

עֶזְרִי מֵעִם יְהוָה,    Ez-ri mei-im Adonai,

עֹשֵׂה שָׁמַיִם וָאָרֶץ.    o-sei sha-may-im va-a-retz.

I lift up my eyes, unto the mountains,
Where will I find my help?
My help will come from my God,
Maker of heaven and earth.

## ידיד נפש

יְדִיד נֶפֶשׁ, אָב הָרַחֲמָן,    Y'did neh-fesh, Av ha–ra-cha-man,

מְשׁוֹךְ עַבְדְּךָ אֶל רְצוֹנֶךָ.    m'shoch av-d'cha el r'tzo-neh-cha.

יָרוּץ עַבְדְּךָ כְּמוֹ אַיָּל,    Ya-rutz av-d'cha k'mo a-yal,

יִשְׁתַּחֲוֶה אֶל מוּל הֲדָרֶךָ.    yish-ta-cha-veh el mul ha-da-reh-cha.

Heart's delight, Source of mercy, draw Your servant into Your arms...

~ ~

## Additional Songs:

Hinei Ma Tov  99

Pit'chu Li  128

Ma Yafeh Hayom  101

Al Sh'losha D'varim 101

David Mehlech Yisraeil 102

Shalom Aleichem  163

Y'rushalayim shel Zahav  182

~ ~

## For the New Month

יְהִי רָצוֹן מִלְּפָנֶיךָ, יי אֱלֹהֵינוּ וֵאלֹהֵי אֲבוֹתֵינוּ וְאִמּוֹתֵינוּ, שֶׁתְּחַדֵּשׁ
עָלֵינוּ אֶת־הַחֹדֶשׁ הַזֶּה, (הַבָּא,) לְטוֹבָה וְלִבְרָכָה. וְתִתֶּן־לָנוּ חַיִּים
אֲרֻכִּים, חַיִּים שֶׁל־שָׁלוֹם, חַיִּים שֶׁל־טוֹבָה, חַיִּים שֶׁל־בְּרָכָה, חַיִּים
שֶׁל־פַּרְנָסָה, חַיִּים שֶׁל־חִלּוּץ עֲצָמוֹת, חַיִּים שֶׁיֵּשׁ בָּהֶם יִרְאַת חֵטְא,
חַיִּים שֶׁתְּהֵא בָנוּ אַהֲבַת תּוֹרָה וְיִרְאַת שָׁמַיִם, חַיִּים שֶׁיִּמָּלְאוּ
מִשְׁאֲלוֹת לִבֵּנוּ לְטוֹבָה. אָמֵן.

Our God and God of our ancestors, may the new month bring us renewed good and blessing

May we have long life, peace, prosperity and health, a life full of blessing, a life exalted by love of Torah and reverence for the divine; a life in which the longings of our hearts are fulfilled for good.

מִי שֶׁעָשָׂה נִסִּים לַאֲבוֹתֵינוּ וּלְאִמּוֹתֵינוּ וְגָאַל אוֹתָם מֵעַבְדוּת לְחֵרוּת,
הוּא יִגְאַל אוֹתָנוּ בְּקָרוֹב, חֲבֵרִים כָּל־יִשְׂרָאֵל, וְנֹאמַר: אָמֵן

Wondrous God, in ancient days You led our people from bondage to freedom; redeem us now out of our exile from one another, making all Israel one united people.

רֹאשׁ חֹדֶשׁ. . . יִהְיֶה בְּיוֹם. . .

The new month of ...... will begin on ......

or

רֹאשׁ חֹדֶשׁ. . . הוּא הַיּוֹם.

The new month of ...... begins today.

יְחַדְּשֵׁהוּ הַקָּדוֹשׁ בָּרוּךְ הוּא עָלֵינוּ וְעַל־כָּל־עַמּוֹ בֵּית יִשְׂרָאֵל:
לְחַיִּים וּלְשָׁלוֹם, לְשָׂשׂוֹן וּלְשִׂמְחָה, לִישׁוּעָה וּלְנֶחָמָה, וְנֹאמַר: אָמֵן.

*God of holiness, let the new month bring for us, and for the whole house of Israel, life and peace, happiness and joy, deliverance and comfort; and let us say: Amen.*

## Bar and Bat Mitzvah Prayers—I

Into our hands, O God, You have placed Your Torah, to be held high by parents and children, and taught by one generation to the next. Whatever has befallen us, our people have remained steadfast in loyalty to the Torah. It was carried into exile in the arms of parents that their children might not be deprived of their birthright.

And now I pray that you, .........., may always be worthy of this inheritance. Take its teaching into your heart, and in turn pass it on to your children and those who come after you. May you be a faithful Jew, searching for wisdom and truth, working for justice and peace. Thus will you be among those who labor to bring nearer the day when God shall be One, and God's children shall be one.

## Bar and Bat Mitzvah Prayers—II

May the God of our people, the God of all humankind, bless and keep you. May the One who has always been our guide inspire you to bring honor to our family and to the House of Israel.

בָּרוּךְ אַתָּה יי, אֱלֹהֵינוּ מֶלֶךְ הָעוֹלָם, שֶׁהֶחֱיָנוּ וְקִיְּמָנוּ וְהִגִּיעָנוּ לִזְמַן הַזֶּה.

Ba-ruch a-ta Adonai, Eh-lo-hei-nu meh-lech ha–o–lam, sheh–heh–cheh–ya–nu v'ki–y'ma–nu v'hi–gi–a–nu la–z'man ha–zeh.

We praise You, Eternal God, Sovereign of the universe, for giving us life, for sustaining us, and for enabling us to reach this season.

# At Home or in the Synagogue

בבית ובבית הכנסת

For fuller Sabbath and Festival home rituals, see:
On the Doorposts of Your House
& Gates of Shabbat

SHALOM ALEICHEM

שלום עליכם

שָׁלוֹם עֲלֵיכֶם, מַלְאֲכֵי הַשָּׁרֵת, מַלְאֲכֵי עֶלְיוֹן,
מִמֶּלֶךְ מַלְכֵי הַמְּלָכִים, הַקָּדוֹשׁ בָּרוּךְ הוּא.

בּוֹאֲכֶם לְשָׁלוֹם, מַלְאֲכֵי הַשָּׁלוֹם, מַלְאֲכֵי עֶלְיוֹן,
מִמֶּלֶךְ מַלְכֵי הַמְּלָכִים, הַקָּדוֹשׁ בָּרוּךְ הוּא.

בָּרְכוּנִי לְשָׁלוֹם, מַלְאֲכֵי הַשָּׁלוֹם, מַלְאֲכֵי עֶלְיוֹן,
מִמֶּלֶךְ מַלְכֵי הַמְּלָכִים, הַקָּדוֹשׁ בָּרוּךְ הוּא.

צֵאתְכֶם לְשָׁלוֹם, מַלְאֲכֵי הַשָּׁלוֹם, מַלְאֲכֵי עֶלְיוֹן,
מִמֶּלֶךְ מַלְכֵי הַמְּלָכִים, הַקָּדוֹשׁ בָּרוּךְ הוּא.

Sha-lom a-lei-chem mal-a-chei ha-sha-reit, mal-a-chei El-yon,
Mi-meh-lech ma-l'chei ha-m'la-chim, ha-ka-dosh ba-ruch hu.

Bo-a-chem l'sha-lom, mal-a-chei ha-sha-lom, mal-a-chei El-yon,
Mi-meh-lech ma-l'chei ha-m'la-chim, ha-ka-dosh ba-ruch hu.

Ba-r'chu-ni l'sha-lom, mal-a-chei ha-sha-lom, mal-a-chei El-yon,
Mi-meh-lech ma-l'chei ha-m'la-chim, ha-ka-dosh ba-ruch hu.

Tzei-t'chem l'sha-lom, mal-a-chei ha-sha-lom, mal-a-chei El-yon,
Mi-meh-lech ma-l'chei ha-m'la-chim, ha-ka-dosh ba-ruch hu.

Shalom Aleichem is translated on page 85

## CANDLE LIGHTING · הדלקת הנרות

Ba-ruch a-ta Adonai, Eh-lo-hei-nu meh-lech ha-o-lam, a-sher ki-d'sha-nu b'mitz-vo-tav v'tzi-va-nu l'had-lik ner shel Shabbat.

בָּרוּךְ אַתָּה יי, אֱלֹהֵינוּ מֶלֶךְ הָעוֹלָם, אֲשֶׁר קִדְּשָׁנוּ בְּמִצְוֹתָיו וְצִוָּנוּ לְהַדְלִיק נֵר שֶׁל שַׁבָּת.

We praise You, Eternal God, Sovereign of the universe: You hallow us with Your Mitzvot, and command us to kindle the lights of Shabbat.

*May we be blessed with Shabbat joy.*

*May we be blessed with Shabbat peace.*

*May we be blessed with Shabbat light.*

## KIDDUSH · קדוש

Raise the Kiddush cup filled with wine or grape juice

(Va-y'chulu is on page 59)

בָּרוּךְ אַתָּה יי, אֱלֹהֵינוּ מֶלֶךְ הָעוֹלָם, בּוֹרֵא פְּרִי הַגָּפֶן.
בָּרוּךְ אַתָּה יי, אֱלֹהֵינוּ מֶלֶךְ הָעוֹלָם, אֲשֶׁר קִדְּשָׁנוּ
בְּמִצְוֹתָיו וְרָצָה בָנוּ, וְשַׁבַּת קָדְשׁוֹ בְּאַהֲבָה וּבְרָצוֹן
הִנְחִילָנוּ, זִכָּרוֹן לְמַעֲשֵׂה בְרֵאשִׁית. כִּי הוּא יוֹם תְּחִלָּה
לְמִקְרָאֵי קֹדֶשׁ, זֵכֶר לִיצִיאַת מִצְרָיִם. כִּי־בָנוּ בָחַרְתָּ
וְאוֹתָנוּ קִדַּשְׁתָּ מִכָּל־הָעַמִּים, וְשַׁבַּת קָדְשְׁךָ בְּאַהֲבָה
וּבְרָצוֹן הִנְחַלְתָּנוּ. בָּרוּךְ אַתָּה יי, מְקַדֵּשׁ הַשַּׁבָּת.

Ba-ruch a-ta Adonai, Eh-lo-hei-nu meh-lech ha-o-lam, bo-rei p'ri ha-ga-fen.

Ba-ruch a-ta Adonai, Eh-lo-hei-nu meh-lech ha-o-lam, a-sher ki-d'sha-nu b'mitz-vo-tav v'ra-tza va-nu, v'sha-bat kod-sho b'a-ha-va u-v'ra-tzon hin-chi-la-nu, zi-ka-ron l'ma-a-sei v'rei-sheet. Ki hu yom t'chi-la l'mik-ra-ei ko-desh, zei-cher li-tzi-at Mitz-ra-yim.

Ki va-nu va-char-ta v'o-ta-nu ki-dash-ta mi-kol ha-a-mim, v'sha-bat kod-sh'cha b'a-ha-va u-v'ra-tzon hin-chal-ta-nu. Ba-ruch a-ta Adonai, m'ka-deish ha-Shabbat.

We praise You, Eternal God, Sovereign of the universe, Creator of the fruit of the vine.

• We praise You, Eternal God, Sovereign of the universe: You call us to holiness with the Mitzvah of Shabbat—the sign of Your love, a reminder of Your creative work, and of our liberation from Egyptian bondage: our day of days. On Shabbat especially, we hearken to Your call to serve You as a holy people.

We praise You, O God, for the holiness of Shabbat.

## Drink

MOTZI

מוֹצִיא

Ba-ruch a-ta Adonai, Eh-lo-hei-nu
meh-lech ha-o-lam, ha-mo-tzi leh-
chem min ha-a-retz.

בָּרוּךְ אַתָּה יי, אֱלֹהֵינוּ מֶלֶךְ
הָעוֹלָם, הַמּוֹצִיא לֶחֶם מִן
הָאָרֶץ.

We praise You, Eternal God, Sovereign of the universe, for You cause bread to come forth from the earth.

Slice or tear the challah
and distribute it to those at the table.

Shabbat dinner is served.

## MORNING KIDDUSH קִדּוּשׁ

וְשָׁמְרוּ בְנֵי־יִשְׂרָאֵל אֶת־הַשַּׁבָּת, לַעֲשׂוֹת אֶת־הַשַּׁבָּת לְדֹרֹתָם
בְּרִית עוֹלָם. בֵּינִי וּבֵין בְּנֵי יִשְׂרָאֵל אוֹת הִיא לְעֹלָם. כִּי־שֵׁשֶׁת
יָמִים עָשָׂה יהוה אֶת־הַשָּׁמַיִם וְאֶת־הָאָרֶץ, וּבַיּוֹם הַשְּׁבִיעִי
שָׁבַת וַיִּנָּפַשׁ.

V'sha-m'ru v'nei Yis-ra-eil et ha-sha-bat, la-a-sot et ha-sha-bat l'do-ro-tam,
b'rit o-lam. Bei-ni u-vein b'nei Yis-ra-eil ot hi l'o-lam. Ki shei-shet ya-mim
a-sa Adonai et ha-sha-ma-yim v'et ha-a-retz, u-va-yom ha-sh'vi-i sha-vat
va-yi-na-fash.

The people of Israel shall keep the Sabbath, observing the Sabbath in
every generation as a covenant for all time. It is a sign for ever between
Me and the people of Israel. For in six days the Eternal One made
heaven and earth, but on the seventh day God rested and was refreshed.

עַל־כֵּן בֵּרַךְ יהוה אֶת־יוֹם הַשַּׁבָּת וַיְקַדְּשֵׁהוּ.

Al kein bei-rach Adonai et yom ha-sha-bat va-y'ka-d'shei-hu.

Therefore the Eternal One blessed the seventh day and called it
holy.

בָּרוּךְ אַתָּה יי, אֱלֹהֵינוּ מֶלֶךְ הָעוֹלָם, בּוֹרֵא פְּרִי הַגָּפֶן.

Ba-ruch a-ta Adonai, Eh-lo-hei-nu meh-lech ha-o-lam, bo-rei p'ri ha-
ga-fen.

We praise You, Eternal God, Sovereign of the universe, Creator of the
fruit of the vine.

# Thanksgiving after the Meal    ברכת המזון

### For fuller and more varied rituals, see
### On the Doorposts of Your House

## ON SHABBAT BEGIN HERE

### Psalm 126

A PILGRIM SONG                          שִׁיר הַמַּעֲלוֹת

בְּשׁוּב יהוה אֶת־שִׁיבַת צִיּוֹן, הָיִינוּ
כְּחֹלְמִים. אָז יִמָּלֵא שְׂחוֹק פִּינוּ,
וּלְשׁוֹנֵנוּ רִנָּה. אָז יֹאמְרוּ בַגּוֹיִם:
הִגְדִּיל יהוה לַעֲשׂוֹת עִם־אֵלֶּה.
הִגְדִּיל יהוה לַעֲשׂוֹת עִמָּנוּ, הָיִינוּ
שְׂמֵחִים! שׁוּבָה יהוה אֶת־שְׁבִיתֵנוּ
כַּאֲפִיקִים בַּנֶּגֶב. הַזֹּרְעִים בְּדִמְעָה,
בְּרִנָּה יִקְצֹרוּ. הָלוֹךְ יֵלֵךְ וּבָכֹה,
נֹשֵׂא מֶשֶׁךְ־הַזָּרַע, בֹּא־יָבוֹא בְרִנָּה
נֹשֵׂא אֲלֻמֹּתָיו.

Shir ha-ma-a-lot. B'shuv Adonai et shi-vat Tzi-yon, ha-yi-nu k'chol-mim. Az yi-ma-lei s'chok pi-nu, u-l'sho-nei-nu ri-na. Az yom-m'ru va-go-yim: hig-dil Adonai la-a-sot im ei-leh. Hig-dil Adonai la-a-sot i-ma-nu, ha-yi-nu s'mei-chim! Shu-vah Adonai et sh'vi-tei-nu ka-a-fi-kim ba-neh-gev. Ha-zo-r'im b'dim-a, b'ri-na yik-tzo-ru. Ha-loch yei-leich u-va-cho, no-sei meh-shech ha-za-ra, bo ya-vo v'ri-na no-sei a-lu-mo-tav.

When God restored the exiles to Zion, it seemed like a dream. Our mouths were filled with laughter, our tongues with joyful song. Then they said among the nations: God has done great things for them. Yes, God is doing great things for us, and we are joyful. Restore our fortunes, O God, as streams revive the desert. Then those who have sown in tears shall reap in joy. Those who go forth weeping, carrying bags of seeds, shall come home with shouts of joy, bearing their sheaves.

## ON WEEKDAYS BEGIN HERE

### Leader:

חֲבֵרִים וַחֲבֵרוֹת, נְבָרֵךְ.

Cha-vei-rim va-cha-vei-rot, n'va-reich

Let us praise God.

168

## Group:

יְהִי שֵׁם יי מְבֹרָךְ מֵעַתָּה וְעַד עוֹלָם.

Y'hi sheim Adonai m'vo-rach mei-a-ta v'ad o-lam!

*Praised be the name of God, now and for ever!*

## Leader:

יְהִי שֵׁם יי מְבֹרָךְ מֵעַתָּה וְעַד עוֹלָם.

בִּרְשׁוּת הַחֶבְרָה, נְבָרֵךְ אֱלֹהֵינוּ שֶׁאָכַלְנוּ מִשֶּׁלּוֹ.

Y'hi sheim Adonai m'vo-rach mei-a-ta v'ad o-lam!

Bi-r'shut ha-chev-rah, n'va-reich Eh-lo-hei-nu sheh-a-chal-nu mi-sheh-lo.

Praised be our God, of whose abundance we have eaten.

## Group:

בָּרוּךְ אֱלֹהֵינוּ שֶׁאָכַלְנוּ מִשֶּׁלּוֹ, וּבְטוּבוֹ חָיִינוּ.

Ba-ruch Eh-lo-hei-nu sheh-a-chal-nu mi-sheh-lo, u-v'tu-vo cha-yi-nu.

*Praised be our God, of whose abundance we have eaten,
and by whose goodness we live.*

## Leader:

בָּרוּךְ אֱלֹהֵינוּ שֶׁאָכַלְנוּ מִשֶּׁלּוֹ, וּבְטוּבוֹ חָיִינוּ.

Ba-ruch Eh-lo-hei-nu sheh-a-chal-nu mi-sheh-lo, u-v'tu-vo cha-yi-nu.

Praised be our God, of whose abundance we have eaten,
and by whose goodness we live.

## Group:

בָּרוּךְ הוּא וּבָרוּךְ שְׁמוֹ.

Ba-ruch hu u-va-ruch sh'mo.

*Praised be the Eternal God!*

169

Ba-ruch a-ta Adonai, Eh-lo-hei-nu meh-lech ha-o-lam, ha-zan et ha-o-lam ku-lo b'tu-vo, b'chein b'cheh-sed u-v'ra-cha-mim. Hu no-tein leh-chem l'chol ba-sar, ki l'o-lam chas-do. U-v'tu-vo ha-ga-dol ta-mid lo cha-sar la-nu, v'al yech-sar la-nu, ma-zon l'o-lam va-ed, ba-a-vur sh'mo ha-ga-dol. Ki hu Eil zan u-m'far-neis la-kol, u-mei-chin ma-zon l'chol b'ri-yo-tav a-sher ba-ra. Ba-ruch a-ta Adonai, ha-zan et ha-kol.

בָּרוּךְ אַתָּה יְיָ, אֱלֹהֵינוּ מֶלֶךְ הָעוֹלָם, הַזָּן אֶת־הָעוֹלָם כֻּלּוֹ בְּטוּבוֹ, בְּחֵן בְּחֶסֶד וּבְרַחֲמִים. הוּא נוֹתֵן לֶחֶם לְכָל־בָּשָׂר, כִּי לְעוֹלָם חַסְדּוֹ. וּבְטוּבוֹ הַגָּדוֹל תָּמִיד לֹא חָסַר לָנוּ, וְאַל יֶחְסַר לָנוּ, מָזוֹן לְעוֹלָם וָעֶד, בַּעֲבוּר שְׁמוֹ הַגָּדוֹל. כִּי הוּא אֵל זָן וּמְפַרְנֵס לַכֹּל, וּמֵטִיב לַכֹּל וּמֵכִין מָזוֹן לְכָל־בְּרִיּוֹתָיו אֲשֶׁר בָּרָא. בָּרוּךְ אַתָּה יְיָ, הַזָּן אֶת־הַכֹּל.

Sovereign God of the universe, we praise You: Your goodness sustains the world. You are the God of grace, love, and compassion, the source of bread for all who live—for Your love is everlasting. Through Your great goodness we never lack for food; You provide food enough for all. We praise You, Source of food for all who live. Amen.

For all this we thank You. Let Your praise ever be on the lips of all who live, as it is written: 'When you have eaten and are satisfied, give praise to your God who has given you this good earth.'

וְעַל הַכֹּל, יְיָ אֱלֹהֵינוּ, אֲנַחְנוּ מוֹדִים לָךְ וּמְבָרְכִים אוֹתָךְ. יִתְבָּרַךְ שִׁמְךָ בְּפִי כָּל־חַי תָּמִיד לְעוֹלָם וָעֶד

Ka-ka-tuv: V'a-chal-ta v'sa-va-ta, u-vei-rach-ta et Adonai Eh-lo-heh-cha al ha-a-retz ha-to-vah a-sher na-tan lach.

כַּכָּתוּב: וְאָכַלְתָּ וְשָׂבָעְתָּ, וּבֵרַכְתָּ אֶת־יהוה אֱלֹהֶיךָ עַל־הָאָרֶץ הַטֹּבָה אֲשֶׁר נָתַן־לָךְ.

170

As it is written: When you have eaten and are satisfied, give praise to your God who has given you this good earth.

U-v'nei Y'ru-sha-la-yim ir ha-ko-desh bi-m'hei-ra b'ya-mei-nu. Ba-ruch a-ta Adonai, bo-neh b'ra-cha-mav Y'ru-sha-la-yim. A-mein.

וּבְנֵה יְרוּשָׁלַיִם עִיר הַקֹּדֶשׁ בִּמְהֵרָה בְיָמֵינוּ. בָּרוּךְ אַתָּה יְיָ, בּוֹנֵה בְּרַחֲמָיו יְרוּשָׁלָיִם. אָמֵן.

Let Jerusalem, the holy city, be renewed in our time.
We praise You: in compassion You will rebuild Jerusalem. Amen.

~ ~

## ON SHABBAT

הָרַחֲמָן, הוּא יַנְחִילֵנוּ יוֹם שֶׁכֻּלּוֹ שַׁבָּת.

Ha-ra-cha-man, hu yan-chi-lei-nu yom sheh-ku-lo sha-bat.
Merciful One, help us to see the coming of a time that is all Shabbat.

~ ~

עֹשֶׂה שָׁלוֹם בִּמְרוֹמָיו, הוּא יַעֲשֶׂה שָׁלוֹם עָלֵינוּ וְעַל־כָּל־יִשְׂרָאֵל, וְאִמְרוּ אָמֵן.

O-seh sha-lom bi-m'ro-mav, hu ya-a-seh sha-lom a-lei-nu v'al kol Yis-ra-eil, v'i-m'ru: A-mein.

May the Source of perfect peace grant peace to us, to all Israel, and to all the world.

Adonai oz l'a-mo yi-tein, Adonai y'va-reich et a-mo va-sha-lom.

יהוה עֹז לְעַמּוֹ יִתֵּן, יהוה יְבָרֵךְ אֶת־עַמּוֹ בַשָּׁלוֹם.

Eternal God: give strength to Your people. Eternal God: bless Your people with peace.

171

# Havdalah    הבדלה

As Shabbat ends, the Havdalah candle is lit.
The following biblical verses are read or chanted.
It is customary to lift the cup of wine or grape juice high
when the last sentence is read and then proceed directly to the
blessing.

הִנֵּה אֵל יְשׁוּעָתִי, אֶבְטַח וְלֹא אֶפְחָד.

כִּי־עָזִּי וְזִמְרָת יָהּ יהוה, וַיְהִי־לִי לִישׁוּעָה.

וּשְׁאַבְתֶּם־מַיִם בְּשָׂשׂוֹן מִמַּעַיְנֵי הַיְשׁוּעָה.

לַיהוה הַיְשׁוּעָה, עַל־עַמְּךָ בִרְכָתֶךָ, סֶּלָה.

יהוה צְבָאוֹת עִמָּנוּ, מִשְׂגָּב־לָנוּ אֱלֹהֵי יַעֲקֹב, סֶלָה.

יהוה צְבָאוֹת, אַשְׁרֵי אָדָם בֹּטֵחַ בָּךְ!

יהוה הוֹשִׁיעָה; הַמֶּלֶךְ יַעֲנֵנוּ בְיוֹם־קָרְאֵנוּ.

לַיְּהוּדִים הָיְתָה אוֹרָה וְשִׂמְחָה וְשָׂשׂוֹן וִיקָר;

כֵּן תִּהְיֶה לָּנוּ!

כּוֹס־יְשׁוּעוֹת אֶשָּׂא, וּבְשֵׁם יהוה אֶקְרָא.

Hi-nei Eil y'shu-a-ti, ev-tach v'lo ef-chad.

Ki o-zi v'zim-rat Ya Adonai, va-y'hi li li-shu-a.

U-sh'av-tem ma-yim b'sa-son mi-ma-a-y'nei ha-y'shu-a.

La-a-do-nai ha-y'shu-ah, al a-m'cha bir-cha-teh-cha, se-la.

Adonai tz'va-ot i-ma-nu, mis-gav la-nu Eh-lo-hei Ya-a-kov, seh-la.

Adonai tz'va-ot, ash-rei a-dam bo-tei-ach bach!

Adonai ho-shi-a; ha-meh-lech ya-a-nei-nu v'yom kor-ei-nu.

La-y'hu-dim ha-y'ta o-ra v'sim-cha v'sa-son vi-kar;

kein ti-h'yeh la-nu.

Kos y'shu-ot eh-sa, u-v'sheim Adonai ek-ra.

172

Behold, God is my Help; trusting in the Eternal One, I am not afraid. For the Eternal One is my strength and my song, and has become my salvation. With joy we draw water from the wells of salvation. The Eternal One brings deliverance, and blessing to the people. The God of the hosts of heaven is with us; the God of Jacob is our stronghold. God of the hosts of heaven, happy is the one who trusts in You! Save us, Eternal One; answer us, when we call upon You. Give us light and joy, gladness and honor, as in the happiest days of our people's past. Then shall we lift up the cup to rejoice in Your saving power, and call out Your name in praise.

## THE WINE OR GRAPE JUICE

בָּרוּךְ אַתָּה יי, אֱלֹהֵינוּ מֶלֶךְ הָעוֹלָם, בּוֹרֵא פְּרִי הַגָּפֶן.

Ba–ruch a–ta Adonai, Eh–lo–hei–nu meh–lech ha–o–lam, bo–rei p'ri ha–ga–fen.

We praise You, Eternal God, Sovereign of the universe, Creator of the fruit of the vine.

(The leader does not drink the wine or grape juice until after the final blessing, when havdalah has been completed.)

## THE SPICES

בָּרוּךְ אַתָּה יי, אֱלֹהֵינוּ מֶלֶךְ הָעוֹלָם, בּוֹרֵא מִינֵי בְשָׂמִים.

Ba–ruch a–ta Adonai, Eh–lo–hei–nu meh–lech ha–o–lam, bo–rei mi–nei v'sa-mim.

We praise You, Eternal God, Sovereign of the universe, Creator of the world's spices.

(The spice–box, symbol of the "Additional Soul" that makes Shabbat sweeter than the weekdays, is now circulated)

## THE LIGHT

### Raise the Havdalah candle

בָּרוּךְ אַתָּה יי, אֱלֹהֵינוּ מֶלֶךְ הָעוֹלָם, בּוֹרֵא מְאוֹרֵי הָאֵשׁ.

Ba–ruch a–ta Adonai, Eh–lo–hei–nu meh–lech ha–o–lam, bo–rei m'o–rei ha-eish.

We praise You, Eternal God, Sovereign of the universe, Creator of fire.

### The candle is held high as the leader says

We praise You, Eternal God, Sovereign of the universe: You make distinctions, teaching us to distinguish the commonplace from the holy; You create light and darkness, Israel and the nations, the seventh day of rest and the six days of labor.

We praise You, O God: You call us to distinguish the commonplace from the holy.

בָּרוּךְ אַתָּה יי, אֱלֹהֵינוּ מֶלֶךְ הָעוֹלָם, הַמַּבְדִּיל בֵּין קֹדֶשׁ לְחוֹל, בֵּין אוֹר לְחֹשֶׁךְ, בֵּין יִשְׂרָאֵל לָעַמִּים, בֵּין יוֹם הַשְּׁבִיעִי לְשֵׁשֶׁת יְמֵי הַמַּעֲשֶׂה. בָּרוּךְ אַתָּה יי, הַמַּבְדִּיל בֵּין קֹדֶשׁ לְחוֹל.

Ba–ruch a–ta Adonai, Eh–lo–hei–nu meh–lech ha–o–lam, ha-mav-dil bein ko-desh l'chol, bein or l'cho-shech, bein Yis-ra-eil la-a-mim, bein yom ha-sh'vi-i l'shei-shet y'mei ha-ma-a-seh. Ba–ruch a–ta Adonai, ha-mav-dil bein ko-desh l'chol.

### Sip the wine or grape juice.
### Extinguish the Havdalah candle in the remaining wine or grape juice, while the following passages are sung or said:

הַמַּבְדִּיל בֵּין קֹדֶשׁ לְחוֹל, חַטֹּאתֵינוּ הוּא יִמְחֹל, זַרְעֵנוּ וְכַסְפֵּנוּ יַרְבֶּה כַחוֹל, וְכַכּוֹכָבִים בַּלָּיְלָה.

Ha-mav-dil bein ko-desh l'chol, cha-to-tei-nu hu yim-chol,
zar-ei-nu v'chas-pei-nu yar-beh ka-chol, v'cha-ko-cha-vim ba-lai-la.

174

Sha-vu-a tov...                                    ... שָׁבוּעַ טוֹב

A good week, a week of peace.
May gladness reign and joy increase.

אליהו הנביא

Ei-li-ya-hu ha–na-vi, Ei-li-ya-hu ha-     אֵלִיָּהוּ הַנָּבִיא, אֵלִיָּהוּ הַתִּשְׁבִּי,
tish-bi, Ei-li-ya-hu, Ei-li-ya-hu, Ei-li-   אֵלִיָּהוּ, אֵלִיָּהוּ, אֵלִיָּהוּ הַגִּלְעָדִי.
ya-hu ha–gil-a-di.
Bi-m'hei-ra v'ya-mei-nu, ya-vo ei-         בִּמְהֵרָה בְיָמֵינוּ, יָבֹא אֵלֵינוּ,
lei-nu, im Ma-shi–ach ben Da-vid,         עִם מָשִׁיחַ בֶּן דָּוִד,
im Ma-shi–ach ben Da-vid. Ei-li-ya-
hu ha–na-vi...                             עִם מָשִׁיחַ בֶּן דָּוִד. אֵלִיָּהוּ ...

  • Elijah the prophet, the Tishbite, the Gileadite:
    come to us soon, to herald our redemption...

175

# Short Hallel

*Psalm 117*

Praise God, all you nations; extol the Eternal One, all you peoples, for great is God's love towards us, and God's faithfulness endures for ever. Halleluyah!

הַלְלוּ אֶת־יהוה כָּל־גּוֹיִם;
שַׁבְּחוּהוּ כָּל־הָאֻמִּים, כִּי
גָבַר עָלֵינוּ חַסְדּוֹ, וֶאֱמֶת־
יהוה לְעוֹלָם, הַלְלוּיָהּ!

*From Psalm 118*

Give thanks to the Eternal One, who is good,
*whose love endures for ever.*

הוֹדוּ לַיהוה כִּי־טוֹב,
כִּי לְעוֹלָם חַסְדּוֹ.

Let Israel declare:
*God's love endures for ever.*

יֹאמַר־נָא יִשְׂרָאֵל:
כִּי לְעוֹלָם חַסְדּוֹ.

Let the house of Aaron declare:
*God's love endures for ever.*

יֹאמְרוּ־נָא בֵית־אַהֲרֹן:
כִּי לְעוֹלָם חַסְדּוֹ.

Let all God–fearing people declare:
*God's love endures for ever.*

יֹאמְרוּ־נָא יִרְאֵי יהוה:
כִּי לְעוֹלָם חַסְדּוֹ.

Blessed are you who come in God's name;
*here, in God's house, may you be blessed.*

בָּרוּךְ הַבָּא בְּשֵׁם יהוה;
בֵּרַכְנוּכֶם מִבֵּית יהוה.

You are my God, and I thank You;
*You are my God, I exalt You.*

אֵלִי אַתָּה, וְאוֹדֶךָּ;
אֱלֹהַי, אֲרוֹמְמֶךָּ.

Give thanks to the Eternal One, who is good,
*whose love is everlasting.*

הוֹדוּ לַיהוה כִּי־טוֹב,
כִּי לְעוֹלָם חַסְדּוֹ.

176

# Chanukah     חנכה

For a fuller home ritual, see: On the Doorposts of Your House
&Haneirot Halalu, These Lights are Holy

The lights of Chanukah are a symbol of our joy. In time of darkness, our ancestors had the courage to struggle for freedom. Theirs was a victory of the weak over the strong, the few over the many. It was a victory for all ages and all peoples.

אַשְׁרֵי הַגַּפְרוּר שֶׁנִּשְׂרַף וְהִצִּית לְהָבוֹת.

אַשְׁרֵי הַלֶּהָבָה שֶׁבָּעֲרָה בְּסִתְרֵי לְבָבוֹת.

אַשְׁרֵי הַלְּבָבוֹת שֶׁיָּדְעוּ לַחֲדוֹל בִּכְבוֹד.

אַשְׁרֵי הַגַּפְרוּר שֶׁנִּשְׂרַף וְהִיצִּית לְהָבוֹת.

Blessed is the match consumed in kindling flame.
Blessed is the flame that burns in the heart's secret places.
Blessed is the heart with strength to stop its beating for honor's
    sake.
Blessed is the match consumed in kindling flame.

| | |
|---|---|
| Zion hears and is glad; | שָׁמְעָה וַתִּשְׂמַח צִיּוֹן; |
| The daughters of Judah rejoice, | וַתָּגֵלְנָה בְּנוֹת יְהוּדָה, |
| Eternal One, in Your judgments. | לְמַעַן מִשְׁפָּטֶיךָ, יהוה. |

The light of our faith burns brightly now; our people Israel has survived all who sought to destroy us. In every generation, we are called, through love and self–sacrifice, to renew ourselves and the life of our people.

*Let the lights we kindle shine forth for the world to see. May they illumine our lives and fill us with gratitude for those who came before us, whose will and courage, time and again, kept the flame of faith from extinction.*

177

## The candles are placed in the Menorah from right to left, and kindled from left to right

We praise You, Eternal God, Sovereign of the universe: You hallow us with Your Mitzvot, and command us to kindle the Chanukah lights.

בָּרוּךְ אַתָּה יי, אֱלֹהֵינוּ מֶלֶךְ הָעוֹלָם, אֲשֶׁר קִדְּשָׁנוּ בְּמִצְוֹתָיו וְצִוָּנוּ לְהַדְלִיק נֵר שֶׁל חֲנֻכָּה.

Ba-ruch a-ta Adonai, Eh-lo-hei-nu meh-lech ha-o-lam, a-sher ki-d'sha-nu b'mitz-vo-tav v'tzi-va-nu l'had-lik ner shel Chanukah.

We praise You, Eternal God, Sovereign of the universe: You showed wonders to our fathers and mothers in days of old, at this season.

בָּרוּךְ אַתָּה יי, אֱלֹהֵינוּ מֶלֶךְ הָעוֹלָם, שֶׁעָשָׂה נִסִּים לַאֲבוֹתֵינוּ וּלְאִמּוֹתֵינוּ בַּיָּמִים הָהֵם בַּזְּמַן הַזֶּה.

Ba-ruch a-ta Adonai, Eh-lo-hei-nu meh-lech ha-o-lam, sheh-a-sa ni-sim la-a-vo-tei-nu u-l'i-mo-tei-nu ba-ya-mim ha-heim ba-z'man ha-zeh.

## On the first night only

We praise You, Eternal God, Sovereign of the universe, for giving us life, for sustaining us, and for enabling us to reach this season.

בָּרוּךְ אַתָּה יי, אֱלֹהֵינוּ מֶלֶךְ הָעוֹלָם, שֶׁהֶחֱיָנוּ וְקִיְּמָנוּ וְהִגִּיעָנוּ לַזְּמַן הַזֶּה.

Ba-ruch a-ta Adonai, Eh-lo-hei-nu meh-lech ha–o–lam, sheh–heh–cheh–ya–nu v'ki–y'ma–nu v'hi–gi–a–nu la–z'man ha–zeh.

## The following may be read or sung

הַנֵּרוֹת הַלָּלוּ אֲנַחְנוּ מַדְלִיקִין עַל הַנִּסִּים, וְעַל הַפֻּרְקָן,
וְעַל הַגְּבוּרוֹת, וְעַל הַתְּשׁוּעוֹת, וְעַל הַנֶּחָמוֹת, שֶׁעָשִׂיתָ
לַאֲבוֹתֵינוּ וְשֶׁעָשִׂיתָ לְאִמּוֹתֵינוּ בַּיָּמִים הָהֵם, וּבַזְּמַן הַזֶּה.

וְכָל־שְׁמוֹנַת יְמֵי חֲנֻכָּה הַנֵּרוֹת הַלָּלוּ קֹדֶשׁ הֵם; וְאֵין לָנוּ
רְשׁוּת לְהִשְׁתַּמֵּשׁ בָּהֶם אֶלָּא לִרְאוֹתָם בִּלְבָד, כְּדֵי לְהוֹדוֹת
וּלְהַלֵּל לְשִׁמְךָ הַגָּדוֹל עַל נִסֶּיךָ וְעַל נִפְלְאוֹתֶיךָ וְעַל
יְשׁוּעָתֶךָ.

We kindle these lights in remembrance of the wondrous deliverance
You wrought for our ancestors at this season, in days gone by.

*During the eight days of Chanukah these lights are sacred; we are not
to use them but only to gaze upon them, so that their glow may rouse
us to give thanks for Your wondrous saving power.*

| | |
|---|---|
| מָעוֹז צוּר יְשׁוּעָתִי, | Ma-oz tzur y'shu-a-ti, |
| לְךָ נָאֶה לְשַׁבֵּחַ, | l'cha na-eh l'sha-bei-ach, |
| תִּכּוֹן בֵּית תְּפִלָּתִי, | ti-kon beit t'fi-la-ti, |
| וְשָׁם תּוֹדָה נְזַבֵּחַ. | v'sham to-da n'za-bei-ach. |
| לְעֵת תַּשְׁבִּית מַטְבֵּחַ | L'eit tash-bit mat-bei-ach |
| וְצָר הַמְנַבֵּחַ, | v'tzar ha-m'na-bei-ach, |
| אָז אֶגְמוֹר, בְּשִׁיר מִזְמוֹר, | az eg-mor, b'shir miz-mor, |
| חֲנֻכַּת הַמִּזְבֵּחַ. | cha-nu-kat ha-miz-bei-ach. |

Rock of ages, let our song
Praise Your saving power;
You, amid the raging foes,
Were our sheltering tower.

Furious, they assailed us,
But Your arm availed us,
And Your word
Broke their sword,
When our own strength failed us.

Kindling new the holy lamps,
Priests approved in suffering,
Purified the nation's shrines,
Brought to You their offering.

And Your courts surrounding
Hear, in joy abounding,
Happy throngs,
Singing songs,
With a mighty sounding.

Children of the Maccabees,
Whether free or fettered,
Wake the echoes of the songs,
Where you may be scattered.
Yours the message cheering,
That the day is nearing,
Which will see,
All go free,
Tyrants disappearing.

# The Sabbath before Purim שבת זכור

We come before You, O God, with words of thanksgiving for the blessing You have been to our people Israel and to all humanity.

Purim brings to mind the suffering we have endured in many generations. Painful trials and bitter struggles, torments of body and soul have often been our portion. But sustained by the hope that goodness and love would triumph over evil and hate, we have perservered.

*Remembering the courage of Esther and the devotion of Mordecai, we give thanks for the women and men of every age who have helped to keep our people alive.*

We shall yet see the forces of destruction—cruel Amalek and vindictive Haman—vanish before the mighty onrush of Your light and Your love. And although many a bitter experience may await us before prejudice and hate will disappear, still we trust that in the end all humanity will unite in love, knowing that they are one, children all of the Eternal God. Amen.

# The Sabbath before Yom Ha-Atzmaut

We turn our thoughts to the land of Israel, cradle of our faith, a land hallowed by memory, a land of prophecy and sacred poems, where mystics and sages taught Torah. In all the ages of our history, and in all the places of our wandering, we have remembered it with love and longing, saying with the Psalmist:

*If I forget you, O Jerusalem, let my right hand wither. Let my tongue cleave to the roof of my mouth if I do not remember you, if I do not set Jerusalem above my highest joy.*

אִם־אֶשְׁכָּחֵךְ, יְרוּשָׁלַיִם, תִּשְׁכַּח יְמִינִי. תִּדְבַּק־לְשׁוֹנִי לְחִכִּי אִם־לֹא אֶזְכְּרֵכִי, אִם־לֹא אַעֲלֶה אֶת־יְרוּשָׁלַיִם עַל רֹאשׁ שִׂמְחָתִי.

And now we are privileged to celebrate Israel's rebirth. We recall with gratitude the vision of its pioneers, the devotion of its builders, and the courage of its defenders. In the desolate spaces of a never-forgotten homeland they have built villages and towns, planted gardens and established industries. We give thanks that out of the ashes of the death-camps there has arisen a land renewed, a haven where broken lives have been made whole again, an affirmation of our people's fidelity to its past and confidence in its future.

ירושלים של זהב

אֲוִיר הָרִים צָלוּל כַּיַּיִן, וְרֵיחַ אֳרָנִים,
נִשָּׂא בְּרוּחַ הָעַרְבַּיִם, עִם קוֹל פַּעֲמוֹנִים.
וּבְתַרְדֵּמַת אִילָן וָאֶבֶן, שְׁבוּיָה בַּחֲלוֹמָהּ,
הָעִיר אֲשֶׁר בָּדָד יוֹשֶׁבֶת, וּבְלִבָּהּ חוֹמָה.
יְרוּשָׁלַיִם שֶׁל זָהָב וְשֶׁל נְחוֹשֶׁת וְשֶׁל אוֹר,
הֲלֹא לְכָל־שִׁירַיִךְ אֲנִי כִּנּוֹר.

חָזַרְנוּ אֶל בּוֹרוֹת הַמַּיִם, לַשׁוּק וְלַכִּכָּר,

שׁוֹפָר קוֹרֵא בְּהַר הַבַּיִת, בָּעִיר הָעַתִּיקָה.

וּבַמְּעָרוֹת אֲשֶׁר בַּסֶּלַע, אַלְפֵי שְׁמָשׁוֹת זוֹרְחוֹת,

נָשׁוּב נֵרֵד אֶל יַם הַמֶּלַח, בְּדֶרֶךְ יְרִיחוֹ.

יְרוּשָׁלַיִם שֶׁל זָהָב וְשֶׁל נְחֹשֶׁת וְשֶׁל אוֹר,

הֲלֹא לְכָל־שִׁירַיִךְ אֲנִי כִּנּוֹר.

אַךְ בְּבוֹאִי הַיּוֹם לָשִׁיר לָךְ, וְלָךְ לִקְשׁוֹר כְּתָרִים,

קָטֹנְתִּי מִצְּעִיר בָּנַיִךְ, וּמֵאַחֲרוֹן הַמְּשׁוֹרְרִים.

כִּי שְׁמֵךְ צוֹרֵב אֶת־הַשְּׂפָתַיִם, כִּנְשִׁיקַת שָׂרָף,

אִם אֶשְׁכָּחֵךְ יְרוּשָׁלַיִם, אֲשֶׁר כֻּלָּהּ זָהָב.

יְרוּשָׁלַיִם שֶׁל זָהָב וְשֶׁל נְחֹשֶׁת וְשֶׁל אוֹר,

הֲלֹא לְכָל־שִׁירַיִךְ אֲנִי כִּנּוֹר.

Your ancient trees all stand in silence,
As though immersed in dream;
Your fragrant breeze now comes to meet me,
As light begins to gleam.
My yearning heart has long remembered
The sun that gilds your face;
Jerusalem, how I have loved you,
How we have been embraced!

יְרוּשָׁלַיִם שֶׁל זָהָב וְשֶׁל נְחֹשֶׁת וְשֶׁל אוֹר,

הֲלֹא לְכָל־שִׁירַיִךְ אֲנִי כִּנּוֹר.

183

# The Sabbath before Yom Ha-Shoah

## All rise

We have lived in numberless towns and villages; in too many of them we have endured cruel suffering. Some we have forgotten; others are sealed into our memory, a wound that does not heal. A hundred generations of victims and martyrs—and still their blood cries out from the earth. And so many, so many at Dachau, at Buchenwald, at Babi Yar, and...

What can we say? What can we do? How bear the unbearable, or accept what life has brought to our people? All who are born must die, but how shall we compare the slow passage of our time with the callous slaughter of the innocent, cut off before their time?

They lived with faith. Not all, but many. And, surely, many died with faith: faith in God, in life, in the goodness that even flames cannot destroy. May we find a way to the strength of that faith, that trust, that sure sense that life and soul endure beyond this body's death.

They have left their lives to us: let a million prayers rise whenever Jews worship; let a million candles glow against the darkness of these unfinished lives.

or

We remember our six million, who died when madness ruled, and evil darkened the earth. We remember those of whom we know, and those whose very names are lost.

*We cherish the memory of those who died as martyrs, those who died resisting, and those who died in terror.*

We mourn for all that died with them: their goodness and their wisdom, which could have done so much to ennoble and enrich

184

humanity. We mourn for the genius and the wit that died, the learning and the laughter that were lost.

*They are like candles that shine from the darkness of those years, and in their light we know what goodness is.*

We salute those men and women who had the courage to stand outside the mob, to save us, and to suffer with us. They, too, are God's witnesses, and a source of hope when we are tempted to despair.

*May such times never come again, and may the suffering of our people not be in vain. In our daily fight against cruelty and prejudice, tyranny and persecution, their memory gives us strength.*

In silence we remember those who sanctified God's name on earth.

## All are seated

## For Our Congregation, our Nation and the State of Israel

### All rise

Eternal God, we pray to You for the whole House of Israel, scattered over the earth, yet bound together by a common history and united by a common heritage of faith and hope.

Bless this holy congregation and all who serve it, together with all other holy congregations, in all lands near and far. Uphold us, shield us, and bestow upon us abundant life and health and peace and happiness. Bring to fulfillment the blessing of Moses: May the Eternal One, your God, make you a thousand times as many as you are, and bless you ...

O God, send Your healing to the sick, Your comfort to all who are in pain or anxiety, Your tender love to the sorrowing hearts among us. Be their refuge through their time of trial, as they pass from weakness to strength, from suffering to consolation, from lonely fear to the courage of faith. *Amen.*

We pray for all who hold positions of leadership and responsibility in our national life. Let Your blessing rest upon them, and make them responsive to Your will, so that our nation may be to the world an example of justice and compassion.

Deepen our love for our country and our desire to serve it. Strengthen our power of self-sacrifice for our nation's welfare. Teach us to uphold its good name by our own right-conduct.

Make us to see that the well-being of our nation is in the hands of all its citizens; imbue us with zeal for the cause of liberty in our own land and in all lands; and help us always to keep our homes safe from affliction, strife, and war. *Amen.*

We pray for the land of Israel and its people. May its borders know peace, its inhabitants tranquillity. And may the bonds of faith and fate which unite the Jews of all lands be a source of strength to Israel and to us all. God of all lands and ages, answer our constant prayer with a Zion once more aglow with light for us and for all the world, and let us say: *Amen.*